Desegregating the City

SUNY series in African American Studies
John R. Howard/Robert C. Smith, Editors

Desegregating the City

Ghettos, Enclaves, and Inequality

Edited by David P. Varady

STATE UNIVERSITY OF NEW YORK PRESS

Published by
State University of New York Press, Albany

© 2005 State University of New York

Printed in the United States of America

For information, address State University of New York Press,
194 Washington Avenue, Suite 305, Albany, NY 12210-2365

Production by Kelli Williams
Marketing by Michael Campochiaro

Library of Congress Cataloging-in-Publication Data

Desegregating the city: ghettos, enclaves, and inequality / David P. Varady,
editor.
    p. cm.—(SUNY series in African American studies)
Includes bibliographical references and index.
ISBN 0-7914-6459-8 (HC)
1. Inner cities—United States. 2. Segregation—United States. 3. United
States—Ethnic relations. 4. United States—Social conditions—1980-
I. Varady, David P. II. Series.
HN59.2.D47 2005
307.76'0973—dc22   2004017710

10 9 8 7 6 5 4 3 2 1

CONTENTS

PREFACE

There is an impressive body of scholarship produced by economists, sociologists, historians, and city planners on the problems of America's ghettos. Highlights of that scholarship include (1) the continuing high levels of racial and income segregation and the concentration of the poor in a relatively small number of high-poverty areas; (2) the root causes of residential segregation including racial discrimination in housing and employment, and the loss of manufacturing jobs; (3) the adverse effects that ghettos have on individuals (e.g., lack of access to good jobs, poor public services, lack of positive role models) and on cities, the spread of high-crime areas outward from city centers, the so-called Detroit scenario; and (4) the difficulties associated with poverty and minority deconcentration strategies, for example, suburban resistance to subsidized affordable housing developments.

Far less attention has been given to what is considered a more positive form of residential segregation—the ethnic enclave—defined as segregation by choice. Since the terrible events of September 11, 2001, segregation in both ghettos and enclaves needs to be reevaluated. According to the ghetto-enclave paradigm, ghettos are bad because people are forced to live there and because they lead to societal tensions. But ethnic enclaves are perceived as good because the choice to live there is voluntary. These ethnic concentrations are considered assets that add to urban vitality; London's Mayor Ken Livingstone declared: "A city's diversity is [its] strength" (Morris 2003). This paradigm is no longer valid and needs to be challenged, because crime and disorder may emanate from both forms of segregation.

The thirteen chapters in this volume are drawn from a subset of more than thirty papers presented at the seminar, Segregation in the City, at the Lincoln Institute of Land Policy, July 25–28, 2001 in Cambridge, Massachusetts, two months before September 11; and are of greatest interest to North American and European audiences. (The concluding chapter was written after the seminar.) While two chapters deal with segregation in South Africa and a third deals with Honduras, these three authors, nevertheless, either locate their scholarly work within the North American tradition, or consider policy questions similar to those faced by North American policy analysts.

I believe the conclusions drawn at the conference now appear to be overly simplistic and possibly even naïve. I make three points in this preface based on recent events and research occurring since September 2001: (1) whether ethnic enclaves are good or bad depends on the circumstances; (2) there is encouraging news about racial and economic segregation; and (3) poverty deconcentration is not a panacea for America's racial and economic segregation.

Enclaves and Ghettos

There was considerable consensus at the conference regarding the evils of ghettos and the virtues of enclaves. In retrospective, the ghetto-enclave distinction seems to be far less valid than previously thought.

Immigration is today a global experience. In America, there are ethnic enclaves of Russians in Brighton Beach, Brooklyn; Dominicans in Washington Heights, Manhattan; Somalis in Minneapolis; Cubans in Miami; Muslims in Dearborn, Michigan; and Portuguese and Brazilians in Newark, New Jersey. Similarly, immigrants from Eastern Europe, the developing countries of Africa, the Middle East, and South East Asia are making homes in ethnic enclaves in Western European cities—African Blacks, Bangladeshis, and Sri Lankans in London (Morris 2003, 9); Algerians in Paris, Marseilles, and Liège; Albanians, North Africans, and Kurds in Rome (*Al-Ahram* 2003); large concentrations of Surinamese in Amsterdam (Musterd 2001), and Somalis in Helsinki (Korva 2002).

While some recent newspaper and magazine articles on American cities report on the positive aspects of ethnic enclaves—"American dream is Ghana home" (Berger 2002),"With an Asian influx, a suburb finds itself transformed" (P. Brown 2001), "Schenectady's Guyanese strategy: Mayor goes all out for a wave of hardworking immigrants" (Kershaw 2002), "Immigrants again renew Sunset Park" (Oser 1996); and "Brooklyn's Russian residents find a 'suburb' in a neighborhood next door" (Yardley

1998)—recent accounts of violence and tension in immigrant ethnic enclaves throughout Europe indicate a worrisome situation.

Theodore Dalrymple provides a vivid description of the physical deterioration and crime that has become commonplace in the Paris cités, the high-rise public housing estates, with large North African, particularly Algerian, immigrant populations.

Fire is now fashionable in the cités: in Les Tartarets, residents . . . torched and looted every store—with the exceptions of one government-subsidized supermarket and a pharmacy. The underground parking lot, charred and blackened by smoke like a vault in an urban hell, is permanently closed. (Dalrymple 2002, 68)

As I write this preface, the French National Assembly voted overwhelmingly to ban all religious symbols from public schools. This move reflects broad public support for the French secular ideal, but may actually increase resentment particularly among the country's Muslim population, Europe's largest. Though media attention has focused mainly on religious attire, the actual legislation addresses and exposes France's inability to integrate Muslims into the broader society. Minister of Education, Luc Ferry, hopes the law "will keep classrooms from being divided up into militant religious communities" noting that "there had been a spectacular rise in racism and anti-Semitism in the past three years" (Sciolino 2004). Some Muslim students have become so disruptive in denying the truth of the Nazi slaughter of Jews that teachers cannot cover the subject of the Holocaust.

In Britain, large-scale immigration from its former colonies on the Indian subcontinent and the West Indies was encouraged by central government to meet labor shortages in the 1950s and 1960s. By and large these immigrant groups were integrated into the larger British society gaining jobs in civil service and entrepreneurial positions. More recent arrivals, however, have faced greater difficulties finding work because of the drop in manufacturing jobs. The rise of Muslim fundamentalist beliefs and practices, even amongst the educated, has impeded their inclusion into the broader society.

Early in the summer of 2001, racial rioting broke out in three English cities with large Asian populations—Bradford, Burnley, and Oldham. Bradford's rioting caused $15 million in damage and left more than three hundred police officers injured (Hoge 2001). These riots shattered

Britain's reputation as one of Europe's more stable multiethnic societies. The Cantle Report (named for Ted Cantle, Chair of the Community Cohesion Research Team (Home Office 2001), asserted that the English riots were caused by the lack of opportunities for minority youths and a deep distrust between white and nonwhite communities, which was seen as a product of voluntary self-segregation, resulting in the sharpening of ethnic segregation.

Whilst the physical segregation of housing estates and inner city areas came as no surprise, the team was particularly struck by the depth of polarization of our towns and cities. The extent to which these physical divisions were compounded by so many other aspects of our daily lives, was very evident. Separate educational arrangements, community and voluntary bodies, employment, places of worship, language, and cultural networks, means that many British communities operate on the basis of a series of parallel lives. These lives often do not seem to touch at any point, let alone overlap and promote any meaningful interchanges. (Home Office 2001, 9)

British Home Secretary, David Blunkett, placed part of the blame on the immigrants themselves, insisting that immigrants must learn English, adopt British values, and drop practices like forced marriages and genital mutilation if they want to reside in Britain (Hoge 2001). Additionally, a recent spate of honor killings throughout the country brought Blunkett's message to the attention of the general public. Honor killings, a practice once unknown outside the close confines of the Muslim community, have now been adjudicated by the British legal establishment, which recently handed down two lengthy sentences for murder. On September 30, 2003, BBC News reported that a Muslim from London was beginning a life sentence for murdering his daughter because he disapproved of her dating a Christian. A month later, the *Dundee Courier and Advertiser* reported that a Muslim father hired a hit man to kill his daughter because she married someone of whom he disapproved (Wilson 2003).

Many immigrants do not feel "British." Abdul Shaif, an educational officer with the Sheffield City Council, quoted a Yemeni teenager, "By day I'm English, but at night I'm Yemeni" (Hoge 2002). Furthermore, a significant segment of the growing Muslim population is hostile or ambivalent to Western values. A poll of Muslims conducted by the ICM Polling agency in December 2001 showed that more than half refused to accept Al Qaeda's guilt in the 9/11 attacks on the United States and more than two-thirds felt that the war on terror was a war on Islam (Shepherd 2004).

Unlike the 1968 report by the National Advisory Commission on Civil Disorders, better known as the Kerner Commission Report, the Cantle Report presents few specific suggestions for dealing with residential separation, which might well reflect the lack of leverage of Britain's central government to alleviating the concentration of minorities in enclaves. Members of the Commission believed that a key factor was that religious schooling reinforced separation of groups and recommended that at least 25 percent of children in faith-based state subsidized schools come from faiths other than that of the institution. Whether this proposal is feasible remains to be seen; Christian parents may be unwilling to send their children to predominantly Muslim schools where Islamic teachings permeate the educational environment.

The policy dilemmas associated with state-funded, faith-based schools are illustrated by a campaign in Glasgow to convert four state-funded primary schools to Islamic teaching (MacLeod 2003); Muslim parents want separate schools because they worry about the influences of secularism on their children; they believe their children would do better in an Islamic atmosphere. Critics worry that the school would reduce the mixing of children from different groups, thereby undermining efforts to promote intergroup tolerance. The proposal is currently a hot issue in Glasgow, because Scotland's first Muslim school, a private one located in a Muslim neighborhood on the city's South Side, was closed in part because the imam who ran the school was following fundamentalist religious principles (Henderson 2004).

Ethnic rioting is not the only problem linked to immigration. Since September 11, 2001, Britain has become a breeding ground for young Islamic radicals connected to terror groups. Here are two examples drawn from recent newspaper accounts. Four young men, known as the "Tipton Taliban," grew up in a Muslim enclave in a small town near Birmingham, converted to Islam, and were later captured with the Taliban in Afghanistan (Waldman 2002). Shamsul Bahri Hussein, one of eight suspects linked to the Bali bombing that killed 180 people in 2002, studied engineering at the University of Dundee in Scotland. Dundee has a relatively small, but growing fundamentalist Muslim population. Nick Meo and Lucy Adams (2003), in an article on Dundee, altered the city's nickname from "Jute, Jam and Journalism" (historically, the city's major products), to "Jute, Jam and Jihad."

This very brief discussion of European immigrant enclaves raises a key question: Does living in an ethnic enclave contribute to the maintenance of traditional religious-cultural practices, which in turn leads to an inability to adopt the mores and values of the larger society? Neighborhood effects theory has been widely cited and used as a basis for a poverty deconcentration strategy for the United States. William Julius Wilson (1987) argues that living in a high-poverty area is a serious burden for the poor over and beyond their low incomes, limited education, poor health, and so forth. A woman dependent on welfare living in public housing and whose immediate friends and/or relatives is, according to this theory, likely to feel strong group pressure not to alter the status quo; her fear of being ridiculed and ostracized by her neighbors would keep her at home.

Neighborhood effects theory would seem to be just as applicable to understanding why ethnic minority immigrants do or do not integrate into the host society. Those living in enclaves where fundamentalism and anti-Western values dominate would feel group pressures to accept and follow these norms (James Q. Wilson 2004). This would be less so among those living outside of immigrant enclaves. I know of no empirical research that has tested the independent impact of "ethnic density" on support for fundamentalism or for the rejection of Western values. Two prestigious journals in the field of city affairs have recently published special issues on urban neighborhoods—*Housing Studies* (Friedrichs, Galster and Musterd 2003) and *Urban Studies* (Kearns and Parkinson 2001) These articles focus on the relation between the level of poverty concentration and the incidence of social mobility; none of these articles links ethnic concentration and cultural isolation. Why this issue is ignored is unclear. Such research is urgently needed.

The foregoing suggests that one must be cautious when discussing the ghetto-ethnic enclave dichotomy. Whether an enclave is good or bad depends on many factors at the global, national, and local levels: the level of immigration; the type of religious beliefs held by immigrants; the numbers and types of jobs available to immigrants; the level of tolerance of long-term residents, and the commitment of the immigrants to the host country. Enclaves can be dangerous to immigrants and to the host society if this ethnic clustering restricts intergroup social interaction, or if it retards integration into the larger society. This danger has taken on increased importance because of September 11.

There is another reason for using caution when discussing the ghetto-enclave typology. In the United States, an increasing number of Blacks are choosing to live in predominantly black areas, like Atlanta or Prince Georges County, Maryland, bordering the District of Columbia (Dent 1992), and racial discrimination is not the cause. Black suburban Atlanta has become a dream destination for those who can afford homes from between $200,000 to $2 million, and since the early 1990s, these upscale subdivisions have been marketed specifically to Blacks. In Atlanta, Blacks that fled north seeking integration in the 1950s and 1960s, are returning to these well-to-do, segregated neighborhoods—enclaves, not ghettos—in the suburbs (60 Minutes 2002).

Rising levels of education and income have enabled upwardly mobile Blacks to choose where to live rather than having the choice imposed on them. A resident interviewed for the 60 Minutes segment recounts:

I remember coming to Atlanta. I was so excited about being at a place where I could just kind of be myself and let my hair down. I didn't have to prove anything to anybody. And I think that's what causes people of any race, any culture, to self-segregate. (60 Minutes 2002)

Isabel Wilkerson, a prizewinning reporter for the New York Times and also interviewed on 60 Minutes, sees the migration from the north to the south as part of a search for one's cultural roots.

There's always a searching to find out what—where did this begin? Why do we eat the food that we eat? Why do we listen to the music we listen to? Why do we speak the way that we do? And this is the way to—to find that out. (60 Minutes 2002)

This trend is, though, not limited to suburban neighborhoods. Afflu-ent black professionals are moving back to urban centers for some of the same reasons that they are moving into upscale Atlanta suburbs. Sections of Harlem are currently experiencing revitalization with building restora-tion and recovery of commercial districts. A diversity of householders in-cludes affluent African Americans, as well as black African and European immigrants (Foderaro 1998; Scott 2001; Waldman 2001a; Waldman 2001b). American black residents, however, feel a sense of ambivalence toward this new diversity. Jonathan Rieder, a Barnard College sociologist attributes this to the Blacks' "long memory of exclusion from white neigh-borhoods [and the fact that they] have much invested in a feeling of com-fort with their own kind" (Scott 2001). John Goering, a Baruch College professor of public affairs indicates that "[t]he current reaction of the African American community in Harlem is like the reaction of many African Americans who since the 80s have begun to question the goal of integration for integration's sake alone . . ." (Scott 2001).

So far, statistics documenting the movement of black professionals back to Harlem are sketchy, but the dramatic rise in housing prices reflects the trend. Howard Sanders, a Harvard Business School graduate, bought a house in Harlem in order to be among others with similar values and outlook on life, and also to reconnect with the black cultural history of the Harlem Renaissance of the 1920s.

I don't have to live next to a white family. . . . I effectively have integrated. I've gone to predominantly white schools. I work in a white firm, and I can live anywhere I want. It really is psychologically soothing for me to be in Harlem. . . . To be honest, there are cultural differences [between whites and blacks], and when you live in your own community, there's not that pressure to assimilate. I'm basking in my own culture when I go to the Schomburg Center [The New York Public Library's Center for Research on Black Culture]. If I lived in the West Village I couldn't do that. I'd have to seek out activities that brought me into contact with black professionals. (Scott 2001)

Thus, in America, researchers must be careful using the terms ghetto and enclave and relying on outdated, simplistic stereotypes. Choice is the key factor distinguishing ghettos from enclaves. Since affluent Blacks moving to upscale Atlanta suburbs are doing so out of choice, these areas are enclaves not ghettos. This type of voluntary self-segregation is not necessarily bad. Living in an ethnic minority enclave is not good—even when segregation is voluntary—if this clustering undercuts social cohesion. The terms have become too nuanced to define so easily. They need to be redefined to reflect our post-9/11 world.

Encouraging News about Racial and Income Segregation

Although levels of racial and income segregation remain unacceptably high, recent research provides encouraging evidence of improvements. A HUD study released November 7, 2002 (U.S. Department of Housing and Urban Development 2002) indicates that housing discrimination nationwide against Blacks and Hispanics, seeking to purchase a home, has decreased more that 25 percent since 1989. For those Blacks interested in renting, housing discrimination is down 18 percent, but it remains unchanged for Hispanics. In addition, Edward L. Glaeser and Jacob L. Vigdor's 2001 analysis of census data indicated that in 2000 black/non-black segregation levels were at their lowest point since about 1920. Of the 291 metropolitan statistical areas analyzed, 272 were more integrated in 2000 than they were in 1990. This decline in segregation was caused primarily by the integration of formerly all-white census tracts.

Ingrid Gould Ellen's neighborhood integration research (Ellen 1997a; 1997b; 1998; 2000; New hope for racial integration 1997) indicates that racially mixed neighborhoods (i.e., ones between 10 and 50 percent black) are more common than most people realize and these neighborhoods are also more stable than is usually assumed. Ellen found that the percentage of Whites remained the same or actually grew during the 1990s in more than half of the racially mixed census tracts in her sample of thirty-four metropolitan areas. Furthermore, a comparison with information from the 1970s shows that integrated neighborhoods became more stable over time. Mixed neighborhoods spatially removed from black inner-city areas or those with a strong institutional presence, like a university or military base, are most likely to remain stable.

Phillip Nyden's research (Nyden, Maly and Lukehart 1997; Nyden et al. 1998) also challenges the widely held perception that "diverse" neighborhoods are inherently unstable. Using both quantitative and qualitative data, fourteen communities in nine U.S. cities were chosen for closer selection. Research teams consisting of academics and practitioners identified two models of urban diversity. Model One, the diverse-by-direction community, developed the institutional structures, social arrangements, and political-social environment that were needed to sustain their diversity. Among these structures are community organizations specifically developed to promote the community as racially and ethnically diverse" (Nyden et al. 1998, 9) The diversity in Model Two, the diverse-by-circumstance community, "is less a product of neighborhood organization intervention and more the product of social and economic forces initially beyond the control of the residents. Such forces include an influx of immigrant groups . . ." (Nyden et al. 1998, 11). The diverse-by circumstance communities represent the newest and fastest growing segment of diverse communities.

Nor is the encouraging news limited to racial integration. A national analysis of high-poverty neighborhoods (Jargowsky 2003), indicated that the number of people residing in high-poverty neighborhoods declined sharply by 24 percent during the 1990s and that the share of the poor living in high-poverty neighborhoods declined among all racial and ethnic groups, especially Blacks.

The preceding "good news" does not mean that efforts to reduce segregation and prejudice should be curtailed. Rather, these findings indicate that antisegregation policies need to build upon the record of success of the last decade.

Poverty Deconcentration and Housing Vouchers Are Not Panaceas for America's Urban Poverty and Segregation Problems

During the 1980s, America's policy for low-income housing shifted away from public housing projects and low-income developments. Rent certificates (also called housing vouchers) were given to households to use in the private housing market. When the program was first introduced in the early 1980s, policy makers hoped it would not only provide access to affordable housing, but that it would enable low-income families to move to low-poverty suburban areas, thereby helping them to move toward self-sufficiency.

In reality, many who received vouchers as part of HUD's regular Section 8 housing voucher program have either stayed put (because their home met housing quality standards), or have made only short-distance moves resulting in little change in the proportion of poor families or minorities in their surrounding neighborhood. (For a detailed review of the literature on the link between housing vouchers and residential mobility see Varady and Walker 2003a, b, c.)

The Gautreaux Assisted Housing Program, which required moves to low-minority neighborhoods and which provided extensive counseling and supportive services, produced some promising results (e.g., higher rates of employment, higher levels of educational attainment for the children, see Rubinowitz and Rosenbaum 2000). Consequently, a number of policy analysts including Myron Orfield (2002), advocate expanding this type of racial/poverty deconcentration strategy to serve all of the urban poor, while at the same time, cutting back on community development programs aimed at helping the urban poor where they live in the inner city.

The Moving to Opportunity (MTO) Demonstration program provides HUD with the ideal opportunity to test for the effectiveness of housing dispersal using a more sophisticated experimental strategy than was possible in the evaluation of the Gautreaux program. Those participating in MTO are randomly assigned to one of three groups: (1) an experimental group provided with vouchers and intensive counseling, who are required to move to low-poverty areas; (2) a control group remaining in public housing; and (3) a group assigned to the regular Section 8 voucher program.

MTO: Interim Impacts Evaluation (Orr et al. 2003) offers mixed evidence regarding effectiveness. While the experimental group achieved improved housing, neighborhood conditions, and safety, the demonstration had virtually no influence on any measure of educational attainment, and virtually no impact on employment, earnings, or receipt of public assistance. It is possible that improvements in employment and education may require more than four to seven years of participation, the amount of time covered in the Interim Report. The final report, which will cover ten years of participation in the program, may provide us with more conclusive results.

Furthermore, even though many of the members of the experimental group were able to move to low-poverty neighborhoods, many of these areas were heavily black or experiencing rapid racial change. "To the extent that racial integration or diversity has a positive impact on any of the outcomes studied here that influence was largely absent in this demonstration" (Orr et al. 2003, p. xvii).

Even if the MTO model is judged successful because of its long-term effects, it will to be difficult to expand it from a demonstration to a national program for the following seven reasons.

- The costs of counseling are high. MTO is an expensive program and it is unlikely that a large-scale national program will be funded in the near future. In fact, it may be more cost efficient to expand the regular Section 8 program to reach more of those who are eligible for participation rather than try to develop a national MTO program (Basgal and Villarreal 2001).

- It may be difficult to convince the poor to participate in an MTO-type program. Many of the poor in the program do not want to move away from relatives or friends, their local church, or accessible public transportation.

- An MTO-type program would not work as well for those who move involuntarily (e.g., those displaced from public housing developments being demolished to make way for mixed income developments) as for those who choose to participate in a housing mobility demonstration. Previous research shows that many of these displacees have characteristics (e.g., physical and mental health problems, poor credit histories, and/or criminal records) which make it difficult for them to conduct housing searches or they appear unattractive to landlords (Goetz 2002, 2003; Popkin et al. 2002; Popkin, Cunningham, and Woodley 2003).

- In tight housing markets, it will be necessary to construct additional affordable housing, but such developments will be strongly resisted by suburban residents.

- Because voucher recipients tend to make short distance moves, they are likely to move into and recluster in fragile neighborhoods experiencing income and racial change, thereby undercutting the viability of these areas.

- To the extent that a national MTO-type program succeeds in helping the stable poor to move to suburban areas, it will be undercutting efforts to revitalize these areas.

- Policies to deconcentrate low-income black ghetto areas may conflict with policies to assist newly arrived immigrants (Goetz 2003). As part of the *Hollman v. Cisneros* desegregation litigation settlement for Minneapolis, HUD and the Minneapolis Housing Authority agreed (1) to demolish nine hundred public housing units located in the Near North Side, one of the highest poverty concentrations in Minneapolis; (2) to construct seven hundred replacements units in the suburbs; and (3) to offer residents a Special Mobility Program (housing vouchers that could only be used in low-poverty neighborhoods, relocation counseling, and other forms of assistance). Southeast Asians strongly resisted the desegregation plan because they believed that moving would mean losing the dense, supportive social networks available to them in the Near North Side. It appears that dispersal advocates were so preoccupied with poverty and black de-concentration that they failed to consider the needs of Southeast Asian residents in a viable ethnic enclave. MTO's unimpressive re-sults, thus far, and the difficulties of expanding the demonstration to a national program, suggests that inner-city ills might be more effec-tively addressed through better education and other social programs aimed at individuals rather than through programs aimed at relocat-ing families to new residential environments (Mac Donald 1997).

Alexander von Hoffman (1998) wisely indicates the need to lower ex-pectations about what housing voucher programs (or for that matter, any particular type of program) can accomplish.

The simple goal of providing decent and safe housing to low-income people where they now live or *where they want to live* is not as lofty as creating modern housing, a high-rise civilization, or a socially heterogeneous society. Yet it is just as worthy and, in these perilous times for social policy, has the advantage of being remotely possible. (p. 19) [Editor's note: Emphasis mine]

All available policy tools to address segregation, including housing vouchers, involve costs as well as benefits. Only by recognizing the weak-nesses and strengths of different approaches and by combining them into comprehensive strategies will it be possible to move forward in reducing income and economic segregation. Poverty deconcentration programs such as housing vouchers cannot alone solve America's segregation prob-lem but must be combined with other approaches including community development in the inner city.

I anticipate that this volume will lead to a spirited discussion about the functions and dysfunctions of ghettos and enclaves, the extent to which progress has occurred in reducing patterns of segregation, and the appro-priateness of different antisegregation policies. The world has changed since 9/11. The debate needs to reflect the new reality.

ACKNOWLEDGMENTS

I would like to express my thanks to Roz Greenstein of the Lincoln Institute of Land Policy, for making the seminar, "Segregation in the City" (Cambridge, Massachusetts, July 25–28, 2001) possible and for initially funding a book based on the seminar; to Xavier de Souza Briggs for offering encouragement and advice (including the title for this book); to Peter McKenna of the Dundee, Scotland Housing Department who provided the ideal environment (a Visiting Scholar position) to work on the final stages of the book between July and December 2003; to Aharon Varady for all his technical assistance in the preparation of the manuscript; and to Managing Editor, Adrienne Varady, who improved the book substantively and stylistically; her encouragement and support proved essential in making this book a reality.

INTRODUCTION

The book is divided into two parts. The six chapters in part I attempt to answer questions specific to enclaves: How do the ethnic enclaves emerging in North American cities today differ from the enclaves occupied by Eastern and Southern European immigrants earlier in the twentieth century? What are the functional and dysfunctional aspects of current ethnic enclaves in cities as varied as Chicago, Toronto, London, and Amsterdam? How can American planners develop policies to deal with the ghetto problem while at the same time recognizing the legitimacy and desirability of most ethnic enclaves? The final six chapters, part II, switch our attention to ghetto remediation strategies and seek to determine how much emphasis should be given to (1) eliminating patterns of housing discrimination, (2) removing zoning and other regulatory devices that restrict low-income housing from the suburbs, (3) creating mixed-income communities in the city, and in the suburbs, and (4) reducing disparities in wealth through, for example, a more progressive income tax structure.

In chapter 1, Peter Marcuse distinguishes between acceptable and unacceptable residential clustering. Clustering that results from voluntary decisions, those that lead to the formation of ethnic enclaves, is generally acceptable, whereas involuntary clustering, that which segregates lower-income people into class ghettos, "is generally objectionable and should be countered by policy measures" (p. 15).

Marcuse notes that in the past, the federal government, as well as state and local governments in the United States, imposed policies that prompted the segregation of low-income people. Examples of such policies included large-lot zoning and prohibitions against multifamily construction, the Federal Housing Administration's (FHA) appraisal criteria, which provided the basis for redlining (the denial of financing to property owners in certain designated areas), and the construction of high-rise public housing in ghetto areas. Therefore, it is "the state" that must play a key role in reducing patterns of segregation. Some of Marcuse's suggestions, such as the dispersal of public housing throughout metropolitan areas, fall within the political mainstream and have a good chance of being implemented. He uses the term "public housing" in its broadest sense to include housing vouchers and subsidized private developments as well as publicly managed projects.

While Marcuse's more radical proposals (an expansion of the welfare state, the banning of competition among cities, and the legalization of squatting) may not be presently politically feasible, they do highlight the need for the federal government to play the leading role in addressing the fundamental causes of poverty and spatial segregation, in particular, limited education and training, unemployment, single-parenthood, among others.

In chapter 2, Ceri Peach criticizes the Chicago School of sociologists for failing to make a distinction between ghettos and ethnic enclaves, and for incorrectly assuming that the ghetto, the enclave, and suburban dispersal are three spatial stages in the inevitable process of ethnic assimilation. The experience of Blacks in Chicago and elsewhere in the United States refutes this three-stage model. First, black residential concentrations have been different in scale and in kind from those of ethnic Whites. White European immigrants typically lived in ethnically mixed areas, while urban Blacks typically lived in predominantly black areas. As for suburbanization, "in the case of African Americans, outward movement did not always equate to dispersal. The ghetto moved out with them like the tongue of a glacier" (p. 37).

Second, the Chicago School failed to predict that some white ethnic groups, such as Orthodox Jews, would continue to maintain high levels of segregation even as they shifted to the suburbs. Unlike Blacks, however, these high levels of residential segregation reflected voluntary choices and were not (as was the case for Blacks) a function of discriminatory practices.

Not only do we need to distinguish between enclaves and ghettos, we need to understand that there are three different types of enclaves apparent in North American and European cities. The first type is the "persistent enclave" as exemplified by Chinatown in New York City. The second type is the "voluntary plural relocated model" an example being the relocation of Jews from the impoverished East End of London to the northern affluent suburb of Golders Green. Finally, the "parachuted suburban" model refers to an area that receives affluent ethnic members directly from the home country; for instance, Hong Kong Chinese in Vancouver, and South Asian Indians in Edison, New Jersey.

Mohammad A. Qadeer's case study of Toronto's metropolitan area (chapter 3) stresses the importance of ethnic enclaves. Toronto, arguably one of the most cosmopolitan cities in the world, continues to draw immigrants from over 150 countries. As one reviewer of this book indicated: "Toronto's socially healthy ethnic enclaves are impressive enough to be a counterpoint to the other North American cities covered in this book."

Immigrant enclaves are found in the newer suburbs as well as in traditional port of entry inner-city areas. These enclaves continue to remain vibrant, according to Qadeer, because members of ethnic groups *want* to live among those who share common cultural values, and moreover, the broader societal environment supports this pattern of self-segregation. Unlike the United States, Canadian culture never supported the notion of a "melting pot." Furthermore, Canada's Charter of Rights and Freedoms (1982) and the Multicultural Act (1988) recognize a person's right to preserve their ethnic heritage, thereby implicitly endorsing the development and maintenance of ethnic enclaves.

Qadeer's research challenges the validity of the assertion made by many scholars and U.S. policymakers that race is always the dominant factor affecting social interaction and residential patterns. In Toronto, where overt discrimination is rare, visible racial minorities, like black Caribbeans, are not as segregated as some white non-English groups. Jews are by far the most segregated group. But, ethnic enclaves have their downside—"they may inhibit immigrants' acculturation into the ways of the housing market and may interfere with an understanding of Canadian social mores" (p. 60).

This chapter raises a number of questions about enclaves that are beyond the scope of his chapter but warrant further exploration. What is the process of ethnic change like? What impact, if any, does ethnic transition have on housing sales prices? Does the inmigration of members of an ethnic group lead existing residents to flee because they no longer feel comfortable in the area? Or does ethnic turnover largely result from a drop-off in demand from all families other than members of the new ethnic group? To what extent is Qadeer's somewhat optimistic picture about intergroup interaction correct? How much physical and social interaction between groups occur in employment, in shopping districts, in public schools (as a result of parental involvement), and through political participation? To what extent does ethnic attachment affect overall civic unity? Are householders, whose lives are circumscribed by their ethnic neighborhood, less likely to identify with the City of Toronto or the Toronto region? Answers to these questions will require large-scale social surveys and detailed analyses of sales price data. Hopefully, Qadeer's chapter will stimulate additional empirical research on these questions.

Frederick W. Boal's (chapter 4) scenarios spectrum would undoubtedly classify Toronto as a pluralistic city, a city where different ethnic groups coexist. Belfast and Jerusalem would be examples of polarized cities. The scenarios spectrum, a heuristic device developed for his students' examination of Belfast, might be helpful to planners and policymakers assessing a city's future. Social mixing in schools and in the housing stock could conceivably shift a city from the polarized category to the pluralistic one. Implementing such strategies in a city like Belfast would be difficult, if not impossible, to accomplish.

Many who write about America's ghettos fail to clarify just why ghettos constitute a problem beyond the obvious one that people are forced to live there. The last two chapters in part I focus on this issue. Xavier de Souza Briggs (chapter 5) asserts that segregation causes spatial isolation which leads to social isolation and economic dependency. "Spatial barriers appear to reinforce social ones that isolate the poor, and the minority poor most of all, from useful connections to job advice, scholarship recommendations, and other forms of aid" (p. 85). Residents in predominantly minority inner-city ghettos (even in the most distressed cities like Detroit) do have access to social networks, but only to those networks that help them cope or get along, not get ahead. In other words, ghetto residents lack access to "social bridges," people, agencies, and companies outside their community who can provide leverage for social mobility.

In the abstract, school desegregation is an ideal solution for building social bridges and for preparing inner-city black youth for living in a racially and socioeconomically diverse society. The reality is that school demographics often work against successful mixing (see for example Varady 1979) particularly when the ratio of white middle-class white students drops and low-income black students increase. Common backgrounds and interests necessary to form friendships and build social bridges no longer exist. Racial tensions and problems of safety may reinforce stereotypes rather than eliminate them. Recently, increasing numbers of urban school districts have shifted their emphasis away from desegregation and busing in favor of neighborhood schools, because parents, regardless of race, believe that neighborhood schools strengthen residential communities, or to use the academic jargon, strengthen social capital. And, in many cases urban school districts lack sufficient numbers of white children to make racial integration demographically feasible.

Briggs points out that the concept of social capital is far more relevant to programs that are relationship driven (e.g., affirmative marketing, job matching, housing relocation counseling, inner-city community development) than those that are mostly institutionalized and routinized (e.g., fair housing enforcement). However, planners need to acknowledge their limited capability to develop social capital in inner-city areas where it does not already exist. Furthermore, and echoing a point made by others in this volume, Briggs emphasizes that social capital should not be viewed as a cure-all for the ills of segregation. Programs that foster the right kinds of social capital need to be implemented in conjunction with macro-level policies aimed at more just and accountable market and government structures to create equal opportunities.

In chapter 6, Glenn Pearce-Oroz turns our attention to Latin America where, in contrast to the United States but similar to housing estates in Europe, low-income ghettos are often located at the edges of cities, distant from jobs, shopping, and good public services. He argues that the new towns of Tegucigalpa (capital of Honduras, population of nine hundred thousand), created in response to the devastation caused by Hurricane Mitch in 1998, illustrate spatial segregation. The dilemmas associated with efforts to reduce spatial segregation in Tegucigalpa characterize urbanization in many other Latin American cities where informal settlements emerge at urban peripheries and where irregular land tenure and the absence of basic urban services are the norm.

Land market forces as well as political and social forces helped to shape the new towns around Tegucigalpa. Because of Honduras' complicated legal framework and dispersed responsibility for land administration, real estate transactions frequently involved disputes over property rights, in effect forcing officials to purchase land some seven to sixteen miles from the city's boundary thereby making access to jobs and shopping a problem. As a result, Tegucigalpa's four macro-shelters, housing approximately twenty-five hundred families, became magnets for social problems, partly because the residents' social networks were destroyed. And while the new towns program appears to have worsened existing spatial segregation, it did improve physical housing conditions, that is, access to potable water, sanitation, and electricity, but "the opportunity to interact with different sectors of the population afforded by public spaces in the urban center will be not readily available to the new inhabitants" (p. 118).

Pearce-Oroz acknowledges that to reduce spatial segregation in Latin America, officials must be willing to address income inequalities and the lack of macroeconomic growth (though it is beyond the scope of his chapter to address these fundamental problems), and proposes a new methodology for problem identification in places like Tegucigalpa, one based on the concept of access deficiency. The proposal includes five elements each linked with corrective instruments: access to jobs, safe and effective transportation, financial services, health care and educational services, and consumer services.

The issue of political feasibility comes up throughout the volume. In part II, we focus our attention on ghetto remediation strategies. What emphasis should be given to incremental, but politically feasible policies (e.g., the enforcement of fair housing laws) versus policies that address the "root causes" of poverty but that have little or no political support at the present time (e.g., a more progressive income tax), or that are considered highly controversial (policies to strengthen families)?

Earlier scholarship offers three different explanations for why racial segregation remains high in U.S. cities: discriminatory private practices and public policies, the low incomes of black families, and the desire of some black families to self-segregate. Gregory D. Squires, Samantha Friedman, and Catherine E. Saidat (chapter 7) use the results of a 2001 survey of over nine hundred families in the Washington DC metropolitan area to obtain empirical support for the first hypothesis mentioned above. Black respondents were more likely to experience discrimination either in locating their home or in arranging financing than their white counterparts. However, it should be noted that only one in ten black families experienced discrimination either in the housing search or in arranging financing, so overt discrimination was by no means a common occurrence.

Whereas this chapter provides a sociological perspective on segregation, the next one offers an anthropological one. Using the United States as a test case, N. Ariel Espino argues that members of higher status, more powerful groups attempt to strengthen their self-identity by distinguishing themselves from members of the lower classes. Until the nineteenth century, members of various social groups lived and worked in close proximity. Types of clothing and other consumer goods allowed members of different classes to identify each other. But improvements in transportation starting in the mid-nineteenth century allowed well-to-do families to suburbanize and, therefore, physically separate themselves from the working classes. The resulting suburban landscape was, and continues "as a patchwork of subdivisions, each of which is targeted to a narrow range of house prices (and, therefore, income groups)" (p. 150). Middle-class families take advantage of planning regulations to maintain the class character of their neighborhoods, to preserve the investment potential of their single-family homes and to keep crime at bay. Espino emphasizes that this patchwork of spatial segregation remains problematic, because it denies lower-income people access to high-quality public services.

He recommends regional land use planning to address existing exclusionary zoning policies. Since single-family home ownership is in itself a fundamental cause of economic segregation, politically moderate policies may not be enough. Therefore, Espino recommends serious consideration be given to the "decommodification" of housing, that is, the elimination of housing as an investment, which could be achieved by regulating housing transactions or by taxing housing profits. Although it is highly unlikely that this strategy will ever be implemented in the United States, since home ownership is considered a basic right and shared value, continuing high levels of economic segregation may be a price Americans will have to pay for the privilege.

Robert W. Wassmer (chapter 9) argues that even if racially bigoted views and practices such as redlining and steering were eliminated, "natural market-based factors would still drive some forms of spatial segregation in metropolitan areas" (p. 159). Planners and policymakers, therefore, need to understand the economic forces that work against spatial integration. Using Charles Tiebout's theory of local expenditures as a starting point, Wassmer focuses on two arguments made by Tiebout and his followers: (1) that residential clustering reflects higher income households being able to pay more for sites with desired amenities; and (2) that an urban area with many governments is ideally suited to respond to the wide variations among householders in their preferences for public services and their ability to pay for them.

America's system of fragmented local governments comes with a high cost: concentrated poverty can serve as a breeding area for crime; high concentrations of low-income children in the public schools can promote poor educational performance; and the spatial mismatch between where poor people live (mainly in the inner city) and where jobs are increasingly located (in the suburbs) can exacerbate unemployment and poverty. Efforts to redistribute property tax funds from better off to poorer school districts are politically feasible, but they are unlikely to reduce inequalities. Wassmer, therefore, recommends providing subsidies to already high-income families to encourage them to accept low-income families as neighbors. He acknowledges that this suggestion is controversial, but given the strong forces promoting segregation, controversy may be unavoidable.

Many observers assume that by facilitating the flight of white, middle-income families from the city, urban sprawl contributes to spatial segregation and to urban distress. As a result, some smart growth organizations attempting to reduce sprawl argue that their policies will also reduce segregation. Rolf Pendall (chapter 10) seeks to improve our understanding of the sprawl-segregation link using econometric models to explain differences in the level of economic segregation across 313 metropolitan areas in the United States. Pendall's findings are exactly the opposite of what smart growth advocates would predict. In 1990, "higher density regions were significantly more segregated by income than lower-density regions; very low-income households were more unevenly distributed and more isolated from other households in metropolitan areas whose density levels were high than in areas where density was low" (p. 189). His explanation for this seemingly surprising finding is quite plausible: "Competition over urban land is more intense when density is higher; in such competitions, people with lower incomes lose, and end up living in a more limited set of less desirable neighborhoods as higher-income people outbid them in the housing market" (pp. 189–190).

Policies to increase overall levels of density will need to be combined with ones at the neighborhood level aimed at achieving mixed uses, compact development patterns, and more choice of housing types. Montgomery

County, Maryland stands out from other American jurisdictions in being able to both protect open space and agricultural land and to promote income-mixed developments through its inclusionary housing program. Pendall reinforces a point made by Marcuse, that local policies are not enough to reduce income segregation: "Policies to produce a more even distribution of population, for example, amendments to make income taxes more progressive, would likely have a much more substantial effect on income segregation than any policy on land development" (p. 198).

To many critics, Los Angeles is the embodiment of urban sprawl with all of its concomitant problems. Up to now, however, there has been little investigation into just how sprawl contributes to spatial segregation, and in turn, to urban inequities. Tridib Banerjee and Niraj Verma (chapter 11) indicate that there is conclusive evidence that sprawl at least promotes environmental injustices. "As Whites and upper-class nonwhites relocate to the periphery, lower-income nonwhite racial groups remain ensconced in the central area and are subjected to greater concentrations of air pollution, toxic hot spots, and other related health hazards" (p. 203). The authors use cluster analysis to determine whether the large number of municipalities in Los Angeles County function as "Tieboutian clubs," that is, whether a small number of groups can be identified based on shared physical characteristics. Applying cluster analysis to a data set, consisting of the land use configurations of various municipalities as well as other variables, Banerjee and Verma identify six clusters: (1) edge cities whose boundaries are defined by deserts, mountains, or the Pacific coast; (2) industrial cities dominated by manufacturing land uses; (3) suburban cities where single-family homes predominate; (4) brownfield cities that contain a mix of extraction sites (oil wells, quarries) and industry; (5) apartment cities dominated by medium- to high-density metropolitan areas; and (6) generic cities.

As an exploratory application of cluster analysis this one, however, suffers from a number of limitations. First, the catchall generic category contains the bulk of both the area and the population of the county. Second, by including the entire city of Los Angeles in the analysis, the authors miss the high level of diversity within Los Angeles with respect to physical layout and also with respect to levels of racial, ethnic, and income segregation. This chapter, nevertheless, could pave the way for future studies that use communities rather than entire municipalities as the unit of analysis.

The final two case studies focus on residential segregation in South Africa. In the past, racist public policies located public housing in minority areas and contributed to the development and maintenance of the ghetto. South Africa's experience suggests that merely replacing white politicians with black ones will not solve the ghetto problem. Since the end of apartheid, black politicians have moved slowly to promote integrative policies. Marie Huchzermeyer (chapter 12) shows how the country's project-linked housing subsidy system first developed under the apartheid regime in 1990, but continued under black governments, has resulted in new, segregated, and poorly located developments. Under this system, developers receive capital subsidies on a project-by-project basis; the completed serviced sites are then transferred to households. In some cases, informal settlements are replaced on the spot by fully standardized and individualized developments, but more typically residents of informal settlements are relocated to a new site. The strategy has achieved impressive numbers in terms of delivery of home ownership. But the residents of the new settlements face long and costly commutes to jobs in city centers or to newer suburban growth nodes. In addition, individual home ownership creates new forms of vulnerability. Many fragile households (especially ones with members suffering from AIDS) are forced to convert their housing asset into cash to pay for drugs. Huchzermeyer recommends a shift in government intervention from the township model (monotonous, standardized dormitory areas on the segregated urban periphery) to mixed-income and mixed-tenure developments in better locations.

In South Africa, as in the United States, politicians face a difficult dilemma. On the one hand they can emphasize high rates of production of affordable housing units, but such a supply-oriented strategy is inherently incapable of eliminating existing ghettos; in fact, such a strategy creates new ghettos. On the other hand, if they adopt an explicit income desegregation strategy, middle-class families would oppose proposals for new developments. The resulting controversy will undoubtedly slow down housing production.

Alan Mabin (chapter 13) highlights the above dilemma by discussing the difficulty of achieving stable racially and income-integrated communities in Johannesburg. Many reformers believed that with the end of apartheid segregation would be reduced, if not completely eliminated, but, in fact, segregation persists in new forms, aided and abetted by suburbanization. The concentration of new activity in the suburbs of larger cities minimizes prospects for close-in housing-jobs linkages; the long commutes, typical of American cities, are being replicated. Although rural townships and suburbs have been brought together under the same political jurisdictions (eliminating the fragmentation found in American metropolitan areas), newer governmental units have not been able to socially integrate new developments. As a result *favela*-like areas exist in close proximity to "American-type" suburbs.

Mabin argues that the values and preferences of suburbanites serve as obstacles to social integration and broader social justice goals. First, although considerable progress has been made in racially integrating formerly Whites-only public schools, this integration necessarily involves white and black children from middle-class homes (see Swarms 2002). The result is that township schools remain all black. Second, the increased ability of upwardly mobile Blacks to move to "the secured compound, the totally automobile-reliant townhouse, or the cluster house complexes of the newest suburbs" (p. 230) has inadvertently promoted segregation. As black-on-black discrimination takes hold, few middle-class Blacks are interested in living in older, gentrified areas close to the city center where they would mix with Whites in public places, and perhaps begin to develop friendships that cross racial lines. Third, members of the new black political elite "are currently not exactly campaigning for an end to social segregation to match their enthusiasm for an end to political separation and oppression" (p. 229). Members of the rising black middle-class accept economic segregation (sometimes living in newly created gated townhouse developments), because it leads to a sense of comfort and a high degree of residential quality. Thus, as in the United States, the quest for neighborhood homogeneity vis à vis values, "leads away from, rather than towards, a wider social justice" (p. 229).

The case studies from the global South as well as those from the global North combine to highlight the difficulties in achieving significant declines in income and racial segregation in both the ghetto and the enclave. To achieve lasting results, both spatially and aspatially, will require policies to decrease inequalities, racial and economic. However, even if such pro-equity policies are implemented, the desire to self-segregate—whether on economic or ethnic grounds—will continue to produce meaningful levels of segregation.

Part I

Defining Segregation and Its Consequences

Chapter 1

ENCLAVES YES, GHETTOS NO

Segregation and the State

Peter Marcuse

Spatial clustering seems to be an inevitable accompaniment of urban life. Spatial processes have resulted in many forms of clustering (ghettos, gated communities, ethnic enclaves, religious communities, developments for the elderly), but the dividing line between those clusters that are of public concern and those of no public policy interest is not always clear. There are two purposes to this chapter. One is to provide a framework in which socially acceptable clustering may be differentiated from clustering that is undesirable. I suggest that segregation, that is, clustering that is involuntary, or better yet, hierarchical (i.e., derived from a ranking system that reflects superiority based on wealth, status, or power), is generally objectionable and should be countered by public policy measures. Clustering that is voluntary, that is, nonhierarchical, clustering, is not in general objectionable.

The second purpose is to illuminate the role that governments play in making various forms of segregation feasible. The forces that produce segregation or undesirable clustering may indeed be strong and are historically dominant. But these forces depend on the state for the implementation of segregation, and it is the state that has the power to end segregation.

The argument is developed with four steps beginning with formal definitions of clustering and segregation, in order to be clear about the terminology used. Second, there is an examination of the origins of clustering, attempting at the same time to be explicit about the existing public policy position and the values that underlie that position. Third, it traces the role of the state in implementing segregation throughout history focusing specifically on the United States. Finally, there is a discussion of how and with what tools governments could end segregation.

What Is Segregation? Formal Definitions

It is very important to be clear about terms, not just for analytic purposes, but to be lucid about desired policy outcomes. In particular, we sometimes hear phrases such as "self-segregation," or "voluntary ghettos," or "upper-class ghettos" (Musterd and Ostendorf 1998). Such formulations are mischievous; analytically they are oxymoronic, and policy-wise, insidious. Clarifying these terms means using "segregation" and "ghetto" for patterns that are undesirable and treating other forms of clustering in a more nuanced fashion.

Operationally, I will use the following definitions. In process terms:

Clustering is the concentration of a population group in space. Clustering is the generic term for the formation of any area of spatial concentration.

Segregation is the process by which a population group, treated as inferior (generally because of race), is forced, that is, involuntarily, to cluster in a defined spatial area, that is, in a ghetto. Segregation is the process of formation and maintenance of a *ghetto*.

Racial segregation is segregation based on race. Most ghettos in the United States are *racial ghettos*.

Market segregation is the parallel process, operating through the real estate market, thereby, segregating those of lower income into *class ghettos*.

Exclusion can be either spatial or socioeconomic. Spatial exclusion is *segregation*. Socioeconomic exclusion accompanying segregation is the process of formation of an *excluded ghetto*.

Quartering is the division of urban space into quarters by the operation of the private market in real estate and housing, based on the income or wealth of households. Quartering is the process of formation of class clusters, and may bring about or reinforce *segregation*.

Congregating is the voluntary coming together of a population group for purposes of self-protection and advancement of its own interests, other than through domination or exclusion. Congregating is the process of formation of an *enclave*.

Withdrawal is the voluntary and deliberate separation of a socially and economically dominant population group. Withdrawal reinforces segregation. Withdrawal is the process that leads to the formation of an *exclusionary enclave*.

Walling out is the extreme physical form of withdrawal. Walling out may be involved in the formation of an *exclusionary enclave,* and is also involved in the formation of a *citadel*.

Fortification is the voluntary coming together of a population group for purposes of protecting, strengthening, and symbolizing dominance. Fortification is the process of forming a *citadel*.

Confinement is the deliberate, intentional separating out of a socially and economically subordinate group and its restriction to a specific location. Confinement is the extreme social, economic, and/or legal form of *segregation,* and may be involved in the formation of a ghetto.

Walling in is the extreme physical form of confinement and may be involved in the formation of a *ghetto*.

Desegregation is the elimination of barriers to free mobility for residents of a *ghetto*.

Integration is the intermixing of population groups with ongoing, positive and nonhierarchical relationships among them.

In spatial terms:

A *cluster* is an area of spatial concentration of a population group. A cluster is the generic term for any concentration of a particular group, however defined, in space, at a scale larger than a building.

A *quarter* is an area of spatial concentration by income or wealth, created by the operation of the private market in real estate and housing, based on the income or wealth of households.

A *ghetto* is an area of spatial concentration used by forces within the dominant society to separate and to limit a particular population group, defined as racial or ethnic or foreign and held to be, and treated as, inferior by the dominant society (Marcuse 1997a).

An *enclave* is an area of spatial concentration in which members of a particular population group, self-defined by ethnicity or religion or otherwise, congregate as a means of protecting and enhancing their economic, social, political, and/or cultural development.

An *exclusionary enclave* is one whose members occupy positions of superior power—wealth, or ethnic, racial, or social status and excludes others from unauthorized entry.

A *citadel* is an area of spatial concentration in which members of a particular population group, defined by its position of superior power, wealth, or status in relation to its neighbors, cluster as a means of protecting, displaying, and enhancing that position.

Empirically, we often find that many spatial patterns share characteristics of more than one of these spatial definitions. The terms defined above should be taken as ideal types. Most enclaves, for instance, have an element that is involuntary, and residence in ghettos is often voluntary for some (see Briggs, chapter 5).

One basis for antisegregation policy is to assume that segregation and ghettos are bad, and that the *involuntary* allocation of space to any group is undesirable in a democratic society, whether this occurs through public or social action (i.e., restrictive zoning, discrimination in selling or renting), or through the market (i.e., differences in income or wealth resulting from discrimination). Antisegregation policy may also be based on the desirability of mixing population groups to achieve integration, as opposed to eliminating segregation. Public policies that promote integration raise complicated issues, issues not involved in efforts simply to end segregation. These issues involve questions of constitutionality, for example, the use of benign quotas (Marcuse 1962) and empirical disputes about the extent to which simple mixing leads to substantive integration (Marcuse and van Kempen 2002). Those issues will not be pursued here; it is enough to ground the critique of segregation and ghettos on the first basis outlined above.

The Origins of Clustering and Segregation

If we look at the broad patterns of spatial clustering in cities historically (Marcuse and van Kempen 2002), we may discern a general pattern that will help us differentiate acceptable from unacceptable forms of segregation.

Cities may be, and have been, divided along a number of lines forming a variety of patterns of clustering. Many, but not all, of those lines reflect social divisions brought about by conscious acts of those clustered or clustering and those who hold power over or among them. Lines of division between those two groups may be based on nationality, class, income, wealth, occupation, religion, race, color, ethnicity, language, age, household composition, personal cultural preference, or life style; other categories can be defined as well. The range of possible categories could theoretically be infinite. For purposes of policy-relevant analysis, the important lines of division are understandable based on three distinguishable groups/ideal types (1) culture (2) functional economic role, and (3) position in the hierarchy of power.

Cultural divisions are, in general, easily discernible: differences in language, in costume, or in architectural style, for instance. Obviously, they may result in divisions by ethnicity, by country or nationality, tribe of origin or parentage or descent, by religion or belief, or by life-style. (I avoid using the term, race, because it conflates cultural differences, falsely defined, with differences of status; see below.) While some of these cultural divisions may appropriately be called "cultural" in the strictest sense, others may be the products of manipulation, idiosyncratic choice, or some combination of these. The key element that differentiates these divisions is culture based on function or status neither on differences in their relationship to economic production nor on relationships of power. One ethnic or religious group may in fact play a different economic role and be socially subordinated to another group, but there are elements of cultural differences that are independent of these economic and social differences; they may reflect them, but are not identical to them. Worship, music, parenting, language, history, holidays, clothing, family relations, are neither dependent on their economic productivity for their hold on people, nor do they require a relationship of superiority or inferiority to outsiders for their strength, although such feelings may easily be incorporated within them. Even the life-style differences that the real estate market might take into account can result in the "spatial segregation of people by household type, family status, and age, so that "the different [age] cohorts take up separate quarters" (Kostoff 1992, 121).

Divisions based on functional economic roles are the result of either physical or organizational economic logic: the divisions between farms and factories and residential areas, for instance. Historically, they included separate locations for different guilds, and later, the separation of service from manufacturing or wholesaling from retailing. The external-ities of certain industries or occupations may require that those involved in them live near each other, or cluster along transportation routes mak-ing them readily accessible to each other. Residentially, the need of workers in particular industries to be located close to their places of em-ployment may create residential divisions, extreme examples of which are company-sponsored housing developments and areas for industrial defense workers. Such functional divisions are essentially independent of cultural differences and do not (at least essentially when status differen-tiations may arise out of functional differences) denote relations of superiority or inferiority to other functions, but simply differences.

Zoning is the accepted legal embodiment of functional divisions. That zoning should be based on the function to which land is allocated, de-fined in terms of economic use (residential as opposed to industrial, light industrial as opposed to retailing, wholesaling as distinguished from of-fice use), is not as self-evident as it might seem. Performance zoning, for instance, attempts to define permitted uses of land, not by their eco-nomic use, but by their environmental impact: traffic generated, shad-ows cast, air circulation impeded, green space occupied, and so forth. And, while "use" may separate manufacturing from retail from residen-tial, it has never been quite clear why residential use for one family should be different from the use by two or three families. Nevertheless, separation by function is generally accepted today as an appropriate di-vision within a city.

Differences in hierarchical status that reflect and reinforce relation-ships of power, of domination, exploitation, state service, are exempli-fied by the imperial enclave in a colonial town or in the black townships of South Africa, to give two extreme examples. But gated communities and security-guarded luxury residences near central business districts reflect and support relationships of power just as much as do working-class quarters or "slums." Class is a widely relevant line of differentia-tion that involves status in the sense used here. Income is often a good surrogate for status, but is not identical with it. The same is true for oc-cupation, and even the cluster of indicators generally known as socio-economic status (SES), are only indicators of an underlying relation-ship, and not descriptive of the relationship itself. Power can exist alongside a multitude of dimensions: military power, political power, economic power, social power, and legal power, of which slavery is the extreme case.

These three divisions, along cultural, functional, and hierarchical lines, overlap and contradict each other; their intertwining is one of the fascinations of the history of cities. *Cultural divisions* may be used to reinforce differences of status to the point that status and culture are at first glance identical; this is notoriously the case with black/white, imperial/indigenous, Jewish/Arab differences, which frequently reinforce differences of status to the point that the two are at first glance identical; but those divisions of status and culture often interfere with the effective lines of *functional division:* groups differentiated by culture and status tied together by economic links need to work and be near each other for efficient production. If Blacks and Whites work together at the same place, it is usually inefficient for them to have widely dispersed and segregated neighborhoods. Relations between *status* and *function* often conflict in their impact on space: employers like to have their employees live close to their work, but they do not want their workers to live close to them. Cultural affinities may contradict status differences: within each group linked by culture, there can be major differences of class as well as of economic function. Interdependence and mutual hostility often go hand in hand. *Function, status,* and *culture* were largely merged in the imperial enclaves of colonial territories in the past, and may be merging once again in today's economies; as Malcolm Cross and Roger Waldinger (1992, 173) point out, "the ethnic division of labor is, in this sense, the central division of labor in the postindustrial city." Since functions are not neutral in the hierarchy of status, the three divisions come together. The permutations are manifold.

As a further complicating factor: the role of space is not constant. Space is socially created; its role changes with shifting social and economic constellations; with different cultural patterns; different economic uses; and the influence of differences in status and power (Lefebvre 1992). Of course, topography and geographical considerations influence the location of spatial divisions and will often correlate with social divisions, for example, upper classes will live in locations with higher environmental amenities. But even such correlations are fluid and subject to social and economic change. Thus, waterfront locations may be put to industrial use and occupied by longshoremen in one society or claimed for luxury housing and recreational use in another. Viewed historically, different patterns of division are differentially reflected, fortified, or contradicted by space; sometimes the powerful separate themselves from the masses in fortresses on hilltops, remove themselves to remote estates or build secure high-rises in central business districts. In 1925, Robert Park overstated this point when he argued that social relations are often inherently linked with spatial relations. Frequently, yes, but inevitably, no. Though certainly not directly, the slave-master relationship can coexist with slaves living next door to masters, as well as if they lived in separate districts of the city. The direction of influence is reciprocal: social relations determine spatial relations, but these in turn generally, but not always reinforce social relations. Where the underlying social relations are in flux or where the allocation and use of space does not closely reflect those relations, there is likely to be conflict in disputes over space and over the underlying relationships themselves. The building of walls to create or enforce spatial divisions may be as much a reflection of the instability of underlying relationships as the strength of the divisions within them (Marcuse 1997b).

Granting these complications, I would suggest clustering that reinforces hierarchical relationships of power is unacceptable from a public policy point of view, and the appropriate targets of state prohibition; cultural or social clustering that does not reinforce such relationships of power is not.

This formulation does not suggest that cultural or functional divisions, even if they are completely voluntary, are necessarily desirable. Measures to lessen their impact, for example, through multicultural programs may indeed be desirable from a public policy point of view to promote understanding, to facilitate economic integration, to increase opportunities, and to enrich culture. But there is, to a lawyer's mind, a sharp difference between penalizing and prohibiting hierarchical discrimination on one side, and promoting various forms of functional economic and social/cultural integration on the other. Measures to reduce segregation should stand on quite a different public policy footing from measures to promote intercultural understanding: programs prohibiting racial discrimination in housing or prohibiting exclusionary zoning have a different standing from programs that provide education about different ethnic groups holidays, music, or cooking.

The State's Role in Imposing Segregation

While divisions on the basis of function and culture are generally voluntary, divisions by status are not, especially for those at the bottom end of the hierarchical order. No group desires low status; it is imposed on them. While those of higher status maintain their separation voluntarily, they need the means to impose low status on others against their wills. Thus, divisions by status require, implicitly or explicitly, the use of force, and in a civilized society such force is (at least in theory) a monopoly of the state. Also, government action may or may not be involved in regulating cultural divisions, and often is involved in shaping functional divisions, but in those cases the state is acting in a purely regulatory role with the consent and for the benefit of all participants. The source of the state's ability to impose upon its residents status divisions with regard to space may have its source in the simple control of physical force, as was true in many early societies when monarchs partitioned space for their own benefit. Or governments may be responding to the desires of the holders of economic or political power, desires that are likewise reflected in parallel market patterns; the powerful benefit both from the state's actions and from private investors' actions in the marketplace outside the direct state apparatus. The state's role in establishing these involuntary lines of division reflecting status/power is, whether it reflects and reinforces market patterns, or establishes those patterns itself, central to the active process I call "partitioning." We are primarily concerned with the role of the state's action in partitioning along lines of power and status, for it is such action that we consider the most threatening to the prospects of a democratic and just city. And such state action may be particularly damaging when it is used and reinforced by divisions of culture and/or function.

Examples from the U.S. experience are many. Historically the black ghetto was created and imposed upon Blacks from the outside, and the instrument of that imposition was the state. The usefulness of division between Whites and Blacks for some employers, as well as the economic advantage of some Whites, continued the racist patterns of behavior by Whites engendered by decades of slavery. The disadvantages suffered by the victims of those decades were all causative elements in the creation of the black ghetto. But indispensable to the ghetto's creation was the ability of those benefiting from segregation to use the instrumentalities of government to impose and enforce patterns of separation on Blacks.

Only a brief account is necessary to show how the government of the United States fostered ghettoization:

- Until the early twentieth century, in city after city, local governments enacted zoning ordinances that explicitly provided that certain areas were to be occupied exclusively by Whites. While these zoning practices used race as a formal criterion, they were finally ruled unconstitutional in *Buchanan v. Warley,* 245 U.S. 60 (1917);
- Nevertheless, "the construction of the ghetto continued apace despite Buchanan, and levels of black-white segregation in U.S. cities rose steadily" (Massey and Denton 1993, 188);
- Zoning devices have long been used to indirectly segregate Blacks from white areas. Some devices include large-lot zoning, prohibiting multifamily construction or limiting areas available for it, and retaining discretionary powers in a local zoning board to permit or reject applications for construction (Abrams 1955);
- Federal courts provided judicial enforcement for restrictive covenants, for many years a major device that excluded Blacks from large parts of cities and confined them to areas with an already high percentage of black residents. Although this practice violated the Civil Rights Act of 1866 (Massey and Denton 1993, 188), it was not until 1948 that it was finally declared unconstitutional by the United States Supreme Court in *Shelley v. Kramer,* 334 U.S. 1 (1948);
- City planning also contributed significantly to limiting the opportunities for the location of residences for Blacks. Designs for "neighborhood unit" developments, the location of boulevards and major roadways, the location and timing of infrastructure provision, often conformed to essentially racist patterns (Thomas and Ritzdorf 1997). For example, Robert Moses' biases, while Construction Coordinator for the City of New York (and public agencies), helped to preserve and maintain existing segregated racial patterns and uses, and in fact, to accentuate them through disproportionate displacement of Blacks through public works (Caro 1974);
- Redlining is the denial of mortgage financing to owners of property in certain designated areas termed "redlined," selected primarily because of the race of the residents. The bulk of private single-family

housing built in the last fifty years has been built with federal mortgage assistance, largely in the form of insurance through the Federal
Housing Administration (FHA). FHA's appraisal of the value of a
home was essential in getting that assistance. The FHA Manual for
Underwriters stated: "important among adverse influences . . . are
. . . infiltration of inharmonious racial or nationality groups. . . ." It
further favored ". . . recorded deed restrictions . . . include the following: . . . prohibition of the occupancy of properties except by the
race for which they are intended" (Citizens' Commission on Civil
Rights 1983; Jackson 1985). This was the classic form of redlining;

- The federal public housing program, adopted in the United States
  Housing Act of 1937, provided for the construction of social housing
  in what is still the major program for government housing construction in the nation. At the outset, and until the 1950s, such housing
  was uniformly constructed on a segregated basis: separate, but rarely
  equal. Since then, housing authorities have frequently built in ghetto
  areas because of strident opposition from white neighborhoods to
  having it built elsewhere. Public housing projects are today often in
  the heart of the black ghetto in major cities (Bauman 1987; Hirsch
  1983; Marcuse 1986);

- The urban renewal program, adopted under Title I of the Housing
  Act of 1949, was the basis for slum clearance and redevelopment in
  the United States, and quickly became known as a "Negro removal"
  program. Although coupled in the same piece of legislation with public housing, urban renewal destroyed more housing than it created in
  its early years. With a widely disparate impact on black housing,
  black residents were often forced from integrated areas into ones
  having an already high concentration of black residents;

- The federal highway construction program, massively subsidized
  with federal funds after 1954, was a sine qua non for the development of the sprawling white suburbs of the postwar years (Gelfand
  1975; Jackson 1985). A significant motivation for Whites to move
  from inner-city areas to the suburbs was to escape the growing black
  population of the inner cities. Whites with cars used the highways to
  separate themselves from inner-city blacks (powell 1999). The movement of employers and jobs to the suburbs only served to aggravate
  the segregation of Blacks.

The preceding examples highlight explicit, affirmative, governmental actions that have fostered segregation. But one could make an argument that goes even further in explaining the state's role, an argument that would apply to most of the countries of the world today. Simply put, no residential pattern, whether fostering or counteracting residential segregation, could exist without fundamental state action. The entire legal structure that makes such development possible is based on laws promulgated and enforced by the state: laws of property ownership, for the formulation and enforcement of financial instruments, evictions, and actions for possession, of prohibitions against trespass, all having state-established courts, police, sheriffs, and law enforcement agencies to back them up. Then there is the laying out of roads, provisions of infrastructure, the granting or withholding of development permissions, levying of taxes, and the provision of municipal services necessary for any type of urban life, which are functions of the state. No private market could function if the state did not enforce the provisions of contracts and afford remedies for their breach. In general, the definitions of those individual rights that will and will not be protected by the state, often contained in constitutional provisions, are functions of the state. Clearly, it is within the state's power to permit or prohibit segregation. If segregation then takes place in any society, it is with the tacit, if not the explicit, sanction of the state.

The State's Policy Responses to Segregation

Having defined types of clustering, which should be the target of public policy, that is, clustering that segregates, what kinds of state action might be considered to effectuate a policy against it? Most of the suggestions advanced fit comfortably within liberal philosophies, although they are generally contrary to the stance of those on the ideological right. Some of the suggestions, particularly for national remedies aimed at reducing inequality, are at the more radical left end of the spectrum. But liberal and conservative measures only contradict each other if they are put forward as substitutes for each other, which is not the view taken here. In practice, I see them as consistent, and as many of each as are feasible should be implemented. But issues of political implementation are not considered here (Dreier, Mollenkopf, and Swanstrom 2001; Sclar 2002), although they are certainly complex. The role of social science, at least in the first place, is analysis and the development of policy recommendations leading from that analysis. Some measures at the local level could have a real impact in combating segregation, since in most countries land use is most directly a matter of local jurisdiction. Some of these measures might include:

- Expanded provision for public housing in different urban areas (not only in areas that already have substantial subsidized rented dwellings), planned as part of an overall program for the mainstream of housing provision (Marcuse 1998). In areas still to be developed, social housing should be included (e.g., units built and managed by community development corporations). In the Netherlands, for instance, 30 percent of new dwellings are on large building sites adjacent to existing cities, 30 percent of new dwellings are provided as affordable units that are managed by housing associations;
- Use of tax incentives to promote local economic development and job creation/ expansion within a broad integrative framework. These tax incentives would open up possibilities for unemployed people to get jobs and higher incomes, and to move to better dwellings away from distressed areas. However, some of those with better jobs may decide to remain in these distressed areas and to participate in efforts aimed at area regeneration;
- Progressive real estate taxes that would make local real-property-based taxes a mechanism for redistributing some of the benefits of land appreciation to the entire community. Porto Alegre, Brazil, for instance, has successfully begun such a practice;
- Capital gains and antispeculation taxes, as have been adopted in some places in the United States. These measures impose a high tax on the profits that result from the purchase and sale of property within a short time and without significant improvement to the property. Such taxes, as have been adopted in Vermont, for example, tend to discourage speculation and reduce displacement due to higher rents in these "gentrifying" areas;
- Intermunicipal agreements with respect to housing low-income households. Such agreements might be especially useful between cities and suburbs. Often lower-income households are located in central cities, while suburban environments house the middle-income

and higher-income households. A possible desegregation plan might include the building of low-rent dwellings in suburban areas and offering high-income suburban households the opportunity to move back to central city areas (see Wassmer, chapter 9). The Mt. Laurel decisions of the New Jersey Supreme Court move in this direction;

- Infrastructure and land use policies that promote physical development desired for its contribution to equity and racial/income integration. Policies that support citadel-like construction of insulated enclaves of the rich and powerful should be discouraged. Provision of mass transportation with stations and stops in different kinds of areas may lead to the increase of economic activities in neighborhoods that did not have good connections before. Inclusionary zoning (as in New York City) that requires a percentage of affordable housing to be included in any newly constructed development, should be adopted. The provision of cheap mass transit (as has been proposed for Los Angeles) could help the poor get jobs, and could in turn, help mitigate segregation;

- Regional planning and land use controls geared to equalizing benefits and burdens of development, so that suburbs are not permitted to escape the costs of urbanization while reaping all of their benefits. Proposals and policies discussed in Minnesota and by the Regional Plan Association in New York are examples of regional planning and land use controls;

- Community information about and participation in public decisions about land use, with broad decentralized control over neighborhood developments, so that local communities can be enabled to resist segregating tendencies, whether gentrification or the dumping of undesired pollutants or other undesired facilities in already neglected ghetto or ghetto-like areas. New York City's Fair Share regulations are intended to be a step in this direction;

- Expansive provision of public space and opportunity for public communication, so that the movement in the direction of private control, with its market-based tendencies to segregate, can be counteracted, and the general sense of a diverse community be reinforced. Planning for Lower Manhattan in New York City is moving in this direction;

- Strong antidiscrimination action, still inadequately used in the United States (see Squires, chapter 7);

- Anti-redlining legislation, and the pro-greenlining provisions that are often part of anti-redlining efforts. Thus, zoning and land use controls can be used to prohibit discrimination in lending and to steer new construction and commercial development to desired areas and limit it in undesired areas;
- Location of public facilities and services at borders between segregated areas (e.g., between predominantly black and predominantly white ones) to help bring residents closer together;
- Control of pollution to achieve environmental justice.

At the national level, the following possibilities might be considered:

- Strengthening national democratic control of the provision of services and goods to meet basic needs in ways that couple the contributions of the traditional welfare state with the efficiencies of the marketplace; for instance, large-scale national public subsidies for housing, with either direct provision by government or by competitive private builders. Though the welfare state has been an almost unquestioned part of the postwar political compromise in every western European country, it is much on the defensive today and is being limited more and more around the world. In some countries, such as the United States, the welfare state was never fully accepted. The result is increased polarization by income and thus, increased segregation;
- Redistribution of nationally generated and collected resources among localities in order to equalize resources and prevent divisions resulting from real or perceived local fiscal self-interest;
- The banning of competition among cities including giving tax advantages, under-cost sales of land, or provision of infrastructure where such competition results in increasing inequalities both among and within cities, as it almost always does. The European Union has provisions adopting such a concept as to competition among countries.

The range of policies that might reduce segregation should in fact include a wide variety of measures, in addition to those listed above that would reduce that inequality, which is the underlying cause of partitioning. In the long run, measures such as steeply progressive income taxes, protection of the rights of women, limitations on the concentration of ownership and control of economic activity, and environmental protection measures that take into account the just distribution of burdens and benefits, would all reduce segregation. To the extent that global/international pressures lead to or accentuate segregation, international agreements establishing standards and limits on private actions from outside national borders should also be considered (Hirst and Thompson 1996).

Chapter 2

THE GHETTO AND THE ETHNIC ENCLAVE

Ceri Peach

Introduction

This chapter is a piece of intellectual archaeology, but it has a potent message for our current understanding of segregation. The key point is that there is a major difference between the ghetto and the ethnic enclave. American sociology for a long time failed to make this distinction and worse still, linked the ghetto, enclave, and suburb as three spatial stages in the inevitable process of ethnic assimilation. The enclave was a stage in the process, but the ghetto was not. The ghetto was an end in itself. The problem of intellectual archaeology is to separate theory and methodology, on the one hand, from models and application, on the other. The theory and methodology developed in the literature are correct; the model of application has been far too restrictive and misrepresents the ghetto.

The central theory in the study of the spatial patterns of ethnic residential segregation is that there is a direct relationship between the social process of assimilation and the spatial pattern of dispersal (Duncan and Lieberson 1959; Massey 1984; Park 1926; Peach 1975). This view is correct. Assimilation leads to the dissolution of socioeconomic and spatial markers of identity over time. The social melting pot also melts the spatial enclave. Assimilation, however, is not the only model for ethnic accommodation. Pluralism, also referred to as multiculturalism, is a different form of accommodation. Social assimilation leads to the melting pot and dissolution; pluralism leads to economic integration but social encapsulation and the mosaic.

It is true that the American belief in assimilation and the melting pot has waned since the 1960s (Glazer 1993, 122; Glazer and Moynihan 1970; Kantrowitz 1969; Marcuse and van Kempen 2000; Ong and Nonini 1997), but in the influential reassessment of the phenomenon, Richard D. Alba and Victor Nee (1999) conclude that it is still taking place in America, albeit unevenly. Moreover there remains a strong lobby in the United States extolling the virtues of assimilation and criticizing multiculturalism for nourishing prejudice and stirring up antagonism (Miller 1998). Since 9/11 this view has strengthened.

Taking the central theory first, in 1925 Robert Ezra Park argued: It is because social relations are so frequently and so inevitably correlated with spatial relations; because physical distances, so frequently are, or seem to be, the indexes of social distances, that statistics have any meaning whatsoever for sociology (18). From this observation developed one of the most fruitful theories of the Chicago School of the 1920s and 1930s and one of the few examples of cumulative social science. The theory equated the statistical levels of residential segregation of minority ethnic populations to their levels of assimilation to the wider society. High levels of segregation were equated with non-assimilation; low levels with high levels of assimilation.

The key process involved was social interaction. Cultural behavior was modified according to whether one interacted more with one's own ethnic group or with the charter (i.e., the indigenous) population. This interaction was controlled by proximity to and intermingling with the respective groups. Residential isolation was hypothesized to minimize social interaction with outsiders while promoting social interaction within the group. Within-group interaction was hypothesized to reinforce the group's identity, language maintenance, in-marriage, and the wearing of traditional dress.

Interpretation and Operationalization

Although the general proposition of the relationship between residential segregation and social assimilation was clear, there were problems of operationalization. Assimilation was difficult to define. Books were written on the topic (for example, Gordon 1964). Stanley Lieberson (1963, 10) provides us with a helpful definition: an assimilated population is defined as a group of persons with similar foreign origins, knowledge of which in no way gives a better prediction or estimate of their relevant social characteristics than does knowledge of the behavior of the total population of the community or nation involved.

Operationalization means taking multidimensional comparisons of the minority population in relation to the target of the core society. Milton M. Gordon (1964, 81) regards structural assimilation or the large-scale entry into the prime group (e.g., into close friendship circles) of the core society, as the key step. Thereafter, intermarriage and other identifiable changes were seen by Gordon to follow inevitably. Thus, operationally, assimilation was treated as a multidimensional phenomenon and its progress was measured by examining the longitudinal change of its many variables (Gordon 1964). Acquisition of the English language, socioeconomic status, out-marriage, and citizenship were some of the variables examined.

Segregation proved problematic to operationalize, largely because of the different ways in which it was conceptualized (Peach 1981). Residential segregation is also a multidimensional phenomenon. A large number of different techniques, differing not only in mathematical formula, but also in the conceptualization of segregation itself have been suggested (Peach 1981). A review paper by O. D. Duncan and B. Duncan (1955) effectively concentrated most subsequent work on the Index of Dissimilarity (ID). ID measures the percentage of a population group that would have to shift its area of residence in order to replicate the distribution of the population with which it is being compared. ID is a measure of unevenness with similar characteristics and values to the economists' Gini Index. An ID of 100 indicates complete segregation; an ID of 0 indicates no segregation at all. Lieberson's P* (Lieberson 1981) is a measure of isolation that has also come into more general use since the 1980s. Unlike ID, it is an asymmetric measure. P* recognizes that the degree of exposure of a small group to a large group is different from the exposure of the large group to the small group. Unlike ID, its use has tended to be descriptive rather than analytical in correlation regressions. More recently, Douglas S. Massey and Nancy A. Denton (1993) have suggested a battery of five measures to quantify what they have termed the hyper-segregation of Blacks.

Segregation and Interaction

O. D. Duncan and Stanley Lieberson demonstrated for Chicago in the 1930s and 1950s that there was an inverse relationship between the level of segregation of foreign national groups and the percent of the group able to speak English. They also showed high degrees of out-marriage correlated with low levels of segregation (Duncan and Lieberson 1959; Lieberson 1963, 156–158). This argument indicated that it should be possible to predict the social interaction between ethnic groups on the basis of their degrees of residential mixing. The Duncan and Lieberson argument was taken further by Ceri Peach (1980a; 1980b) who demonstrated that Ruby Jo Reeves Kennedy's (1944; 1952) triple melting pot (Protestants, Catholics, and Jews) in New Haven Connecticut did not exist. The Irish, Poles, and Italians in the supposed Catholic melting pot were all highly segregated from each other. If high segregation levels suggested low social interaction, it would also suggest low, not high, marriage rates between the groups. Peach demonstrated that the claimed intermarriage rates between these groups were in fact lower than statistically expected, while Irish intermarriage with the (Protestant) British, Germans, and Scandinavians, from whom they had low levels of segregation, were higher than statistically expected. There was no Protestant melting pot, but an old European melting pot that included the Irish. There was no Catholic melting pot, but two separate, in-marrying Catholic groups of Italians and Poles. Residential mixing or integration was the clearest predictor of group intermarriage. In time, as segregation rates for all European groups with each other have fallen, there has arrived a white melting pot.

Thus, residential mixing was hypothesized as the key to social interaction. If residential mixing is limited to one's own ethnic group, then the values and taken-for-granted nature of the group's beliefs will be reinforced. If mixing takes place with outsiders, then taken-for-granted values, language, and expected marriage partner choice is likely to become modified. Residential mixing is a necessary, but not sufficient condition for social interaction. However, where residential mixing takes place, it is likely to promote social interaction. It is important to distinguish between *spatial mixing* and *spatial proximity*. Northern Irish Protestants and Northern Irish Catholics live side by side separated by "peace walls."

This is proximity not mixing. Similarly Hasidic Jews, Blacks, and West Indians live in close proximity in Crown Heights in Brooklyn, but there is a clear boundary between black and white and total social separation.

The assimilation hypothesis formed itself into what we may conceive of as a simple three-stage cycle. The first generation of immigrants clustered together in high concentrations and high segregation in the central city. There they were unassimilated, few spoke English; overwhelmingly they married their own ethnic group. The second generation moved a little away from their inner-city port of entry; they were less segregated; a higher proportion spoke English; a greater proportion married out. The third generation suburbanized, spoke English and intermarried fully. They were assimilated.

But Assimilation Is Not the Only Model

However, one should not assume that assimilation was the desired outcome for all groups. On the one hand, social assimilation is enhanced by residential dispersal, while on the other hand residential segregation has the opposite effect. Therefore, a group wishing to assimilate will tend to disperse; however, to a group, wishing to maintain its ethnic identity, clustering is an important strategy. It is also true that a group that disperses tends to assimilate whether or not the group as a whole is in favor of assimilation.

There are, thus, two basic ways in which minorities are accommodated into a wider society: assimilation and integration. *Assimilation* argues for the disappearance of difference either through conforming to a dominant structure (as in Anglo conformism) or through merging (as in the melting pot). *Integration or plurality or multiculturalism* means accommodation while maintaining a separate identity. Integration is often economic while maintaining social closure. This model also accords with the 'acculturation' stage of Milton M. Gordon's assimilation process, a stage at which the process could freeze (Gordon 1964, 77). Gordon argued that this was the position, for very different reasons, of Jews and African Americans in the United States.

The two models, assimilation and plurality, therefore, will be expected to produce different spatial outcomes. Assimilation requires spatial diffusion.

The minority and majority become socially and residentially intermixed. Multiculturalism or integration or plurality (as opposed to assimilation) posits a society in which social encapsulation and residential concentrations and separation, through higher degrees of segregation, remain.

Not All Plurality Is Voluntary

However, the ghetto model may come about from totally different causes. Low levels of segregation imply high degrees of social interaction; high levels of segregation suggest high degrees of social encapsulation. Segregation may be either voluntarily embraced or negatively enforced (Boal 1981). A hegemonic group, wishing to separate itself from its perceived inferiors, will attempt to enforce segregation upon the lower group (Lemon 1991; Massey and Denton 1993).

There are, therefore, two diametrically different reasons for ethnic segregation. Ethnic segregation may be either voluntarily adopted as a strategy for group survival or else it may be negatively imposed upon a weaker group.

While there are two different models of accommodation, key points of the interpretation of the levels of social integration represented by the degree of spatial segregation of groups from one another remain the same. Low levels of segregation imply high degrees of social interaction; high levels of segregation suggest low degree of social interaction. Thus, interpreting the probable outcomes of given levels of segregation, it is not critical to know whether those levels are the net result of positive or negative forces.

The Problem with the Chicago School

The central problem with the Chicago School was that while it correctly conceptualized the relationship between spatial pattern and social process, it failed to recognize that the unidirectional transition from the highly concentrated inner city to suburban dispersal was neither an inevitable process nor was it the only process. The Chicago School, in other words, did not distinguish between the melting pot and the mosaic. They did not distinguish between the assimilationist and the pluralistic models.

They did not distinguish between the ghetto and the enclave. The ghetto and the immigrant colony were conceptualized as interchangeable terms.

> The Chinatowns, the Little Sicilies, and the other so-called ghettos with which students of urban life are familiar are special types of a more general species of natural area, which the conditions and tendencies of city life inevitably produce.
> The keener, the more energetic and the more ambitious very soon emerge from their ghettos and immigrant colonies and move into an area of second immigrant settlement, or perhaps into a cosmopolitan area in which the members of several immigrant and racial groups live side by side. (Park 1925, 9)

Worse still, not only did the Chicago School fail to distinguish between the ghetto and the enclave, it believed that the ghetto was a stage within the melting pot model. It saw the ghetto as the first stage of three-generational progression of (1) ghetto, (2) enclave, and (3) suburb. In this fundamental misunderstanding, the Chicago School falsified the ethnic history of long settled groups, misunderstood the processes affecting blacks and mistakenly forecast their future in American cities.

For the Chicago School, the terms "ghetto" and "enclave" were not problematized. Furthermore, it was assumed that the outward movement of minority ethnic populations away from the inner city equated to dispersal. A series of researchers in the lower foothills of the Chicago School busied themselves demonstrating the unstoppable outward diffusion of minority groups from their inner city segregated ports of entry to their inevitable suburban diffusion (Cressey 1938; Ford 1950; Kiang 1968). While they demonstrated the progressive shift of the center of gravity of ethnic groups away from the CBD over time, in the case of Blacks, however, outward movement did not always equate to dispersal. The ghetto moved out with them like the tongue of a glacier.

The Flaws of the Three-Generational Model

While the basic hypothesis of the equation of high segregation with non-assimilation remains valid, interpretations of the model were flawed by the mistaken belief that the hypothesis had universal validity: that all groups would conform to this three-generational cycle. Even in the 1950s, Philip M. Hauser, head of the Chicago School, declared with confidence that Blacks would inevitably follow this model.

The Negro migrant to the city will, without question, follow the same pattern of mobility blazed by the successive waves of immigrants who settled our central cities. Just as the immigrant underwent a process of "Americanization" the inmigrant Negro is undergoing a process of "urbanization." The Negro is already rising and will continue to rise on the socialeconomic scale as measured by education, occupation, income and the amenities of urban existence. Furthermore, the Negro, in time, will diffuse through the metropolitan area and occupy outlying suburban as well as central city areas. (Hauser 1958, 65)

This view was deeply mistaken. It equated upward mobility with spatial diffusion. It regarded the process of ghetto formation and dispersal as the same as the three-generation process of other immigrant groups. It regarded time as the independent variable for ghetto dissolution. It was wrong on all counts.

In reality, the African American ghetto was different in kind from the ethnic enclave of the European as well as other ethnics. Park's casual equation of Chinatowns, Little Sicilies, and other so-called ghettos with the black ghetto was deeply flawed (Park 1926, 9). The black ghetto was dually segregated; nearly all Blacks lived in urban areas; almost the whole population in such areas was black. The enclaves, on the other hand, were dually diluted. Only a minority of ethnic groups lived in areas that were associated with them. Rarely did they form even a majority of the population of what were supposedly "their" areas. Thomas Philpott's (1978) book, *The Slum and the Ghetto,* hammered the point home (Table 2.1).

TABLE 2.1. "Ghettoization" of Ethnic Groups, Chicago, 1930

Group	Group's City Population	Group's Ghetto Population	Total Ghetto Population	Percentage of Group Ghettoized	Group's percentage Ghetto Population
Irish	169,568	4,993	14,595	2.9	33.8
German	377,975	53,821	169,649	14.2	31.7
Swedish	140,913	21,581	88,749	15.3	24.3
Russian	169,736	63,416	149,208	37.4	42.5
Czech	122,089	53,301	169,550	43.7	31.4
Italian	181,861	90,407	195,736	49.7	46.2
Polish	401,316	248,024	457,146	61.0	54.3
Negro	233,903	216,846	266,051	92.7	81.5

Source: Data from Thomas Philpott, *The Slum and the Ghetto* (New York: Oxford University Press, 1978), p. 141, table 7.

In 1930, while 93 percent of the black population lived in the black ghetto and the black population formed 82 percent of the population of the black ghetto, only 3 percent of the Irish lived in Irish areas; they formed only one third of the population of Irish areas. The two most concentrated white groups were Italians and Poles. Just under half of the Italians lived in Italian areas, and they formed just under half of the population of Italian areas. The Poles were a little more concentrated: 61 percent lived in Polish areas, and they formed just over half of the population of Polish areas.

However, even these levels of concentration were different in *kind* rather than different in *degree* from the situation of Blacks. All the European minorities lived in truly mixed areas. Hardly any of the Blacks did. Table 2.1 shows that over 92 percent of the Blacks lived in areas where over 80 percent were Black. This means, of course, that 92 percent of Blacks lived in areas containing up to 20 percent of Whites in their population, but this is not what might be termed "truly mixed" areas. While truly mixed districts like Oak Park or Rogers Park in Chicago were important, they were not typical. While white ethnic enclaves dissolved over time, black ghettos intensified and expanded territorially in a compact form. Even in 1990, the massive concentration of the African-American population into black areas of Chicago continued. Two thirds of the African-American population lived in areas that were 90 percent or more black; 82 percent were in areas that were 50 percent or more black.

If one compares the Chicago situation in 1930 and 1990 with London in 1991 (see Peach 1996, table 2.2), the difference in kind rather than degree between the situation of Blacks in the United States and Britain is vividly illustrated. The column heading "Percentage of group ghettoized" simply copies Philpott's category, but refers to the proportion of a group living in areas arbitrarily defined as those where they form 30 percent plus of an enumeration district (block).

The British experience of racial segregation has so far been very different from that of the United States. The black-Caribbean population (the British 1991 census categorization) is the nearest equivalent of the African-American population. Caribbean segregation levels are about half those of Blacks in U.S. cities. The Caribbean ID against the white population in 1991 in the seventeen cities that contained at least one thousand Caribbeans was forty-five (Peach 1996). This compares with an

TABLE 2.2. "Ghettoization" of Ethnic Groups at ED level in Greater London
30 Percent Cutoff

Group	Group's City Population	Group's Ghetto Population	Total Ghetto Population	Percentage of Group Ghettoized	Group's percentage Ghetto Population
Non-white	1346119	721873	1589476	53.6	45.4
Black Caribbean	290968	7755	22545	2.6	34.4
Black African	163635	3176	8899	2.0	35.6
Black Other	80613	—	—	—	—
Indian	347091	88887	202135	25.6	44.0
Pakistani	87816	1182	3359	1.4	35.2
Bangladeshi	85738	28280	55500	33.0	51.0
Chinese	56579	38	111	0.0	34.2
Other Asian	112807	176	572	0.2	30.8
Other	120872	209	530	0.2	39.4
Irish born	256470	1023	2574	0.4	39.8

Source: Ceri Peach, *Good Segregation, Bad Segregation, Planning Perspectives 11*
(1996) 379–398.

average of seventy-eight for Blacks in the sixteen metropolitan areas in
the United States in 1990 covered by Denton's research (Denton 1994,
58). Not only is this the case for the Caribbeans in Britain, the levels of
segregation have shown a steady decline over time. At ward level in London, which contains 60 percent of the British Caribbean population, IDs
had decreased from fifty-six in 1961 to forty-one in 1991 (Peach 1996).
The Caribbean population seems to be following a traditional melting
pot trajectory of outward movement from the inner city coupled with
high degrees of intermarriage or cohabitation with Whites (Peach 1996).
The South Asian populations (Indians, Pakistanis, Bangladeshis), on the
other hand, were following a more pluralistic path of intensification of
the existing areas of concentration. Even so, their degree of concentration
in London does not approach ghetto levels.

The American literature, by failing to distinguish between the ghetto
and the ethnic enclave, linked the two distinct phenomena together as the
first two stages of the three-generational model: ghetto, enclave, suburb.
From here it was an easy step to envision groups occupying these three
positions as occupying places on an escalator. Those at the bottom of the

staircase, in the ghetto, were new arrivals; those at the top, in the suburbs had been on the staircase longest and had reached their destination. Those who were half way up had previously been at the bottom and were now on their way to the top.

From this conceptualization, it became easy to see time/space substitutions in the three-generational model. If, for the sake of argument, the Irish were suburbanized, the Poles were still in an enclave, and the Blacks in the ghetto, then it became possible to argue that a generation previously, the Irish were in the enclave and two generations ago, they were in the ghetto. The Blacks and the Poles were envisioned as representing stages one and two of the Irish past. In the same way, the contemporarily suburbanized Irish, predicted the Polish future in the next generation, and the African American future in two generations. This, after all, was what Hauser (1958) was predicting. However, while the Polish/Irish time/space substitution was correct, the Irish future did not exist for the black population. Nor did the contemporaneously ghettoized black situation represent the Irish past. No other group had experienced the hypersegregation of the Blacks.

While Hauser in 1958 could confidently predict the inevitability of black diffusion and assimilation, seven years later the whole optimistic edifice collapsed with the publication of Karl and Alma Taeuber's book, *Negroes in Cities* (1965). Using the first large-scale availability of census block data from the 1960 census, the Taeubers demonstrated the overwhelming segregation of Blacks in American cities. On a scale from 0 (no segregation) to 100 (total segregation), the Taeubers showed that the mean segregation index was 86.2 for the 207 cities for which block level data were available in 1960. They showed that the index was high in all regions (1965, 37), that it was high irrespective of whether city populations were large or small, whether the nonwhite population was large or small, whether the nonwhite percentage was high or low. They showed that indexes had been high in the past and had remained high. Hauser's comforting expectation of decreasing segregation with time was a delusion.

The Taeubers also dealt a deathblow to another American myth. This was that economic progress would dissolve racial segregation. Using Lieberson's (1963) technique of indirect standardization, they calculated how segregated the black population of Chicago would be from Whites, if income differences were the only variable affecting their distribution.

This is achieved by applying the percentage that Blacks form of each income band in the city population to the appropriate number of persons in each income band in each tract in the city. For example, if Blacks formed 10 percent of the middle-income group in Chicago, then 10 percent of the middle-income group would be expected to be black, wherever the middle-income group lived, and so forth. Having calculated the expected distribution of black and white in the city, the degree of segregation between the two groups could be calculated and compared with the observed level of segregation. On this basis, the observed level of segregation in Chicago in 1960 was 83 and the expected index was 10. In other words, only 10/83 or 12 percent of the observed level of segregation could be attributed to differences in income (Taeuber and Taeuber 1964). Economic differences did not explain the segregation of Blacks from Whites.

Subsequent work by Massey and Denton (1993, 86) showed that the intervening years since the Taeubers' work (despite William Julius Wilson's 1978 book) had not produced a decline in the significance of race. Massey and Denton demonstrated that the overall average levels of black/white segregation had declined by only 7.5 points between 1970 and 1990 (Massey and Denton 1993, 222).

Massey and Denton also showed that irrespective of income level, poor blacks were segregated from poor whites, middle-income blacks from middle-income whites, and rich blacks from rich whites by the same massive amounts, with indexes over eighty, almost without exception.

Thus, we arrive at the realization that there is not one model of American minority accommodation but two: the assimilationist and the pluralist; the enclave and the ghetto. The great error has been to force the pluralist model of African-American segregation into the assimilationist framework and to graft the contemporary ghetto model onto the historical European settlement patterns in cities. The ghetto was different in kind; the ghetto was distinct from the ethnic enclave. We can summarize some of the differences (table 2.3).

Is All High Segregation for Negative Reasons?

However, because the disproving of the universality of the Chicago School's three-generational model was demonstrated through the example

TABLE 2.3. Summary of Differences between the African-American Ghetto and the Ethnic Enclave

African-American Ghetto	Ethnic Enclave
Dually segregated: Large majority of blacks are in it; large majority in it are black.	Dually dilute: Only a minority of the group is in it; they form only a minority of the population of the area associated with the group.
Negative	Positive
Enforced	Voluntary
Expanding	Residual
Real	Symbolic
Threatening	Tourist
Permanent	Temporary

Source: Author

of the African-American ghetto, another error was created. This error was the belief that all high levels of segregation were produced by negative discrimination.

The reasons for this belief are not hard to find. First, the expectation of decreasing levels of segregation over time led to the belief that a high segregation level was an early and primitive feature of minority settlement. Second, nearly all of the available examples of high segregation were related to groups that were disadvantaged. Third, the key minority group, the Jews, on whom the plural model of socioeconomic-progress-but-continuing-ethnic-segregation could be tested, is not counted either as a group of national origin or as an ethnic group in the U.S. census. The term "Russian-born" was treated by some analysts as a surrogate for Jewish origin (Lieberson and Waters 1988, 10–11), but of course not all Jews were of Russian origin nor were all of Russian origin Jewish. U.S. census data for Russians in Chicago in 1930 does not indicate an exceptional degree of segregation. Nathan Kantrowitz (1969) had hinted at segregation as a viable strategy for groups that wished to maintain their ethnic identity, but in a fairly oblique way arguing only that decreases in the level of European segregation in American cities should not be expected to continue forever.

While the U.S. government identified the Jewish population as a religious rather than ethnic group, and thereby prevented the census from enumerating them, however, the Canadian census harbored no such delicacy.

The Canadian census counts the Jewish population as both a religious and as an ethnic group. There are markedly high levels of Jewish residential segregation in Canadian cities. In terms of the ID, Jewish segregation is as high as African-American segregation in American cities. In Toronto and Montreal, which in 1991 contained the two largest concentrations of the Jewish population of Canada, the IDs were seventy-five and eighty-two respectively (see Qadeer, chapter 3). The Canadian Jewish population is extremely successful on a socioeconomic scale and although there is evidence of growing anti-Semitism in Quebec (Small 2000, 24–26), there is no indication that the levels of Jewish segregation are not the result of positive wishes for association (Darroch and Marston 1972; Hiebert 1995; Small 2000, 23).

Perhaps even more interesting about the Jewish patterns of segregation is the suggestion that it has come about accompanied not only by upward social mobility, but also by suburbanization as well.

However, while the IDs for the Jewish population in Toronto and Montreal are similar to those for Blacks south of the border, the Jewish population lives in enclaves rather than ghettos on the black model. The highest percentage that the Jewish population formed of any Toronto tract was 70 percent in 1991, and only 2 percent of the population lived there. Only a third of the Jewish population lived in areas in which they formed a majority of the tract population and all of these tracts held a mixed (i.e., non-Jewish population) as well. In Montreal, the highest percentage, which the Jewish population formed of any tract, was 90 percent. Like Toronto, a third of the Montreal Jewish population lived in tracts where they formed a majority of the population.

In London, although we do not have ethnic census data, it is apparent from other sources that the Jewish population which originally settled in the working-class East End at the end of the nineteenth century, suburbanized, notably to the northwestern outer fringes of the city during the twentieth century, but remained concentrated (Newman 1985; Waterman and Kosmin 1986a, 1986b). Such patterns of ethnic pluralism may be referred to as relocating enclaves.

There is also evidence from the European experience that some affluent minority ethnic populations manifest high levels of segregation. Both G. Glebe's work on the Japanese in Düsseldorf (1986) and Paul White's work on the Japanese in London (1998) indicate IDs in the 70s. These groups differ, of course, from settled minorities in that they are largely composed of sojourners who have been seconded by their firms for a period of years. New wave Chinese settlements of the 1990s in Canadian cities (Ley 1995, 2003; Li 1988) have moved directly to the suburbs. Such concentrations may be thought of as parachuted communities.

Summary of Types of Enclaves and Ghettos

We may now summarize the five types of enclaves and ghettos. The *traditional assimilation-diffusion* model of the Chicago three-generational schemas is the most widespread and general type. Settlement begins in the inner city; the second generation moves out a little and becomes more assimilated; the third generation is suburbanized, diffused and totally assimilated. Even in its early days, the center is not the exclusive preserve of one group.

The *American ghetto* model is involuntary and plural (non-assimilatory). It starts in the inner city, but with almost exclusive concentration of the minority. A high proportion of the inner-city black population live in such areas; nearly all in such areas are black. It expands outwards in a segmented shape over time, but remains dually exclusive. Nevertheless, there are attractive neighborhoods on the edge of black clusters to which black professionals move through choice rather than discrimination. Such neighborhoods may be spatially linked to the dominant cluster, but their residents would object to their being termed ghettos.

The *voluntary plural* model *is* the persistent enclave. It is the San Francisco or New York Chinatown model. A high proportion of the population of the areas may be of a given ethnic group, but the Chinese population of Chinatown forms only a minority (often a small minority) of the total Chinese population of the city. It is a symbolic or tourist center; it is an institutional or market center; it may remain and persist over time, but it is not the exclusive center of the ethnic group.

The voluntary plural relocated model describes Jewish residential spatial patterning, that is, a Jewish population concentrated in the inner city relocates en masse to the suburbs. The London Jewish shift from the East End to the northwestern suburbs is the best-studied example in the United Kingdom. Although segregation levels measured by the ID may be high, the areas are not the exclusive preserve of the Jewish population, but are mixed. Nor are all Jews living in such areas.

The *parachuted suburban* model applies to concentrated areas of affluent, often transitory sojourners. The Japanese in London and Düsseldorf or the Hong Kong Chinese in Vancouver are good examples.

Conclusions

The United States has had an unparalleled, successful history of assimilating minorities. Buoyed by this success, the theorization of this process has been cast into a single model, which I have characterized as the three-generational model. However, the theory has ignored the multicultural or plural model, and worse still, tried to make this essentially contrasting model part of the assimilation model itself. Put crudely, the assimilation model is a brick-in-the-pond model. The group begins as concentrated, segregated, and unassimilated in the inner city; it speaks a foreign language; it marries its own kind; it is unassimilated. The second generation ripples out a little, mixes more with the charter group, learns English, and begins to marry out. The third generation, replicates the socioeconomic structure of the population as a whole; it speaks English; it is highly intermarried. It is suburbanized and assimilated.

The theory states that there is a direct relationship between the degree of residential, spatial segregation and the degree of social distance: high spatial segregation, high social distance between groups; low segregation, low social distance (and high degree of social interaction, marriage, etc). The methodology of using the ID to measure the degrees of spatial segregation is correct. High ID gives an excellent and consistent measure of group social distances. The problem lies in assuming that there is only one model. The single model argument is for an inevitable, unidirectional change from high to low segregation over time. This model does work for a large number of groups in a large number of situations. *But, it is not the only model.* The African-American population does not fit into this model nor does the Jewish population. For a long time, attempts were made to interpret the African-American experience in terms of the single model when the evidence pointed in a totally different direction. Black segregation was high and remained high. The Jewish pattern escaped notice, because the data were not collected in the United States. But, if we can extrapolate Canadian experience, where such data exist, the Canadian data show an unmistakable pattern of high and long-lasting segregation. But Jewish concentration does not constitute a ghetto, but a voluntary enclave.

Because the U.S. sociological analysis operated for so long on the single model, it had a massively distorting effect on both historical analysis and on contemporary policy. Historically, it was assumed that all groups were previously as segregated as the contemporary African-American population. There was a mythological back-projection of current levels of black segregation onto the nineteenth-century history of European immigration. The ghetto came to be seen as a *stage* through which *all immigrant groups* went, hence the Chicago School references to "Irish" ghettos, "German" ghettos, and so forth. Since there was only one model, it was assumed that it was only a matter of time before Blacks would diffuse through the urban system and assimilate like the Irish and Germans. This process for different groups was viewed as a time/space substitution, with old groups representing the future positions of new groups and new groups representing the past position of old groups.

The black ghetto, however, was *different in kind* from the degree of segregation experienced by other groups. It was massively more concentrated and dually segregated: nearly all Blacks were in the ghetto and nearly all of the ghetto population was black. The black ghetto did not dissolve with time. The Jewish high levels of concentration seem not to have dissipated over time in Canadian cities, though precise locations did change. U.S. patterns may show more dispersal, but comparable data are lacking. There was movement from the inner city to the suburbs, but it was an en masse relocation rather than diffusion. Unlike black segregation, however, these concentrations were voluntary and by no means as dually segregated as the black experience. Not all of the Jewish population lived in Jewish areas nor was the population of Jewish areas all Jewish. Both the African American and the Jewish populations were following *plural rather than assimilatory* models. The assimilation model was not the only one.

If we look at the contemporary experience of Britain, we can see both the plural and the assimilatory models in existence. The black-Caribbean population has followed the assimilatory trajectory. Its levels of segregation in London have fallen census by census since 1961. The areas of greatest concentration have experienced the greatest losses of Caribbean population. The movement has followed the classic pattern of outward movement from the center towards the periphery. However, when we look at the Indian, Pakistani, and Bangladeshi populations, changes in population have tended to reinforce rather than reduce existing areas of concentration.

Both the assimilation and the multicultural models equate dispersal, diffusion, and low segregation with assimilation. However, the dominant model of the Chicago School considered the assimilation model to be the only one and considered its process to be inevitable. It recognized the existence of the ghetto, but did not distinguish it from the enclave. It conceptualized the ghetto as the first stage of the sequence of the three-generational model. It incorporated its very antithesis as part of the model itself.

The failure to distinguish between the ghetto and the enclave has had a pernicious effect on the understanding of ethnic areas in American cities. First, it has conceptualized the ghetto as a temporary phenomenon. In reality, the ghetto has become permanent. Second, it envisioned socio-economic improvement as the mechanism for the dissolution of the ghetto; in reality, rich Blacks are as segregated from rich Whites as poor Blacks are from poor Whites. Economic differences are not unimportant, but they do not explain black segregation. Third, it encouraged academics to identify the ghetto as a product of wealth difference rather than race (Harvey, 1973, 120–152; cf. Peach, 1998; Wacquant, 1997). Fourth, it has falsified our view of ethnic history in the United States by envisioning a ghettoized past for the early years of all groups; it has led to the assumption that Irish, Italian, and other ethnic enclaves were homogeneously made up of the Irish, Italians or whatever. They never were. Fifth, it encouraged the belief that the African-American ghetto would dissolve in a "natural" and inevitable way. Finally, it encouraged the belief that all segregation was bad and negatively superimposed on groups. In reality, for those groups who choose it and for whom it is not enforced, concentration has many benefits. However, we need to be able to recognize the difference between the chosen enclave and the enforced ghetto.

Chapter 3

ETHNIC SEGREGATION IN A MULTICULTURAL CITY
Mohammad A. Qadeer

Introduction: The Social Context of Segregation

Segregation is a word soaked in the history of racial discrimination and colonialism. The word conjures up images of African townships, black ghettos, and native reservations contrasted with colonialist estates, white suburbs, and exclusivist neighborhoods. These places represent not only residential separation by race, color, religion, and/or class, but also a fragmentation of the social order through domination and subjugation sustained by compulsion and ideology. But what if residential separation were not accompanied by enforced social inequality? Would this condition make segregation more tolerable or acceptable? These two questions are critical with regard to the phenomenon of residential segregation found in North American cities in general, and Canada in particular. This chapter examines the social implications of such ethnic concentrations in residential neighborhoods through a critical analysis of their development in the Greater Toronto Area (GTA) and proceeds from the distinction that Peach (see chapter 2) draws between the ghetto and the ethnic enclave.

The ideology of racism was the social context within which racial residential segregation in the United States was forged in the eighteenth, nineteenth, and first half of the twentieth centuries. Although this burden of history still survives in various forms, there has been a paradigmatic shift since the 1960s. The Civil Rights movement and subsequent antidiscrimination legislation in the United States helped to break down the racial barriers that had fostered segregated urban neighborhoods.

Canada's Charter of Rights and Freedoms (1982) and the Multicultural Act (1988) conferred equality rights on all citizens as individuals on the one hand, and recognized their entitlement to preserve their ethnic heritage as communities and groups on the other (Kymlicka 1998). As in the United States, Canada made discrimination on the basis of race, color, religion, or culture and, more recently on gender and sexual orientation illegal. No longer can a landlord or a property owner openly refuse to rent or sell to a person on the basis of race, culture, or gender. Fair housing laws and antidiscrimination provisions of civil rights legislation made it illegal to deny access to housing to persons of color or single women. This legislation has had some impact on the structure of urban residential markets in North America although there is little question that more forceful implementation of this legislation is needed (see Squires, chapter 7).

Although overt forms of discrimination have declined, Americans continue to buy and rent in areas where their neighbors come from the same ethnic background. Once one ethnic group becomes predominant in a neighborhood, businesses and institutions are established to support the needs of this particular group, thereby reinforcing the neighborhood as a culturally distinct ethnic enclave (Portes and Bach 1985, 203). Little Havanas, Indian bazaars, Japanese malls, or Mexican barrios bring variety, color, and economic vibrancy to a city giving it an air of cosmopolitanism.

The differences between the old and repressive versus the new and expressive forms of residential segregation have not been fully acknowledged by scholars despite the fact that ethnic enclaves are commonly observable in North America. More specifically, sociologists have not shaken themselves loose from the assimilatory perspective of the Chicago School (see Peach, chapter 2; Glazer and Moynihan 1970, and Greeley 1971). European and Canadian scholars are more attuned to differences in the various forms of segregation (Reitz 1980; Van Kempen and Özüekren 1998).

Recently, a new theoretical perspective has begun to emerge from studies of ethnic economies and the contribution of immigrants to the economic revival of declining neighborhoods and cities (Portes and Rumbaut 1996; Waldinger 1990; Winnick 1990). Ethnic enclaves and economies are credited with fostering entrepreneurship primarily on the strength of the areas' social, cultural, and economic networks. Enclaves play an important role in promoting flows of capital and labor (both professional and managerial) across national and continental borders.

These new realities require that residential segregation be assessed on the basis of its role in a local social system instead of its being viewed simply as a product of racism and discrimination.

Canadian Multiculturalism and Ethnic Segregation

Canada has always been a country of diverse cultures, from the Inuits in the north to the mixed blood Metis on the prairies to the Mohawks along the United States border. European and Asian immigration in the nineteenth and twentieth centuries transplanted ethnic communities across the Canadian urban and rural landscape. Though mainly bilingual and bicultural, Canada remained indifferent to its cultural diversity until October 1971 when the Trudeau government formally proclaimed Canada a multicultural society.

Canada is a "lived-in" multicultural society like the United States, but unlike the United States, it has never subscribed to the ethos of assimilating cultures into a national "melting pot" (Lipset 1986). While recognizing the territorial dominance of the French in Quebec and the British throughout the rest of Canada, the country has, nevertheless, accommodated Ukrainian, Irish, Italian, Finnish, Jewish, Japanese, and Chinese communities, among others.

"New" Immigration and Cultural Diversity

Until 1976, Canadian immigration policy explicitly favored Europeans. Japanese, Chinese, and East Indian immigrants who arrived in the early twentieth century were treated as aliens and were confined to ghettos. From 1966 onward, a series of measures opened up immigration, culminating in the Immigration Act of 1976, which did away with the quota system and introduced nondiscriminatory criteria for the selection of migrants (Troper 2000). At the same time, Canadian demography was changing; the birth rate was steadily declining to the point where the total fertility rate was below the replacement level. Today, Canada is increasingly dependent on immigration to avoid population decline.

Since the mid-1970s, increasing numbers of immigrants have come from China, India, the Caribbean, Latin America, and Africa. These immigrants are racially, linguistically, religiously, and culturally visible. Economically, there are two distinct streams of immigrants: (1) entrepreneurs and professionals who enter directly into the middle and upper strata of Canadian society, settling in comfortable suburbs and affluent neighborhoods of central cities; and (2) working-class immigrants who fill low-level positions at or close to the minimum wage, congregating in low-rent apartments and filtered-down homes in both central cities and suburbs.

Most immigrants settle in the metropolitan areas, particularly Toronto, Vancouver, and Montreal, the three metropolitan hubs of Canada's modern economy. These three metropolitan areas have almost 30 percent of Canada's population, indicating a top-heavy urban system in a country of only thirty-one million people.

Multiculturalism: Old and New

Historically, multiculturalism was a private affair with immigrants speaking their languages, cooking their exotic foods, and forming their own neighborhoods and communities reminiscent of their homelands. Toronto and other major Canadian cities have a long history of Blacks, Jews, Italians, and Chinese, and as of late, Polish and Portuguese immigrants, clustering in neighborhoods and communities, creating private "little homelands" through individual and group initiative (Harvey 1985, 11).

But a new multiculturalism was forged during the 1970s and 1980s. Japanese corporations built cars in Canada and Canadian dot-com companies recruited software engineers from India and China, and Canadians were living and traveling abroad in millions. Canada's traditional, normative, uniform of way of life began to break apart. The demand for new and diverse foods, dress, music, art, recreation, and ethnic products services increased. This diversity was valued and cultivated by many urban Canadians, particularly the young.

This new multiculturalism accommodated not only the individual's right to organize his private life in accordance with his culture, but also supported the group's right to build communal institutions and to maintain its heritage and language in the public domain within the limits prescribed by the Canadian constitution and the charter. The new multiculturalism does not prevent or impede integration, but renegotiates the terms of integration (Kymlicka 1998, 58).

The Greater Toronto Area (GTA)

The boosters of Toronto (city population 2.48 million, GTA population 5.16 million in 2001) claim it to be the most multicultural city in the world (Doucet 2001). Whatever the truth of this claim, in the past two decades the GTA has become a place of striking ethnic and racial diversity. The GTA draws the largest number of immigrants, about 43 percent of all who come to Canada each year (Lo et al. 2000). Between 1991 and 1996, for example, a staggering four hundred fifty thousand immigrants settled here (Bourne 2000, 2).

Outgrowing its reputation as a clean, decent, but dull city, Toronto is home to approximately 169 different ethnic groups (forty-eight ethnic groups have more than five thousand members). About 30 percent are visible minorities (people of color) (Siemiatycki et al. 2001). The GTA is dotted with ethnic enclaves. Bathurst and Lawrence West is a Jewish enclave and one of the most enduring ethnic districts. Dundas West is the spine of the Portuguese community. The Crescent Town apartment complex has become a Bangladeshi/South Asian concentration. A few blocks east along Dawes Road are apartment buildings predominantly inhabited by Serbs and Russians. Agincourt, in suburban Scarborough, is an acknowledged "third China Town," while a fourth has emerged in the affluent northern suburban municipalities of Markham–Richmond Hill. Sikh enclaves are found in Malton, near the airport, and in Brampton, a sprawling municipality on the northwestern periphery of the GTA.

The GTA comprises twenty-nine municipalities with the Toronto Metropolitan Municipality (TMM), the core, and ringed by suburban municipalities and edge cities. The TMM was only recently consolidated through the merger of historic Toronto city and five inner suburbs.

The Scale and Pattern of Ethnic Segregation

Ethnic segregation results from the convergence of households of a particular ethnicity in a specific neighborhood. As these households combine to form a majority of an area's residents, they invest the area with their particular identity and institutions. Eventually, the cluster may evolve into an enclave, if ethnic businesses and services develop and dominate the area. Toronto's growth and social ecology have been profoundly affected by recent immigration with the resulting emergence of numerous ethnic residential concentrations and enclaves. Almost "every municipality, every neighborhood, every block" has been changed (Bourne 2000, 3).

An analysis of census data (detailed results not included here because of space limitations) shows that Toronto's ethnic enclaves are not large; few concentrations even fill the equivalent of one tract in area or population; those extending over two or more tracts are even less common. Often, an ethnic concentration is an area of perhaps two or three residential streets or in a cluster of apartment buildings. Ethnic segregation in the GTA is not on a large enough scale to produce neighborhoods the size of Harlem, the South Bronx in New York City, or Watts in Los Angeles. Ethnically segregated neighborhoods in the Toronto region are also not large enough to result in segregated public schools or community facilities. Seldom are members of ethnic groups so spatially separated as not to encounter people of other ethnicities in their daily routines and activities.

Jews are the most highly concentrated group based on the percentage of metropolitan census tracts in which 50 percent of an ethnic groups population live; about half of the Jewish population lives in 3 percent of the tracts. Jews are followed by Scandinavians, Aboriginals, Chinese, South Asians, Ukrainians, and Blacks (Balakrishnan 2000, 127, table 9.1). Visible minorities are not as segregated as some of the white non-English groups, that is, Jews and Scandinavians.

Jews are also the most segregated group based on the Gini index (Balakrishnan 2000). The Gini index is derived from Lorenz curves. The vertical axis on a graph shows the cumulative percentage of the population of one group, the horizontal axis shows the census tracts arranged in the decreasing order of the group's population. The distance of the curve from the diagonal of the graph (Lorenz curve) is the measure of its geographic concentration. Like the Index of Dissimilarity, it varies between 0 and 1, where zero indicates no segregation and one means complete segregation. For examples of research using this measure for 1991 and 1996 see I. R. Balakrishnan and Feng Hou (1999), Abdol Mohammad Kazemipur and Shiva Halli (2000), and Brian Ray (1999).

Ray concurs that the "lower levels of concentration among visible minority immigrant groups compared with long-established European groups remain an enduring feature of Canadian cities" (Ray 1999, 82). Balakrishnan and Hou (1999) found that between 1981 and 1991 residential segregation remained the same for all ethnic groups. However, occupational segregation decreased significantly, which may be the result of the recruitment of immigrants for their education and skills. Yet, the pattern of residential segregation between European and non-European immigrants remained, following the order described above (Balakrishnan 2000, 129). Regardless of what measure is used to measure ethnic segregation, it appears that an immigrant's culture, language, and country of origin are more potent forces for drawing people together than racial or ethnic discrimination.

Structural Features of the Ethnic Segregation in Toronto

In the early nineteenth century, English and Irish settlers were socially and spatially separated from one another, and both were separated from a small group of black freemen who had fled from the United States. In the post-World War II period, ethnic neighborhoods began to emerge in newly developing suburbs with the movement of middle-class residents out of the city. Jews and Italians led the way in forming secondary residential concentrations. More recently, the new multiculturalism and more liberal immigration laws have spawned ethnic residential enclaves/concentrations in the outer suburbs and edge cities while reinvigorating central city "homelands." Thus, these suburban ethnic enclaves have not replaced Toronto's older ethnic neighborhoods, since many of these remain "reception areas" for new immigrants. Immigrant professionals and business entrepreneurs often buy homes in areas where co-ethnics have settled, thereby creating "ethnoburbs." Sikhs in Malton, Chinese and South Asians in Markham and Mississauga, Caribbeans and Somalis in northern Etobicoke, Italians in Woodbridge, and Jews in North York are examples of such concentrations.

Fine differentiations within ethnic groups are reflected in different patterns of residential clustering. Chinese immigrants from Hong Kong tend to live on different blocks, and sometimes even different neighborhoods, from those emigrating from Taiwan or mainland China. Similarly, Blacks from Jamaica tend to cluster around the western end of Eglington Street, while Ethiopians and Ghanaians choose the Bloor-Ossington area. In suburban Mississauga, apartment buildings are nicknamed *begum pura* due to the predominance of wives (*begums* in Urdu) and children of Pakistanis working in the Gulf Emirates and Saudi Arabia. As a result, Pakistani expatriates know in advance about these buildings. Likewise, Bosnian Serbs tend to congregate in different parts of the city from other Serbs.

Housing Markets and the Process of Ethnic Segregation

Typically, the concentration of an ethnic group in a particular area reflects the aggregation of thousands of householders' choices framed by their income and class. These concentrations are not dictated, planned or coordinated by any authority or agency, but arise from market transactions, one by one.

As stated earlier, Canadian housing markets are subject to antidiscrimination provisions specified in the Charter of Rights and Freedoms, the Human Rights Codes, and the Landlord-Tenants Acts. Overt acts of discrimination are prosecutable offences and are relatively rare. Undoubtedly, incidents of ethnic and racial discrimination occur in buying and selling, but most occur in the rental sector against new and/or poor immigrants. The Centre for Equality in Accommodation (CERA), a tenant's rights advocacy agency, receives between five hundred to six hundred complaints a year, half or more of which turn out to be landlord-tenant disputes gone sour.

Families may be hurt, however, by the existence of tight-knit enclaves. They may not be able to move into certain areas because vacancies are never formally advertised in newspapers or similar sources.

Discrimination on the basis of source of income (i.e., welfare status) does, however, occur to a significant degree. Families may be denied accommodation because they cannot afford the security deposit or advance rent, or because they have a poor credit history.

Variations in housing costs (reflecting differences in quality and location) divide the metropolitan housing market into distinct submarkets. Many of these markets are further divided by the ethnicity of residents. Once a submarket emerges, other groups tend not to buy or rent in the area. This pattern of "invasion and succession" is most evident in the rental submarket. Buildings that were rented by Greeks a decade ago may be rented mostly to Gujaratis or Somalis today. Thorncliffe Park, northeast of downtown, is an example of such ethnic succession.

Ethnic concentration is an outcome of two intersecting factors: (1) immigrants' housing search behavior, and (2) the structure of the local housing market (the type, cost and quality of housing available). On the basis of some published accounts, case studies (Bourne 2000; Carey 2001; Grover 1995; Harvey 1985; Kazemipur and Halli 2000; Murdie and Teixeira 2000; Myles 2002; Ray 1999), and field observations in the Toronto region, the following three-stage process for the formation of ethnic residential concentrations can be identified:

In stage 1, the nucleus of the enclave is formed. When immigrants arrive in Toronto, they typically contact friends, relatives, or acquaintances for help in finding housing. It is not uncommon for them to lodge with co-ethnics temporarily while searching for a permanent abode. Refugees and other sponsored immigrants may stay in motels, shelters, or institutional facilities at first, but when searching for permanent housing they tend to turn to their sponsors and other co-ethnics for information and guidance on search strategies, frequently for cosigning and other forms of guarantees requested by landlords. Often, home-owning ethnics may rent out basements or rooms to new arrivals. New immigrants in the home-buying market seek advice and information from those already settled. These are the mechanics of establishing an ethnic enclave.

In this first stage, immigrant access to housing is influenced by vacancies and rental costs. A recession may cause rents to decline opening up an area to new immigrants, thereby turning it into their "neighborhood." A Somali concentration in a high-rise apartment complex on Dixon Road in suburban Etobicoke is such an example. The influx began with a few refugees renting vacant condominium units during the real estate bust of 1990–1995. Within three to four years of the initial influx, Somalis had rented 59 percent of the rental stock, thereby forming the nucleus of what now is a large Somali concentration (Grover 1995).

As a particular group grows, a tipping point is reached, stage 2, transforming the area into an enclave. When this occurs, households of other ethnic backgrounds begin to move out. Demand for the housing stock largely comes from the new majority ethnic group. In rental buildings, landlords take advantage of this emerging ethnic concentration by relying on the channeling strategies of the group to fill any vacancies. Thus, landlords are spared the costs of advertising. In the home ownership sector, the ethnic concentration creates a niche submarket of distinct price, quality, and symbolic values. The concentration of an ethnic group facilitates the development of religious, cultural, and community institutions. A building with a sizable number of Muslim tenants, for example, allows the pooling of funds to rent a room for daily prayers or, in the case of Chinese Christians, a room for services in Cantonese. Additionally, public schools, community centers, and health services can offer programs for women, the elderly, or children specifically tailored to their linguistic and social needs. Finally, groceries, restaurants, and video stores that cater to an ethnic group round out the process of creating an enclave.

The time required to consolidate an enclave, stage 3, varies by ethnic group and is influenced by the group's population size, rate of immigration, economic status, and degree of organization. Once an enclave establishes services and institutions, it tends to persist and evolve. The community becomes a segmented subhousing market sustained by real estate agents, businessmen, lawyers, and community and religious leaders. They act as "gate keepers" by facilitating the movement of ethnic households into and out of the community, all the while sustaining its continuity.

Toronto's ethnic groups exhibit social class differentiation; poorer and richer members of particular groups are found living in different areas. The GTA has pockets of "high-rise ghettos," where concentrations of poor Indians and Pakistanis, Caribbean, and African Blacks as well as white immigrants from eastern Europe can be found. These ethnic poor are dependent on the availability of poor quality, but affordable housing (Kazemipur and Halli 2000), a commodity that is constantly and continually in demand. In Toronto, such housing is in short supply.

Eric Fong (1996) maintains that residential segregation of visible minorities in Canada is lower than that among Blacks, Hispanics, and Asians in the United States. Furthermore, he contends that Canadian cities do not show a clear color hierarchy. John Myles (2002) has traced spatial assimilation of immigrants of visible minority background by analyzing census data. He found that in Toronto, Blacks and South Asians move out of disadvantaged immigrant enclaves in low-income housing areas and move into ethnically mixed neighborhoods. In contrast, Chinese immigrants continue to buy in Chinese neighborhoods regardless of their social mobility and retain their ethnic affiliations (Myles 2002).

Thus, members of some ethnic groups choose to live among their own, although they have the income to live elsewhere. Affluent Chinese, Italians, Jews, Sikhs, religious Muslims, and eastern Europeans have "by choice" reconstituted subdivisions and neighborhoods in their respective ethnic and/or religious idiom. One can look at parts of Markham, Mississauga, and North York where home owners have communities with distinctive ethnic identities. The territorialization of ethnic communities is not a transitory phase of immigrant settlement; it appears to be a mode of development in the Toronto region.

The three-step process of ethnic enclave formation described above oversimplifies reality somewhat. Given the numbers of ethnic groups, variations from this evolutionary path are to be expected. For example, ethnic cooperatives and coplanned subdivisions skip steps one and two and proceed directly to stage three. An example of this is Crescent Village, a not-for-profit, 170-unit townhouse cooperative developed by the Jaffaria Islamic Society for its members. Some concentrations dissipate at stage two with the infiltration of other groups.

All in all, the GTA's social landscape remains a mosaic of affluent and poor ethnic communities interspersed with large swaths of mixed neighborhoods where no one group dominates. Exclusively white-Anglo neighborhoods are rare, although elite neighborhoods such as Forest Hill, Bridal Path, Rosedale, and Mississauga Road, come close to being overwhelmingly white.

Toronto's Ethnic Clusters are Not Ghettos

Typically, these enclaves are not necessarily classical ghettos where housing blight is intertwined with poverty and social disadvantages. In general, the housing stock in these enclaves is good with "relatively few dwellings in Toronto . . . in need of major repairs" (Murdie and Teixeria 2000, 46). Ironically, immigrant housing conditions are slightly better on the whole than for the Canadian-born, perhaps because most new arrivals settle in relatively new housing stock in suburbs, though there are pockets of ill-kempt rental apartment complexes that have become ethnic neighborhoods (Murdie and Teixeiria 2000, 46).

On the criterion of household density, immigrants fare better than the Canadian-born. The occupancy ratio for immigrants is about 1.1 persons per room, though immigrants from Asia, Africa, and Latin America live in more crowded conditions because of larger households. Immigrants do fall behind the Canadian-born with respect to the affordability of their homes. Nevertheless, GTA's relatively good housing stock provides a safety net of tolerable living conditions in ethnic enclaves.

Public housing developments are true multicultural communities where households of diverse ethnic backgrounds live side by side. For example, the largest public housing complex in the Toronto region, the Jane/Finch high-rise corridor in the northwest corner of Metro Toronto, has 137 nationalities. Regent Park, in downtown Toronto, is home to Jamaicans, Pakistanis, Anglo-Canadians, Tamils, and Somalis along with a sprinkling of other nationalities.

Conclusions

Because Toronto's ethnic clusters reflect voluntary choices and because they benefit both residents (due to mutual support networks and strong community organizations) and the metropolitan area as a whole (through tourism-induced economic development and the more intangible benefits associated with cultural diversity), these areas need to be accepted on moral and pragmatic grounds (see Marcuse, chapter 1). Nevertheless, these enclaves may have a downside; they may inhibit immigrants' acculturation into the ways of the housing market and may interfere with an understanding of Canadian social mores. These are "potential" problems; there is no hard evidence that they exist. If and when evidence becomes available that these problems do exist, ameliorative policies will need to be developed.

Today, social segregation, including its spatial manifestations, has a different meaning than it did in the early twentieth century. In Canada, social identity, personal roots, and cultural differences are valued and diversity is regarded as an asset for a city and the nation as a whole. Cities are not only being carved into ethnic enclaves, but also into areas defined by life style (e.g., gay districts). Multiculturalism is the social ideology of the times. Transnational citizenship and globalization are overriding notions of national homogeneity. In the United States some black community leaders are resisting gentrification (which could lead to greater integration), because they place more emphasis on maintaining the historic, ethnic character of these areas. Thus, for a variety of reasons there is decreased support for assimilationist and secularist views of modernism and increased backing for sustaining diverse communities and for preserving a variety of subcultures.

Social integration has a new meaning, that of constructing a common ground of institutions and services for civic engagement of diverse communities. Extending equal citizenship to diverse communities, and not aiming to homogenize their differences, is, according to this perspective, in the public interest. In the spatial arena, it means pursuing policies for adequate and affordable housing for all as well as providing infrastructure and services for viable community life. Rather than focusing on residential segregation, the focus ought to be on greater mixing in schools, work places, recreation and sports and the political arena, and providing public and commercial facilities at the boundary between different ethnic/racial clusters (see Boal, chapter 4). These policies could form the common ground for the social integration of diverse communities.

Chapter 4

URBAN ETHNIC SEGREGATION AND THE SCENARIOS SPECTRUM

Frederick W. Boal

Introduction

I think it is appropriate to start by quoting the distinguished New England poet, Robert Frost (2002). In one of his best-known pieces, "Mending Wall," he writes:

> . . . there where it is we do not need a wall:
> He is all pine and I am apple orchard.
> My apple trees will never get across
> And eat the cones under his pines, I tell him.
> He only says, "Good fences make good neighbors."
>
> Why do they make good neighbors? Isn't it
> Where there are cows? But here there are no cows.
> Before I built a wall I'd ask to know
> Who I was walling in or walling out.

Why quote Frost? My reasons are threefold. First, the poem is suggestive of the presence of segregation. Second, it questions why there should be segregation and third, it hints at interventions that could reduce or indeed reinforce segregation.

I will return to these matters in subsequent sections of this chapter.

My interest in urban ethnic segregation derives from living and working in Belfast for the past thirty-eight years. I now realize that my interest developed through five sequential stages. First, I attempted to quantify the degree of segregation that existed in Belfast. Second, I began to explore what functions ethnic residential segregation might perform, particularly in urban environments characterized by severe intergroup conflict. Third, I began to focus on change and stability in the degree of segregation that existed. Here, I became increasingly aware that segregation levels at one point in time were not necessarily an indicator of likely future levels or, indeed, of levels in the past, though I also had to note that segregation levels *could* remain nearly constant for many years. Fourth, I became increasingly concerned to place the ethnic segregation I observed in Belfast in a wider, comparative context. Was the Belfast experience unique or was it something that was part of a much bigger story? And finally, I sensed a growing need to consider the impact of segregation on other aspects of urban function and to explore policy initiatives that might be targeted at reducing segregation. While my initial concentration was on Belfast, as comparative work came to the fore it became necessary to broaden the range of cities examined. Contextualizing Belfast in this way offered the opportunity to develop generalizations applicable to an ever-widening field of urban centers.

So, five aspects of segregation have, at different times, been at the top of my agenda—the measurement of segregation; the functions of segregation; stability and change; intercity comparisons; and policy and action. I will now build the rest of my discussion round these key points.

Aspects of Urban Ethnic Segregation

The Measurement of Segregation

The first question we ask about ethnic segregation is how much? Thus, in my early work in Belfast, I became concerned to measure the degree of residential segregation that existed between Catholics and Protestants. Three aspects of this task required attention (Boal 1987; Poole and Boal 1973):

- How was membership in the two categories to be defined? For instance, were we to treat the population of the city as falling into one of three categories, Protestant, Catholic, and "others," or was our categorization to be simply binary, with Catholics in one "box" and everyone else in the other? Also, was there a danger that we might be imposing an unreal internal homogeneity on the groups we were labeling Catholic and Protestant? We also needed to be aware that ethnicity is a continuous variable rather than an inherent attribute of persons. Thus, the intensity of identification both by the persons concerned and by "others" varies between individuals and over time. This identification may be highly situational in that group membership may be instrumental for individuals at one time or of minor practical value at another. That said, the data available for measuring segregation does not usually permit such subtleties to be taken on board.

- How were we to measure the degree of segregation? In other words, what index or set of indices was to be employed? Arguments here have been designated "the index war" by Ceri Peach (1975, 3). Because of its wide use, we adopted the Index of Dissimilarity as our main measure. However, we also made considerable use of an index based on the percentage of all households in the city residing in what we defined as "segregated" streets, that is streets where at least 90 percent of the occupants were Catholic or 90 percent Protestant.

- Perhaps most critically of all, what was to be the scale of the spatial units to be used, in the analysis? How large, how were the boundaries to be defined, and so on? We were aware that segregation indices tended to be scale-dependent: the smaller the size of the spatial units (census tracts, enumeration districts, electoral wards, etc.) used the higher the resultant indices, and vice versa. We were also concerned that the pattern of segregation on the ground should be "caught" in our spatial net. Was some segregation in the form of many small pockets, while elsewhere it was constituted as one or more extensive areas? Finally, what was the extent of the overall spatial analysis unit—the inner city ("central city"), central city and suburbs, the whole metropolitan area or what? Again, the decision made here could have a profound effect on the degree of segregation observed.

Later, when we moved to comparative intercity work, we became highly sensitized to the need for standardization in the techniques employed. Were the same indices available for each city? Was the overall unit of analysis (the central city, city plus suburbs, metro area) the same in each case, and most critically of all, was the scale of the areal units consistent between the comparator cities? (Poole and Boal 1973)

The Functions of Segregation

I think there is a general inclination to view segregation as "bad." This is not surprising, bearing in mind many of the negative consequences that segregation generates. It tends to isolate, it can reduce housing, educational and employment opportunities, and it can help delimit easily identifiable areas for containment and control purposes and even for physical attack (Boal 2002, 693).

On the other hand, in specific circumstances, segregation may have positive functions. I was pointed in this direction when I began to explore the functions of segregation in urban environments where intergroup conflict was severe and where violence was a recurrent theme (Boal 1972). To start with, we can note that conflicting situations in cities lead people to feel threatened. The perceived threat may materialize in the form of physical violence, or it may remain as psychological threat. In both instances, it is reasonable that the individuals or groups concerned should attempt to cope with such threat. The psychologist Richard S. Lazarus identified two main classes of coping: direct action tendencies and individual or defensive forces. It is the former, which we note here, in that the term implies that "coping effort is aimed directly at eliminating or mitigating the harmful condition" (Lazarus 1969, 210). As Lazarus has suggested, four different direct action tendencies have been distinguished. These are: preparing against harm, avoidance, attack, and inaction or apathy. Each tendency, except for apathy, is an attempt to take the individual or community out of jeopardy. From this standpoint, the spatially concentrated urban ethnic community can be interpreted as a mechanism for coping with threat. Following Lazarus, I recognized three basic ways in which urban communities cope with threat: by specific preparation against harm, by avoidance of the source of the harm, and by attacking (politically and/or physically) the perceived sources of the threat.

1. *Preparation against harm—physical defense.* The clustering together of a group within a city can provide the basis for defense against external attack. By joining the cluster, members of a particular group no longer find themselves residing in isolation, and the existence of the group itself within a clearly defined area enables an organized defense to be developed. The long history of communal conflict in

Belfast illustrates time and time again the importance of the community-segregated cluster as a defensive arrangement.

2. *Avoidance.* The psychologically supportive role of the ethnic residential concentration has been referred to in many contexts. Classically, Louis Wirth referred to "the tolerance that strange ways of living need and find in immigrant colonies, in Latin quarters, in vice districts and in other localities. . . . [This] is a powerful factor in the sifting of the population and its allocation in separate cultural areas where one obtains freedom from hostile criticism and the backing of a group of kindred spirits" (Wirth 1928, 19–20). The avoidance of "the other," a desire for comfort and a relaxed atmosphere amongst one's own all accentuate the search for neighborhoods congenial to one's own ethnic predispositions.

3. *Attack.* The residential segregation of a particular ethnic group can provide it with a base for action in the struggle of its members with society in general. This struggle may take a peaceful political form or it may become violent. In terms of political action, spatial concentration of a given group may enable it to elect its own representatives who can then attempt to fight their group's battles in the political arena. This wish was expressed, among others, by a number of American Blacks concerned that residential dispersal might be employed against their community as a means of weakening their electoral strength. However, the significance of group residential concentration can extend beyond institutional politics in that such areas can potentially provide the base for urban insurrection or guerrilla warfare. They provide a milieu closely equivalent to the classic guerrilla situation favored by Mao Tse-tung—the guerrilla is the fish and the sympathetic population is the sea. Certain areas in Belfast have functioned in this way from time to time; rioters and insurrectionary groups "disappear" into such areas, protected by the silence of the inhabitants, a silence based on sympathy or on intimidation or on a mixture of both.

Cultural Preservation

Starting from this conflict perspective, it became clear that a broader view of segregation was required (Boal 1987, 103–109). Thus, though ethnic group solidarity and spatial concentration (segregation) may be promoted by outside pressures, there also appears to be a desire among many urban ethnics to preserve and promote their own cultural heritage. Again, Louis Wirth's comments on the immigrant Jewish "ghetto" are apposite here:

. . . to the Jews the geographically separated and socially isolated community seemed to offer the best opportunity for following their religious precepts, of preparing their food according to the established religious ritual, of following their dietary laws, of attending the synagogue for prayer three times a day, and of participating in the numerous functions of communal life which religious duty imposed upon every member of the community. (Wirth 1928, 19)

Dahya provides a more recent example in his discussion of Pakistani ethnicity in the industrial cities of Britain:

. . . the immigrant community's ecological base serves several important functions, which are related to the community's need to create, manifest, and defend its ethnic identity. During the early stages of the community's settlement, the ecological base is closely interwoven with the immigrants' participation in ethnic socioeconomic institutions and mutual aid, and with the community's need to define its identity, both for its members and outsiders. Reinforced by endogamy, the ecological base with its concomitant institutions serves as an instrument for the transmission of the community's culture to the second generation and for maintaining ethnic boundaries and for avoiding (or minimising) ambiguities with regard to ethnic diversity. (Dahya 1974, 95)

As Dahya notes, in the cultural preservation process, endogamy (marrying within one's own group) can play a significant role. Endogamy, of course, can be enforced with varying degrees of success by the operation of a set of ethnic rules and norms. In addition, it can be further enhanced by the geographical proximity of potential partners, who are themselves set within a relatively homogeneous ethnic residential geography, in a word—segregation. Schools perform important roles in cultural maintenance and ethnic residential segregation may ensure a particular group's dominance in a given catchment or may enable a group to sustain schools of its own. Other institutions, such as churches, synagogues, mosques, and temples can also contribute significantly to the cultural preservation process. Indeed, in a completely complimentary way, not only do these institutions help sustain the group, group concentration helps sustain the institutions.

I would stress that the cultural preservation function of ethnic residential segregation serves a socioemotional or "expressive" purpose. However, as well as serving an "instrumental" purpose in cultural preservation, segregation may also function instrumentally in the development of mutual aid networks and the enhancement of group solidarities. The latter strengthens the ethnic group's hand in its bargaining and in its confrontation with the wider society.

Ethnic Entrepreneurship

A further aspect of the functionality of ethnic segregation should be noted. Here we refer to the idea of "ethnic entrepreneurship" in which the ethnic space provides a context for the development of ethnic businesses, professional services (such as lawyers, teachers, doctors, and travel agents), and so on, all oriented to the specific needs of particular ethnic groups. Again, as with the cultural aspect, it is a matter of mutual sustenance whereby the ethnic concentration provides a base for the entrepreneurs, while the presence of the "ethnic friendly" entrepreneur becomes a component of the ethnic group's support structure.

The View from Beyond the Group

This examination of the functions of segregation has viewed it from the perspective of the segregated group. However, segregation has functionality for the wider society as well. Just to briefly illustrate the point, we can see that the "attack" function has its mirror image, where segregation of certain groups serves as a containment or control device for the wider society. For instance, where the ethnic vote is herded within a small number of electoral units, continued majority control of neighboring wards is secured. Segregation also sets up an ethnic group as a clearly defined target for attack, as was starkly the case of the Warsaw ghetto during World War II.

Segregation also provides an "avoidance" function for dominant groups, reducing members' contact with what may be perceived as undesirable or alien "others" (see Peach 1996). Finally, we may note that segregation contributes to majority group cultural preservation by reducing the probability of intermarriage and helping to ensure majority group dominance in neighborhood schools.

Negative Functions

Up to this point, my approach appears to stress the positive aspects of segregation. I will only briefly rehearse the negative dimensions, since these will undoubtedly be fully examined by others in this volume. Suffice to say, as noted earlier, we are all aware of the lack of choice confronting many segregated groups particularly in terms of housing, schools, and employment opportunities. We know that segregation can mean entrapment and exclusion and we also know that the low intergroup contact environments are conducive to a surfeit of negative stereotyping of the ethnic "other."

So my first exploration of segregation through the lens of "function" has indicated clearly that the spatial separation of ethnic groups has positive as well as negative dimensions. However, sometimes positive functions are responses to negative contextual factors, in this case segregation appears positive at one level, but negative when a broader view is taken. For instance, we have noted the utility of the defensive function, but we must query the negative environment that makes such defense necessary. And, to follow the comments on recent riots in a number of English cities, it may be that segregation provides the very environment for riotous intergroup behavior (Home Office 2001; Oldham Independent Review 2001).

In all this, I want to stress that my functional exploration of ethnic segregation encouraged me to get behind the picture presented by the simple spatial distributions, whether these distributions indicated segregation or mixing. Thus, we cannot make judgments on pattern alone. Rather we must understand what drives the underlying processes. Do these processes involve voluntary behavior on the part of the residents concerned or are they the consequence of external pressures or perhaps some mixture of the two?

The functional analysis also made me aware that when we carry out these investigations and make statements about what we observe, we are telling "stories." These stories are an attempt to obtain an ordered sense of what goes on. But there are various stories to be told. They may reflect different realities or they may be a product of the different ways different people see things. In an earlier paper (Boal 1996), I suggested that there are four basic stories to be told about ethnic residential segregation; as a transitional device on the road to assimilation, as a long-term situation selected by choice, as a prolonged phenomenon constituted by opposed nationalisms, and as a ghetto that corrals unwilling people, probably on a long-term basis. Whatever our stories we must remain vigilant to the fact that, as the historian William J. Cronon puts it, our interpretations "become covert exercises in power—sanctioning some voices while silencing others" (Cronon 1992, 1350). Moreover, some of our interpretations may be shaped as much by our objectives for the future as by our readings of the present or the past.

Stability and Change

I, like many others, was raised on the Chicago model (Park 1926; Park, Burgess, and McKenzie 1967; Wirth 1928) where the assumption was that most ethnic differences that existed in cities were transitional phenomena. In this, ethnically specific institutions were considered to be valuable as part of the transitional arrangements, if, and only if they assisted the movement towards assimilation (Grillo 2000). Thus, ethnic segregation was a changing, dynamic, and in the Chicago case, a short-term characteristic of cities. However, it could also be observed in the United States' case, that not all segregation appeared to have an assimilationist end point. Here the black ghetto clearly suggested that assumptions about change in segregation levels and about the unidirectionality of such change were, at best, only part of the story. Indeed similar continuities in segregation, albeit at a lower level, could be observed within the Jewish community, though here segregation was retained even during inner-city/ suburban relocations (see, for instance Rosenthal 1961 on Chicago; for a more detailed discussion of the Chicago model, see Peach, chapter 2).

An awareness of the temporal dynamics of segregation provided by the Chicago model made me conscious of the need to also examine stability and change in Belfast. Did Belfast, for instance, fit the U.S. immigrant model, or did it conform to the Jewish (predominantly voluntary) or the black (predominantly involuntary) "ghetto" models? The answer turned out to be none of these! With Belfast, we found that ethnic segregation levels had actually increased very significantly over a period of some 150 years. We also discovered that this increase had not taken place in a gradual fashion, but rather as a series of sharp jumps. This pattern of change was subsequently labeled the "ratchet" mode (Smith and Chambers 1991).

This tendency for segregation to increase in Belfast over the past 150 years, points to the fact that the city, which we might have expected to follow the assimilationist model, actually became locked in an ethnonational struggle. Ethnonational conflict, and the associated opposed sovereignty claims not only locked in the ethnic segregation of the early and mid- nineteenth century, but it also provided the motor that has driven segregation levels to heights not previously experienced in the city.

What do we conclude from this? First, that we must be sensitized to the temporal dynamics of segregation. Second, that we cannot make assumptions about whether change will occur or not. Third, that we cannot make assumptions about the direction of change. Where ethnic patterns have become mixed (suggesting, therefore, a desegregating trend), we need to distinguish between those situations where the mixing will continue to exist for a significant period of time (what I call "stable mixing") and those where the mixing is merely a stage between two highly segregated conditions ("transitional mixing").

Thus, just as we must be open to acknowledge the contextual variability of the functions of segregation and the interpretations we give to these functions, so we must also be open to acknowledge that temporal change in segregation is a varied and context specific phenomenon where we can find rapid increase on the one hand, rapid decrease on the other, with slow change (or even stability) in between.

Intercity Comparisons

Issues of stability and change in degrees of segregation and the presence of different kinds of temporal change in different cities opened up another field for development and exploration. Initially my concern was to place Belfast in a wider frame. Could Belfast, for instance, be placed in a category composed of cities that have served as immigrant reception centers? Some useful comparisons could be made here, such as when Anthony C. Hepburn (1996) suggests that the Catholic community could be considered "the Irish in Belfast," comparable to the Irish immigrants in Glasgow, Liverpool, and Boston. But the model did not seem to fit particularly closely, or more precisely, the immigrant model fitted only so far, there being additional dimensions to the Belfast "immigrant" experience. This something more was provided with a comparative frame when I became aware of a categorization being developed by Meron Benvenisti (1987).

In the late 1980s, Benvenisti outlined conditions in a composite city he labeled JEMOBESIA (Jerusalem, Montreal, Beirut, Belfast, Berlin, and Nicosia), where micro-conflicts over service delivery are intensified by larger national macro-conflicts. When national conflict intensifies local cleavages, a "divided" city is transformed into a "polarized" one. A crucial element of a polarized city is when governing takes place (or is at least attempted) without the presence of consensus on the overall issue of sovereignty. Two competing groups exist in a twilight war, attempting to act both as neighbors and as enemies—an intolerable situation as Benvenisti quite rightly sees it (Benvenisti 1987). He concluded that Jerusalem encapsulates the Palestinian-Israeli conflict. I had previously claimed, in like manner, that Belfast encapsulated the conflict in Ireland between those who identified as British and those who identified as Irish (Boal, Murray and Poole 1976).

More recently Joël Kotek, researching out of Brussels, has attached a more helpful label to cities designated "polarized" by Benvenisti. Kotek, calls them "frontier cities." According to him a frontier city is a territory for two (or more) dreams. They are disputed spaces because of their location on fault-lines between ethnic, religious, or ideological wholes (Kotek 1999, 228). Kotek concludes, "as it is, above all, a question of sovereignty, one can understand why the notion of frontier city cannot be mistaken with the notions of multicultural, pluri-ethnic or multiethnic cities" (Kotek 1999, 229).

The polarized city/frontier city categorization offered a useful frame for broadening our understanding of the nature and dynamics of a specific set of cities, one of which was Belfast. However, a second level of comparison was called for: where do frontier cities fit in the wider scheme of things? This is where I introduced the concept of the *scenarios spectrum* (Boal 1999).

Before outlining this perspective, honesty requires that I admit that the scenarios spectrum was originally developed, not as a frame for comparing frontier cities with other forms of divided city, but as a heuristic device for use with my own students in our examination of Belfast itself. The idea was that we would attempt to develop a range of future scenarios, future Belfasts, if you like. Five scenarios were offered: "assimilation," where intergroup differences would disappear; "pluralism," where difference would be accommodated in a positive manner, with segregation existing to a degree, but where opportunities to move beyond the segregated enclaves would be widely available; "segmentation," where differences would be sharply retained, desegregation being difficult to achieve even if desired, though in a context where competing sovereignty claims would not be present; "polarization," which basically would be the current frontier city situation of competing sovereignty claims; and finally "cleansing," where ethnic differences would be eliminated by removal of one of the sources of the differentiation (Boal 1999). The scenarios spectrum stresses the unsegregated conditions present both under "assimilation" and under "cleansing," though the processes leading to these two states are as unlike as night and day (Figure 4.1).

This teaching device pointed us in two further directions. First, while recognizing that Belfast, as currently constituted, resided in the "polarized" category, it could also be recognized that some other cities were in the same category (for instance Jerusalem) while others, again, could be located somewhere else on what we came to call the "scenarios spectrum" (Toronto under "pluralism" [see Qadeer, chapter 3], Chicago, as recognized by Robert E. Park and Ernest Burgess, under "assimilation," black segregation in U.S. cities under "segmentation," Sarajevo under "cleansing," and so on). The scheme consequently encouraged us to compare Belfast with like "polarized" cities, while at the same time placing the "polarized" category alongside, and in contrast with, other urban ethnic situations.

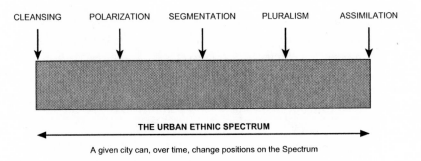

THE URBAN ETHNIC SPECTRUM

A given city can, over time, change positions on the Spectrum

Figure 4.1. The Scenarios Spectrum
Source: Author

Our exercise, however, goes a stage further than this. In setting up a number of different Belfasts in our modeling exercise, we also raised two questions. Was Belfast showing any evidence of movement along the spectrum, for instance from "polarization" towards "pluralism" on the one hand, or towards "cleansing" on the other? This suggested that we should explore what is happening with other cities that can be placed on the spectrum—are they remaining static in position or are they moving in a more integrationist or a more separatist direction? The second question stimulated by the use of the spectrum entails more than observation—it calls for intervention. The question here basically is whether the current spectrum position of a given city is a desirable one, or should attempts be made to steer it towards one of the alternatives? The pro-active implications of this question mean that policy concerns need to be addressed.

Policy and Action

Whatever position a city has on the scenarios spectrum, it will be important to monitor what is going on. Is the city retaining a fixed position or is it evolving from that position towards a different one on the spectrum? For instance, Belfast became more polarized in the 1970s and 1980s. More importantly, have judgments been made as to where it is considered desirable for the city to be found on the spectrum? If, for instance, it is considered desirable for the city to become more pluralistic (moving perhaps from segmentation), then judgments can be made regarding the acceptability or unacceptability of observed change underway in spectrum position. Policy (housing, planning, etc.) can then be reactive, encouraging the direction of change or trying to check or even reverse it, depending on circumstances. More proactively, however, policy can be evolved that attempts to steer the city in the desired direction. What, for instance, can be done to reduce housing segregation or to provide urban arenas conducive to ethnically integrated interaction?

Of course economic factors must be included in any assessment. To what extent is segregation a product of the economic position of the segregated group or groups? At a more micro-level, policies such as the re-differentiation and the physically restructuring of the urban housing stock can help reduce ethnic division, particularly where such actions increase the residential mixing of different income groups. The Netherlands provides a good example of a situation where major efforts are underway to retain or to create neighborhoods with a range of tenure types and a range of rents and/or prices. This is aimed at encouraging a good mix of income levels in individual neighborhoods, rather than having neighborhoods that are sharply differentiated from each other in terms of the incomes of their households (Priemus 1998; 2000).

Reducing urban division, that is, moving to the right along the spectrum (see figure 4.1), can also be aided by a policy focus on social institutions. Here two strategies can be suggested. The first is one where, in any given set of neighborhoods, institutions appropriate to the needs of a range of ethnic groups are encouraged through the application of appropriate land use planning measures, development control decisions, and financial subsidization (Krishnarayan and Thomas 1993). In this way, members of a given ethnic group will be encouraged to take up (or continue) residence in the neighborhood concerned, because institutions supportive of their way of life will be found nearby (religious institutions, schools, community centers, etc.). The second approach, also having the objective of encouraging neighborhoods of mixed ethnicity, is to aid the development of integrated (shared) institutions such as integrated schools.

Further inputs aimed at moving cities in a more integrated direction along the scenarios spectrum will focus on housing policy. In this, the public *and* the private sectors must be part of the overall effort both in terms of fairness and in terms of cultivating ethnic sensitivity in their operations. Mixed neighborhoods can be encouraged in the social housing sector both by allocation policies and by the removal of what in Belfast are known as "ethnic chill factors" (certain types of graffiti, many wall murals, nationalistic flag flying, etc.), while householders can be offered incentives (both monetary and housing quality [Murtagh 2002]).

Policy Appraisal

Whether policy is reactive or proactive, monitoring should not only track the urban dynamics; it should also focus on policy appraisal. Thus, in Belfast it has been proposed that Policy Appraisal for Separation and Sharing (PASS) should be initiated (Hadden, Irwin, and Boal 1996). The objective of PASS would be to ensure that all official policies are assessed for their contribution to ethnonational sharing and the avoidance of any increase (whether intentional or not) in the extent of separation. The same theme has been highlighted by Brendan Murtagh (1995) when he called for monitoring and evaluating the implementation of local planning governmental development initiatives and their impact on the sensitively balanced "cultural communities" with the results of such monitoring being fed back to inform the planning process. Murtagh (1995) uses the term "cultural community" as a substitute for "ethnic" or "ethnonational" group. Such language tends to soften some of the brutal realities experienced on the ground. Indeed, I think we can begin to talk of "ethnic impact statements" becoming required elements of all major planning and housing proposals.

Here I am reminded of the earlier writings of Brian McLoughlin (1969) who, following W. Ross Ashby, talked of "error controlled regulation." He saw four central features of such control:

- The system to be controlled;
- The intended state or states of the system;
- A device for measuring the actual state of the system and, thus, its deviation from the intended state;
- A means of supplying correcting influences to keep the system within the limits set or to steer it in the right direction.

For the scenarios perspective, the system to be controlled encompasses the ethnic dimensions of the city concerned (most particularly levels of segregation). In the second case, the intended state would be the desired ethnic arrangements (where should the city be on the spectrum?), though one has to admit that there might well be a lack of consensus as to what is desirable. Third, monitoring, as suggested by Tom Hadden, Colin Irwin, and Frederick W. Boal (1996) and Brendan Murtagh (2002), would provide the measuring devices, while "error controlled regulation" would be attempted by proactive intervention in the planning system, the housing market, the pattern of school provision and so forth. In McLoughlin's (1969, 86) diagram, the "disturbance" could be any development proposal that might impact on the spatial dimensions of ethnic relations, while the "decision" would be whether or not (or to what extent) the "disturbance" should be permitted to go ahead.

Urban Professionals

There is one other matter I would like to refer to, that is the role of urban professionals in all this. Here a very thought provoking categorization can be introduced. Again I draw on Meron Benvenisti (1987) who first applied such a scheme in the urban ethnic context. This scheme has been further developed and applied by Scott A. Bollens (1999). Four urban policy strategies are recognized: "neutral," "partisan," "equity," and "resolver." Urban professionals operating under one of these ideological rubrics approach their tasks in quite distinctive ways. Ethnically neutral planning, for instance, attempts to apply a color blind approach (Bollens 2000, 23) where the objective is to seek the depoliticization of territorial issues by framing urban problems as value-free, technical matters soluble through planning procedures and the operation of professional norms. A partisan urban strategy, in contrast, chooses sides and, according to Bollens, is a regressive agent of change. With this, the city's governing ideology merges with the empowered group's ideology. Domination strategies are applied to land use planning and regulation in order to entrench and expand territorial claims or to enforce exclusionary control of access (Bollens 2000, 24). The third model, the equity strategy, gives primacy to ethnic affiliation in order to decrease rather than perpetuate intergroup inequalities. Because they seek remediation and compensation for past hurts and wrongs, equity-based criteria will often be significantly different from the financial and technical criteria deployed by the ethnically neutral urban professional. Finally, there is the resolver model. Here an attempt is made to connect urban issues to the root political causes of urban polarization, power imbalances, subordination, and disempowerment. Resolver is the only strategy of the four that attempts to resolve the conflict rather than just manage it. It goes beyond the equity-based allocation of urban resources (the latter with its focus on urban symptoms) to pursue urban empowerment for all ethnic groups in the city (Bollens 2000, 26).

If we relate these four approaches to urban segregation, we can suggest how this might work out. With the neutral model, little would be done that would intentionally increase or decrease segregation, but attempts would be made to deal with each group in a fair manner. Partisan planning, on the other hand, would entail manipulation of segregation as a management tool in the repertoire of the dominant group. Equity planning would recognize inequalities in the segregated environment and would attempt to rectify perceived imbalances. Affirmative action in the housing and land markets, allocation systems, and in land use planning would be important. Finally, there is resolver role. Here urban professionals would recognize a need for intervention at the higher structural levels of society, acknowledging that segregation itself is a reflection of that structure. Bollens suggests that the resolver strategy would entail planners and others pursuing urban empowerment for all ethnic groups in a given city, challenging, thereby, the existing power structures. He suggests that nongovernmental planners adopting advocacy roles may be most successful (Bollens 1999, 28–29).

The point being made here is that planners and housing professionals (and academics for that matter!) are operating from particular ideological perspectives (whether they admit it or not and whether they are aware of it or not). Consequently, it is necessary to recognize what these perspectives are and how they shape our thoughts and actions; in the present case, how issues of segregation are confronted or, indeed avoided. This also raises the question as to how urban professionals are to be trained. Leonie Sandercock (1998) suggests that future planners (and other urban professionals) should be equipped with a set of five literacies: technical, analytical, multicultural, ecological, and design. The third of these, the multicultural, impinges most directly on segregation and has profound implications not only for the formal training of planners and other urban professionals, but also for the ways in which we approach issues of segregation. It does not, however, provide ready answers. Rather it sensitizes.

Chapter 5

SOCIAL CAPITAL AND SEGREGATION IN THE UNITED STATES

Xavier de Souza Briggs

Introduction

The now ubiquitous concept of *social capital*—in essence, the resources stored in social connections—sheds light on both the causes and consequences of segregation in the United States. Social capital also highlights some critical but often overlooked dimensions of the most common efforts to undo segregation or mitigate its effects, that is, to reduce various types of spatial inequality or to live with them at lower social cost. Social capital thus hints at how we might do both more effectively.

Understood as the value stored in social networks, group membership or "community" variously defined, social capital has generated enormous, if sometimes confusing, interest from scholars, practitioners, and policymakers over the past decade. The scale and variety of interest are thanks in large part to the influential work of political scientist Robert D. Putnam (1993; 2000) and the cottage industry of social capital studies and commentaries that his work has inspired and provoked.[1] The notion that key features of social connectedness, such as personal and institutional networks, pro-civic norms, and social trust, can help actors accomplish a variety of objectives has gained considerable new legitimacy and attention both in the United States and around the world. Recent research has provided considerable empirical support for, and promoted much broader public understanding of, ideas about social connection long taken for granted in certain branches of social science, particularly in sociology.

As Alejandro Portes (1998, 2) notes, the formal concept that membership in groups or networks can generate positive as well as negative effects for the individuals involved is a "staple notion" of social theory dating back over a century. Putnam's evidence has helped make the idea commonly acceptable but also something of a cause célèbre, since in the case of the United States, he chronicles a sharp decline in almost every measurable form of social capital over the past generation.

Whatever the conceptual emphasis, from high-performing business clusters to healthy and well-educated children, from effective and accountable government to safer city streets, social capital is increasingly "implicated" in the most positive sense of that word.[2] Notably, the largest known online source of studies, commentaries, measurement tools, and other resources related to social capital is the World Bank. The Bank has declared social capital a key tool for both understanding poverty and reducing it worldwide, particularly through locally based and "community-driven" initiatives.[3] Discussions of social capital are increasingly common, from international policy groups to the chambers of lawmakers and meetings of grassroots advocates for community improvement.[4]

Less common, however, is the recognition that social capital is a *means,* that is, a resource that enables productive action, just as other forms of capital do, and not an end in itself, that it possesses no right or wrong until some judgment is made about the ends to which we put it. We covet social capital for the reasons that many people covet money: not for what it is, but for what we can do with it. And so, social capital, in the metropolis and rural village alike, can be employed to exclude, dominate, and cheat, not just to promote the common good, however a given group of stakeholders may define that good.

More broadly, social capital's origin in relationships conveys the benefit as well as the burden of sustaining human relationships and of being a member of any group. As Portes (1998, 16–17) reminds us, groups may make "excessive claims of . . . members" and even promote a "downward leveling of norms" within the group, making achievement in the wider society less attractive and more difficult for group members. The labeling of school achievement as an unattractive "white thing" by some minority youth is one hotly debated example of the leveling by peer groups (Ogbu 1978; Small and Newman 2001), though by no means an example that excuses the structures of discrimination and unequal access to resources that do so much to drive educational inequality. Finally, influential poverty research that highlights the resilience of many poor people's networks has also born eloquent testimony to the overwhelming obligations and strains that chronically resource-poor social ties—endlessly needy others—can place on individuals and families struggling to get ahead (Stack 1974).

If these "dark sides" of social capital offer one brake on the social capital rush, another is the fear that political conservatives are turning to social capital, as they often have to self-help and volunteerism, for confirmation that community bonds make an effective substitute for government action. *More community available, less government required,* or so the theory goes.

Notwithstanding such important concerns, the public and scholarly debates have shifted somewhat from whether social capital is beneficial in measurable ways to precisely how and why social bonds matter for particular behavior and outcomes that society cares about. We have also begun to focus more intently on whether an understanding of such how's and why's is actionable in any reliable way at any significant scale, that is, the how-do-you-leverage-it question. Observers and would-be change agents wonder whether we can create more social capital of the kinds that serve important public interests—what Robert D. Putnam and others have termed "public-regarding" social capital—and how to do so through formal instruments of public policy and planning or more informal means of collective action.[5] Creating more social capital, but only of some kinds, implies being both systematic and selective and implies *formalizing,* somewhat, the means for enabling, creating, or sustaining an intrinsically *in*formal resource.

Segregation Meets Social Capital: A Preview

We might think of social capital as having two quite distinct purposes in discussions of segregation and the city. First, social capital is an *analytic lens* that helps clarify cause and effect relationships that link race to space and both to persistent patterns of social inequality. Social capital enriches economic and other perspectives on the city that rely too exclusively on individual choice and calculus to explain spatial and other patterns of inequality. Specifically, social capital provides a flexible way to understand the social context or "embeddedness" of individual choices and rationality (Coleman 1990). Second, social capital is a deployable asset, if not often an easily measured or easily directed one, through which particular agents seek to accomplish purposes that matter to them, at least some of which also matter to the wider society. The first purpose helps us take stock of the second and, if we are lucky as well as wise, make better decisions about the types of social capital worth cultivating and where and how to deploy that capital.

If the case for social capital's importance to human life is stronger and more empirically grounded than ever, the testing of our capacity to produce and allocate more of the right kinds of that capital is much weaker, more nascent, and less amenable to the prescriptions of traditional social research and the professions. The subject of urban spatial segregation, and along with it *social* segregation among groups who live in cities or metropolitan areas, thus pose important reality tests for the charismatic concept of social capital.[6]

Census 2000 provides a mixed picture of segregation in the United States at the turn of this new century. On one hand, rates of segregation in the most hypersegregated metro areas—rates of black segregation from Whites, most of all in older cities of the Northeast and Midwest—continue to fall (Lewis Mumford Center 2001a). This continues a three decade-long trend and represents an overall drop in black/nonblack segregation to its lowest point since 1920 (Glaeser and Vigdor 2001). At the same time, those rates remain distressingly high in absolute terms. The rate of decline is minimal in a number of large and hypersegregated metros and, over the past two decades, these high-level/slow-decline cities have shown some of the highest rates of concentrated minority poverty in the nation. We know extreme racial isolation to be a marker for extreme social and economic distress. In an interview on NPR's All Things Considered (2001), sociologist John Logan put the decline in black-white segregation in perspective: "It's at a rate that my grandchildren, when they die, will still not be living in an integrated society."

The average white in U.S. cities and suburbs lives in a neighborhood (census tract) that is overwhelmingly white (about 84 percent) and thus offers little exposure to other racial/ethnic groups (Lewis Mumford Center 2001a). Asians, Hispanics, and Blacks are more exposed to other groups; all three groups live in more integrated neighborhoods than Whites do, on average, though high rates of immigration are combining with concentrated settlement patterns to increase rates of Asian and Hispanic segregation from Whites in some of the fastest growing metro areas. There is strong evidence that predominantly white neighborhoods offer minorities better schools and services, lower crime, and better amenities, that on average, people of color in America "pay a price" for living in largely nonwhite neighborhoods (Wilson and Hammer 2001, 272).

This chapter will begin by outlining the distinct analytic concerns and levels of analyses that have shaped contemporary research on social capital, emphasizing social capital's implications for inequality. Of particular importance is the concept of "bridging" social ties (Briggs 2003a), which spatial segregation undermines both directly and indirectly. Next, more specific arguments are explored linking spatial segregation to social capital—ironically, separation to connectedness. These arguments include long-posited links, such as those between physical isolation and social isolation, but also more overlooked relationships, such as that between political power and social capital (how social capital in *networks of influence* contributes to spatial segregation) or between social capital and human capital (the network and social-psychological benefits of integrated school environments). Third, the commonly prescribed "cures" for segregation are reconsidered in light of social capital. The conclusion reviews the claim that social capital teaches us important things about the causes, consequences, and cures of segregation. It is a hopeful, but mixed, claim and one with important surprises for those who believe that more "community" will mean less, or at least less damaging, segregation.

Social Capital and Inequality: Three Analyses

With respect to the themes of this volume—space, inequality, and important patterns of urban and regional change worldwide—three relatively distinct analytic uses of social capital have emerged in contemporary research (table 5.1). The first focuses on the benefits and costs of particular types of *personal* networks. Social capital, in its guise as an "individual

TABLE 5.1. Social Capital and Inequality: Three Analytic Emphases

Tradition/Features of Social Relations Emphasized	Level(s) of Analysis	Principal Action Problems for which Social Capital is a Resource (exemplars)
1. *Individual Support and Status Attainment:* personal networks, proximate (particularized) trust.	Micro (individual to small group)	Individual and proximate network coping (Wellman and Frank 2001), individual and proximate-network status attainment (Briggs 1998, Hannerz 1969, Kleit 2001, Lin 2001)
2. *Collective Efficacy or Community Capacity:* proximate trust, social cohesion, personal and organizational networks, presence of "indigenous" organizations or other institutional capacity in a group.	Micro (small group) to Meso (neighborhood or larger "community")	Small-area social organization, informal social control and proximate trust (Sampson, Raudenbush, and Earls 1997); capable neighborhood-level institutions and functional networks (Chaskin et al. 2001, Gittell and Vidal 1998)
3. *Civic and Economic Performance:* generalized trust, broad associational participation, personal and organizational networks.	Meso to Macro (community to nation)	Economic performance and democratic function (Fukuyama 1995; Keyes et al. 1996; Putnam 1993, 2000; Woolcock 1998; Woolcock and Narayan 2000).

Note: The exemplars included here are limited to empirical research in which the term "social capital" is employed. Many earlier and more varied works, including pioneering ethnographic work, treated social resources as central to poverty and inequality problems. See for example, Jeremy Boissevain, *Friends of Friends* (Oxford: Blackwell, 1974); Clyde Mitchell, *The Concept and Use of Social Networks* (Mancester: Mancester University Press, 1969); Carol Stack, *All Our Kin* (New York: Harper and Row, 1974).

good," is understood to be a key source of social support (coping or "getting by") as well as status attainment (mobility or "getting ahead"). Decades of research in varied methodological traditions has underlined the importance of both, particularly for the very poor (Briggs 1998, 2003a; Putnam 2000; Stack 1974). Among other functions, personal networks can act as bridges across spatial barriers in the divided metropolis. That is, social ties help determine our ability to compensate for spatial disadvantage, the uneven "geography of opportunity" in metro areas (Briggs 2003b; Galster and Killen 1995; Pastor 2001).

While many important social ties in city, town, or suburb are not based in one's immediate neighborhood, a variety of studies indicate that access to social resources can vary widely by geography, particularly in metropolitan areas deeply segregated by race/ethnicity, income level or related factors (Briggs 2003a). Causality is tricky in this picture. It is not always clear, for example, to what degree observed spatial differences reflect mere aggregation of those personal or household traits in particular geographic areas and to what degree access to useful social capital is promoted or constrained by spatial factors per se. The best evidence is that these factors are interdependent (Massey and Denton 1993). For example, spatial barriers appear to reinforce social ones that isolate the poor, and the minority poor most of all, from useful connections to job advice, scholarship recommendations, and other forms of aid. But it is also true, that neighborhoods of concentrated minority poverty "select on" families (in-movers) who possess relatively weaker connections on arrival. The pattern is self-reinforcing.

Within this first approach, the *status attainment* line has focused largely on job networks and occupational attainment (Granovetter 1974; Lin 2001) and to a lesser extent on political influence (Boissevain 1974). *Social support* researchers focus on care provision, confiding, and companionship, and other informally provided resources that contribute to mental and physical health, family management, and economic survival (Wellman and Frank 2001). Social supports do not necessarily do double duty, that is, provide opportunity-enhancing leverage to improve economic circumstances or secure influence over others' decisions. But informal coping resources no doubt help us take advantage of opportunities that entail risk and exertion. They are especially vital to the chronically poor, who lack formal alternatives (Stack 1974). For most people, social support tends to come from socially similar others, often though not always in "strong ties" of friendship or kinship. Ties to *dis*similar others—social bridges—are often essential for getting ahead, and these are often, though not always, weaker, such as ties to civic and professional acquaintances. The association between bridges and getting ahead seems to be especially pronounced for racial minorities and the poor for whom socially similar peers are often not well positioned to provide leverage (Briggs 1998, 2003a; Wacquant and Wilson 1993).

The second approach defining social capital research and application emphasizes unequal access to collective capabilities, described as *collective efficacy* (Sampson, Raudenbush, and Earls 1997) or *community capacity* (Chaskin et al. 2001). While the empirical evidence is emergent, the collective-good role of social capital is implicated in both inequality problems and responses. That is, researchers and advocates have linked social capital (or lack of the same) to the reproduction of inequality and some of its most devastating symptoms, such as high and spatially concentrated rates of crime in many metropolitan areas, and to processes and outcomes of community development and or alternative responses to crime, unemployment, and other persistent spatial inequalities. Like the personal networks approach, the newer collective efficacy approach owes an important debt to William Julius Wilson's (1987) evidence on poverty concentration and the effects of massive social and economic changes in U.S. cities and suburbs on the isolation of poor racial minorities in inner-city neighborhoods.

The third approach scales up the collective-good aspect of social capital to consider the economic performance and democratic functioning, or the nonperformance and dysfunction, of entire regions or nations (Woolcock 1998). While much of Putnam's most recent work emphasizes individual-level benefits of social connection, his concern for civic engagement and societal well-being have consistently posited such scaled-up effects, first in comparisons of regions in Italy (Putnam 1993) and more recently in the United States (Putnam 2000) in analyses of health, civic engagement, economic performance, and other indicators against state-level measures of social capital. Portes (1998) and others have criticized strongly the analytic "stretches" entailed in such scaling up, recommending that we focus our attention on meso- or micro-level analyses (but see Woolcock and Narayan 2000).

In this third tradition, social, economic, and political inequality are an indirect concern conceived as societal dysfunctions, a failure to "make democracy work" to paraphrase the title of Putnam's first volume on social capital (1993). Certain types of social capital are recommended as partial cure. Here, space is decidedly a two-edged sword *facilitating* the development of strong communities of interest and face-to-face exchange, as in the formation of regional and national networks, neighborhood organizations, and even urban social movements (Fisher 1994) or *preventing* such contact, as in the case of segregated public schools whose enrollment tracks residential segregation. There is some evidence that residential segregation by race acts as a key barrier to the formation of bridging social ties (across diverse social groups) and more cross-racial political engagement (Briggs 2003b; Massey and Denton 1993; Putnam 2000).

Across all three levels of analysis, bridging ties, which spatial segregation appears to thwart, are important for two key reasons. First, such ties mitigate against economic inequality and enhance productivity by improving access for excluded or historically disadvantaged "out-groups" to information, endorsements (wherein an individual or institution vouches for someone's talent, reliability, or other traits), preparation, mentoring, and other keys to career success. Politics is the second reason that bridging ties matter so much, especially for a large society becoming more socially diverse and institutionally complex. In the classic rendering, crosscutting ties are essential to the development of broader political identities and broader communities of interest (Blau and Schwartz 1984; Simmel 1955). Beyond mere representation of all groups in elected office, the more basic diversity challenge is evident in a wide variety of regions and nations around the globe, from the immigrant Turkish minority in German or Dutch cities to Los Angeles' large, but largely disenfranchised, Hispanic majority. Crosscutting ties are thought to be key social foundations of power sharing without which the formal machinery of democratic government—organized political parties, open and competitive elections, civil liberties, and more—tend to falter (Lipset 1994).

Space as a Factor: Linking Spatial Segregation to Social Capital

The main arguments linking segregation and social capital are straightforward, but decidedly mixed:

- *Socially organized "avoidance" behaviors:* that social ties and group cohesion help produce segregation;
- *Space as a barrier:* that physical separation helps create social isolation;
- *Opportunity as spatially organized:* that physical and social isolation help generate and perpetuate inequality in a very uneven geography of opportunity;

- *(Conversely) "enclavism"*: that physical and social isolation also help
  beget solidarity attitudes, and behaviors, intensifying social and economic organization to promote sense of identity, confidence, and individual and group attainment.

Socially Organized Avoidance

First, the causes of persistent segregation are hotly debated, especially
where segregation by race is concerned. Segregation by income is more
easily explained away by affordability differences across neighborhoods
in metropolitan housing markets. But most analysts agree that beyond
differences in ability to pay and patterns of discrimination in the marketplace, self-segregation and the ethnic "bounding" of housing choices
along networks, plays some role in perpetuating racial/ethnic segregation
(reviews in Briggs 2003b; Charles 2001; Ellen 2000). In survey after survey, people of all racial backgrounds want some neighborhood diversity
but not too much. Networks and group attachments create a preference
for having some same-race (or co-ethnic) neighbors. This limits housing
choice in ways that contribute to segregation.

Space as a Barrier

There is some empirical evidence that spatial segregation by factors such
as class and race/ethnicity undermines social support and truncates job
networks and other useful social leverage. Segregation also creates social
divides more indirectly by perpetuating prejudices and discrimination,
and creating sharper and more persistent inequality than might exist
were status divisions not so strikingly compounded by spatial ones
(Briggs 2003b; Massey and Denton 1993; Peterson and Harrell 1992;
Wilson 1987).

Opportunity as Spatially Organized

Unequal social capital contributes to unequal social and economic opportunity and unequal outcomes, as well as political division, in a spatially
segregated society. Calling spatial segregation by race the "missing link"
in contemporary explanations of urban poverty, Douglas S. Massey and
Nancy A. Denton (1993) argue that segregation be treated as the central

force perpetuating social inequality, especially that suffered by Blacks. Beyond the stunting of interracial social and political relationships per se, the researchers point to a particularly strong emphasis on local governance and finance of critical public services, such as public education, through local policymaking bodies and local property taxes. This localism, in turn, generates sharp spatial divisions in access to quality schools and other key institutions, a sharply uneven "geography of opportunity," at a time when educational attainment is increasingly important in the economy (Briggs 2003b; Galster and Killen 1995).

Enclavism: The Benefits of Boundaries

As Peter Marcuse defines it in this volume, an enclave is "an area of spatial concentration in which members of a particular population group, self-defined by ethnicity, or religion, or otherwise, congregate as a means of protecting and enhancing their economic, social, political, and/or cultural development." Spatial segregation, by limiting opportunities for contacts and influence within the wider society and by promoting enclavism of groups thus excluded, has historically been a boon to within-group solidarity and the associated patterns of mutual aid on which the disadvantaged, from inner-city Chicago to the *favelas* of Rio de Janeiro, have often relied significantly (Stack 1974; Woolcock and Narayan 2000). Ethnic enclave economies bear this imprint as well, from Chinatown in New York to Little Havana in Miami (now a largely Central and South American enclave that retains the name coined by an earlier wave of entrepreneurial Cuban immigrants). Patterns of exclusion in the wider locale create boundaries with mixed effects. Exclusion imposes costs by limiting opportunities for social and economic "mainstreaming" while forging stronger, denser, and often richly beneficial patterns of exchange within the enclave, from lower cost capitalization of firms to labor savings and access to restricted consumer markets (Portes 1998; Waldinger 1986; Zhou 1992). Ethnic ghettos that are largely involuntary tend to feature the costs without the benefits (Glaeser and Cutler 1997).

These common arguments are specific instances of the more general links posited by the three analytic traditions in social capital research, outlined above, about the costs and benefits of social ties at individual, small group, and societal levels. Clarity on the broad approaches helps one assess these more specific arguments about space, social connection, and opportunity in a critical light.

For example, a frequent blind spot in the application of solidarity concepts to social inequality, and to the study of poverty, specifically, is in the failure to think about the quality or *contents* of social ties and the specific types of action for which social resources are needed. Take arguments about the "community building" potential in very high poverty areas, which often fail to distinguish the social resources that help the poor cope with conditions of chronic scarcity from those that act as opportunity generators, helping the poor "get ahead" through improved access to a good job opportunity, for example, or a critical loan or life-changing educational scholarship. Even rotating credit pools and other small-scale self-help models among the poor, such as the now world-renowned Grameen Bank, typically rely on outside infusions of capital, consumer demand, and technical assistance (Servon 1999). In effect, they rely on what scholars of international development have termed *synergy* among the state (government action), private market, and civil society (private nongovernmental or "community" initiative) (Woolcock 1998).

Within-group solidarity, if the group in question is chronically poor, is typically a much better generator of getting-by support than getting-ahead leverage, a finding that underlines the critical importance of effective and durable social bridges. Given that there are benefits and costs depending on what is inside the enclave as well as what lies without, the *net* value of an enclave turns out to be a function of several things:

- The benefits of social resources available within the enclave compared to those available on the outside (an opportunity cost of relying on particular connections and foregoing the work of establishing others);
- The specific coping and attainment uses for which social resources may be useful to enclave members in particular niches at particular points in time, for example, start-up businesses have needs that mature ones do not, and networking rewards are not equivalent across all types of professions (Lin 2001); and
- The cross-group stigmas, within-group social obligations, and other potential burdens associated with belonging to an identifiable physical and social enclave.

Politics, Education and the Embedded Character of Social Capital

The main arguments linking social capital to segregation cover quite a range of urban and metropolitan phenomena and stand on solid empirical ground, even if they emphasize dangerously partial views of what individuals and communities need to survive and thrive, and even if the arguments rarely suggest simple choices for public policy or public action. On closer examination, however, social capital and segregation reveal other powerful, and in some ways more complex, associations than the important ones outlined above:

- Social capital is actively employed as a political resource, whether for exclusionary or inclusionary ends: to reinforce spatial segregation and other mechanisms of exclusion, but also to forge progressive alliances to combat such mechanisms; and
- Social capital effects should not be simply treated as "net" of education (human capital) or other factors shaping status and well being, but as operating to shape inequality through those factors.

Social Capital and Politics

By flourishing among groups that mobilize to protect their status from perceived threats, social capital is a resource actively cultivated and employed by political actors in the United States and elsewhere around the globe to promote spatial segregation and other mechanisms of social exclusion. Think of South Africa's apartheid-sustaining white minority (a white enclave insisting on forced black ones), but also of exclusionary not-in-my-backyard (NIMBY) opposition to desegregation and mixed-income housing in local U.S. policymaking.[7] Social capital is also evident in progressive efforts to link poor and racially isolated neighborhoods to external resources, often through civic and philanthropic networks or metro-wide coalitions of neighborhood-based organizations. In this political view, social capital is developed and deployed along local influence networks that sometimes become durable coalitions or "regimes" or that challenge regimes by pressing claims (Stone 1989). Finally, social capital can be defined to include broad psychological attachments to a region or nation-state and civic norms that bind its citizens in a sense of shared fate, promoting the kind of social consensus needed to make sustained progress on inequality and other problems (Putnam 1993, 2000).

Why do social capital and politics need each other? Contrary to the wishful portrayals of social capital as mere we-feeling or community attachment or to specifications of the concept as indicated by organizational membership in lieu of political interest or participation (Fuchs, Shapiro, and Minnite 2001), establishing patterns of trust and reciprocal obligation is crucial in any society or social group, not because trust and reciprocity eliminate important conflicts of political interest, but because they make it easier to manage conflict in creative and sustainable ways. Social capital is a vital resource for cities, neighborhoods, and individuals in part because of power and politics and not in place of them (Briggs 1998; Warren, Thompson, and Saegert 2001). Our efforts to analyze this basic idea formally and empirically are in their infancy, though studies of the local politics of development have persuasively distinguished cities high in such forms of social capital (where collective action and conflict resolution seem to be more successful) from cities that lack it (Keyes et al. 1996).

Closer to the themes of this volume, the evidence in much social research of the past few decades is that social capital, though often not by name, is both cause and effect of the politics of segregation. As cause, social capital is crucial to the network and other influence strategies through which some political actors win spatial and other goods—a decision to add desired recreational facilities to a neighborhood, a decision *not* to site a waste treatment plant there—more often and more richly than other actors, sometimes triggering organized response that draws on and generates social capital. As effect, and as outlined in the previous section, the politics that helps produce and sustain the segregated metropolis helps deprive our community problem solving, via that segregation, of the boundary-spanning, bridging relationships, and greater social trust we need to play the political game more equitably (Briggs 2002; Putnam 2000). Parochial communities of interest, in acting to defend their status or "way of life," may generate an adversarial, and even violent, politics (Danielson 1976).

But a larger point concerns the political nature of social connections themselves. Human relationships are significantly interest driven. Beyond the need for affiliation itself, we try to get tangible problems solved with and through other people, as early ethnographic analyses of personal networks emphasized (Boissevain 1974; Mitchell 1969). In this way, an enormous number of the social interactions and other network-building phenomena of which social capital is derived, are, at least in part, "political" in the broad sense of the word.

Beyond everyday or personal interests, though, it is civic interests, collective action, and power that are at issue. Here, social capital meets two traditions of urban political theory. In the first, early studies of community power and elite influence by sociologist Floyd Hunter (1953) launched a focus on influence network, on how relationships are formed and deployed, in specific issue areas, to influence decisions, and other events. As David Knoke (1994) notes in a review of this tradition, network patterns per se seem to matter most where access to information and decision makers is not highly institutionalized, but rather more fluid and informal. This simple insight confirms the conventional wisdom of those who, by analogy to the role of networks in the job market, recognize that influencing political events is not just about what you know (as an expert), but about who you know—at city hall, on the foundation board, in the real estate developers' roundtable, or in the more informal networks along which political influence is had.

In a second line of urban political analysis, regime theory, much research in the 1980s and 1990s has focused on "power to, not power over" (Stone 1989, 229). That is, rather than analyze who wins particular decisions, such as in urban redevelopment or education debates, and who loses or does not participate at all, analyses of urban regimes focus on how durable coalitions are built to accomplish important, contested purposes over time through sustained political programs. Interests are not treated as given, for they "emerge through action, social relationships, and experience" (Stoker 1995, 61). The world of politics is seen as messy and uncertain with fragmented decision-making authority and a highly dispersed capacity to produce outcomes that stakeholders value.

Is such a context for local politicking unique to the United States or increasingly the way of the world? Analysts have offered some comparisons to cities in Europe and other parts of the world (Dowding 2001). But regime analyses are still centered on the United States, with its high level of government decentralization (localism) and long-standing preference for private, nongovernmental initiative in social policy and problem solving—a preference that contributes mightily to "disperse" capacity and legitimacy to act.

In the regime conception, cooperation and competition in local political arenas are carried out along networks that are not simple hierarchies or egalitarian chains composed of claimants of equal status. Most studies in the regime theory tradition find that coalitions of leading (might we say elite?) business and government players dominate most localities (Dowding 2001; Stoker 1995; Stone 1989). Except in rare contexts (DeLeon 1992), such dominant coalitions make selective concessions to progressive coalitions or lower-status stakeholders and engage public life in ways that defy the image of constant collusion and seamless coordination suggested by the phrase "power elite."

To theorists, the focus on elite-dominated versus pluralistic access to power, and the validity of methods that emphasize relationships (structure) versus those that emphasize behavior (action) and trace influence through relationships, are importantly different (Altshuler and Luberoff 2003). But from the standpoint of policy and political options, the differences may not be so important. The picture that emerges from the last several decades of research on local politics in America is one that, regardless of discipline or analytic approach, emphasizes a number of structural traits that call for the cultivation of advantage through strategic social connections or social capital. These traits include the increased informational complexity of public life, interdependence among issue domains, the presence of more varied political actors and networks of the same, coalition structures as the basis for short- and long-run influence, interjurisdictional fragmentation, fluidity introduced by changing economic fortunes in cities and suburbs, and the devolution of authority from the federal government to states and localities.

In recent years, researchers have used social capital to illuminate a variety of political phenomena relevant to the themes of this volume, showing how social capital is employed as a political resource for or against spatial inequality and associated patterns of disadvantage. It may be too early to posit "traditions" per se, but at least four potentially distinct emphases are evident thus far:

- Exclusion by a cohesive political elite: close to the Hunter line of community power analysis, some research shows how social capital is employed by a cohesive citywide or regionwide elite, often in small towns and cities and in rural areas, to preserve segregated economic, political, and social life (e.g., Duncan 2001; Hunter 1953);

- Social resources across two-level games: a growing body of research shows how social capital functions through a kind of two-level game in its political and other dimensions, serving as an instrument of influence within neighborhoods (bonding people of similar interests) and bridging to create access to financial and other needed resources concentrated and brokered elsewhere, in the wider politics of the city or region. In concrete terms, this bonding and bridging happens through important interorganizational networks, as well as interpersonal ones (Briggs and Mueller with Sullivan 1997; Gittell and Vidal 1998; Marwell 2000). Two sides can play at this two-level game, of course. The affluent and exclusionary do so in the politics of NIMBY-ism, as the overtly prosegregation white neighborhood associations and their allies at city hall did almost a century ago (Massey and Denton 1993);

- Shared control and joint capacity: as one study puts it, social capital can be developed and applied to create the shared "commitment, capacity, and control" needed to enable partnerships for community development (Gittell and Vidal 1998) or the "community capacity" needed to mitigate the high costs of spatial inequalities, such as concentrated neighborhood poverty (Chaskin et al. 2001; Keyes 2001; Keyes et al. 1996). This emphasis does not assume a simple convergence of political interests. Rather, it offers a view of the community-as-system in which both political will and productive means must be assembled, across a wide variety of political, physical, and other divides, to tackle important social problems. Consistent with the broad claims of regime theory, this vein of analysis considers social capital as a resource in the ongoing project of amassing "the will and the way" needed to get things done in society (Briggs 2002);

- Relationship-building and resource use via new structures of participation: some analysts emphasize the danger of treating social capital as a disembodied network resource. Instead, they probe institutional structures, and, in particular, the nongovernmental or civil society institutions that organize relationships and channel power (Cohen 2001) in keeping with a long tradition from De Tocqueville to Putnam that explores the link between associations and democracy. Much recent analysis in this tradition appears to be rediscovering the representation, co-optation, and other dilemmas of "poor people's organizations" that the community action era highlighted (Marris and Rein 1967). Like the two-level game concept, structural arguments offer no special leverage to the disadvantaged: the affluent and the exclusionary can strategically enhance their channels of deliberation and influence, too.

Social Capital, Education, and Housing Mobility

Some of the huge social costs attributed to spatial segregation turn out to bear the imprint of social capital. The clearest example reflects spatial inequalities in public education in the United States. The most aggressive, and arguably the least popular, policy responses to such school segregation include desegregative efforts that span entire metropolitan areas, beyond the central cities where racial minorities and the poor are disproportionately concentrated. The best evidence on long-run effects of such metro-wide school desegregation suggests that low-income black youth educated in mostly black and poor schools located in inner-city neighborhoods are denied a critical social resource relative to comparable black youth educated in racially and socioeconomically diverse schools in higher income neighborhoods (Crain and Wells 1994; Eaton 2001). This resource is a product of the diverse and useful social networks, cross-cultural skills, and even the psychological resources for managing one's minority status in the presence of a majority group, all of which have significant and enduring positive effects on life and career. Notably, such effects depend on a level of meaningful social contact that can be undermined in a wide variety of ways: by "tracking" (ability grouping) students of different racial/ethnic backgrounds in separate classes or schools within a school; by failing to develop extracurricular bridges across groups; by encouraging exclusionary peer groups (cliques) that thwart bridges; and so on.

Institutional structure aside, self-segregation (within the ethnic group) thwarts bridging no matter how integrated a school or other environment appears to be in the aggregate. One cannot mandate bridging friendships or other positive peer relations, but they can be fostered, and schools are especially promising contexts for this. Schools work with the young (whose attitudes and relationships are more fluid and malleable than those of adults); schools organize productive work for which a diversity of contributions and contributors may be required; and schools are well positioned to instill active curiosity, including a respectful curiosity about "the other." More diverse social networks, a broader repertoire of interpersonal skills, and psychological resources for managing social life are all factors for which ongoing social interaction and close observation across borders of race and class are important—something more than media-provided images of ethnic style or stylized narratives that often entertain without educating.[8]

Perhaps more powerfully than any other evidence in the social policy research arsenal, these findings on desegregation's impact or, more usefully, on the mechanisms of such impact, lend support to the familiar adage on the limits of human capital: "It's *who* you know, not what you know." It is not at all that human capital benefits from better and more socially diverse schools are unimportant for segregated youth in American cities and suburbs but that the measurable, *independent* effects of those benefits may not outweigh the social capital benefits of attending such schools. More precisely, good schools generate useful social contacts, credentials, *and* tangible knowledge and skills (human capital). The network, signaling, and human capital benefits of "better" schools interact and are compounded in ways that statistical models of mobility tend to obscure (controlling on education to test supposedly independent effects of networks).

Given these findings on how social capital is embedded in political capital and human capital, each a vital resource for combating inequality, it is noteworthy that area-wide school desegregation, which often involves busing young people across town, has often faced intense opposition from white and minority advocates for neighborhood schools. As Putnam (2000) notes, beyond the family inconveniences associated with busing, such advocates typically emphasize the notion that schools embedded in neighborhoods with vibrant social capital, that is, active parent networks, neighboring, and more, can better monitor children, coordinate advocacy efforts, and otherwise support the educational enterprise than "placeless" school communities of parents and teachers who rarely interact. These are the very factors that led Coleman and Hoffer (1987) to propose social capital as the key *social* advantage that private schools have over public ones, once financial and other resource differences are taken into account.

Beyond the neighborhood schools counterargument, school desegregation faces three huge obstacles. The first is a general loss of support for race-based or affirmative social policy (Edley 1996). The second is demographic: the still-shrinking proportion of Whites among families with children in central cities, due to strong white preferences for the safety and better schools in the suburbs, and also to rapid minority immigration in many cities where housing is typically more affordable. Given these changes in the demographic pool to be distributed, some metropolitan areas offer no prospects for racially integrating schools within a single political jurisdiction and metro area-wide solutions are politically unpopular. The third obstacle is reform-based: new "choice" programs are creating charter schools and magnet programs that are often more segregated than assigned public schools. Not surprisingly, overall rates of racial segregation in public schools have increased steadily over the past decade and are now higher for Hispanics than for Blacks (Frankenberg, Lee, and Orfield 2003).

Recent housing policy demonstrations offer more hope. There is compelling, if incomplete, evidence that housing mobility programs that encourage and enable poor urban families to move to nonpoor neighborhoods, often in more racially mixed areas and sometimes in suburbs, may have significant social and economic benefits for participating families. Benefits include enhanced feelings of safety, improved mental and physical health, and possibly long-run gains in education and employment by children in these families (Del Conte and Kling 2001; Rubinowitz and Rosenbaum 2000). In at least some instances, and especially for young movers, benefits include new ties to socially dissimilar others. But our evidence on these effects is piecemeal at best thus far, and it is not clear what positive effects of new neighborhoods depend on (i.e., the causal pathways) or how quickly they register. Early evidence on the Moving to Opportunity (MTO) program, a five-city experiment launched by the U.S. government in 1994, suggested major life improvements by parents and children who moved to low poverty areas (the experimental group) and confirmed that many such movers can adjust effectively and do value safer, more racially mixed environments (Goering, Feins, and Richardson 2003). Yet at the five-year mark, MTO's effects on this experimental group appear more mixed: some of the families have moved back to higher poverty areas, health effects persist but few if any education effects have registered for young people, some increases in delinquent behavior are evident for experimental-group boys, and no effects on employment or reduced dependence on public assistance are evident for parents (Orr et al. 2003). Even allowing for the fact that MTO's experimental group is no longer uniformly residing in low-poverty areas (due to the moved-on pattern), the mixed results suggest that expanding the housing choices of the minority poor has the most immediate effects on safety and feelings of well-being rather than human capital or job success. A poor black or Hispanic single parent without a car or job who moves from a poor area to a nonpoor one still faces all of the barriers to getting ahead that those nonlocational traits imply.[9]

Re-thinking Segregation's "Cures" in Light of Social Capital

The last fifty years of public policy and community initiative reflect two responses to spatial segregation: target the root problem or mitigate its symptoms (see table 14.1). In the first instance, we have made limited efforts to reduce rates of spatial segregation despite the extensive case on its social costs. These "cure" efforts have focused on segregation in housing, and they have relied on affirmative recruitment, structured choice, or regulatory mechanisms of various kinds, each targeting some part of the larger problem.

Second, we have used a much wider variety of tools to live with or retrofit segregation, accepting that it will continue for some time to be unacceptably high—or even worsen for some groups, given rapid immigration and limited housing choice. Live-with efforts count on mitigating the social costs of segregation. Efforts of this type include: in-place community development strategies to enhance quality of life where the disadvantaged already live and often to attract a wider income mix to distressed areas; fiscal reform to reduce funding disparities among school districts or local governments; reverse commuting, job matching, and other workforce programs to connect workers in those areas to job growth at a distance; school desegregation (to break the link between neighborhood and school segregation); and other strategies.

Over the past decade, both cure and mitigate strategies have focused increasingly on income rather than race, particularly in the domain of housing assistance programs for low-income families. Income mixing and poverty deconcentration have become the watchwords. Race-based strategies are rarely pursued outside of court-ordered desegregation, and for a variety of reasons, these court-ordered efforts typically show troubled implementation and limited impacts (Briggs 2003c; Popkin et al. 2003). Notably, a major deconcentration element of the 1998 Quality Housing and Work Responsibility Act, the biggest reform in federal public housing in years, strenuously avoided mention of race.[10]

Neither type of effort—cure or mitigate—reflects a consistently applied, coherent national strategy resting on a stable political consensus. Quite the opposite: Our responses to spatial segregation have been episodic, fragmented across a patchwork of public agencies and private actors, inconsistent in content and objectives, misunderstood, highly localized in the details, hotly contested, and often forced to compete with other policy objectives or public ideals. One example of the latter would be the classic juxtaposing of the ideals of *integration* (even where choice must be constrained) and of *individual choice* (even at great cost to integration). Current debates over racial quotas in college admissions and the earlier feuds over racial stabilization policies in federally subsidized housing or in court-ordered housing desegregation programs attest to how divisive and disabling these controversies can be (Haar 1996; Varady 1979). Starrett City, a federally subsidized multifamily rental complex in New York City that was developed to promote racial integration, is an infamous case in point. Affordable housing advocates argued that minority families should not be kept on a waiting list so that "underrepresented" white families could move into vacant units. Reformers could find no way to promote racial balance in the housing complex without forcing one group of families (racial minorities) to wait longer for affordable housing. Back in the courts, affordability trumped integration.

I have already made the case for social capital's place in these difficult politics of segregation. But as a "deployable asset," can social capital help us either cure or mitigate, reduce rates of segregation, or lower the social costs? That is, can it help us deliver on whatever we manage to develop and sustain some political will to authorize? "Delivering" well seems especially important given the difficulties of implementing integrative strategies, as David P. Varady and Carole C. Walker's three articles on housing vouchers illustrate (2003a, 2003b, 2003c).

In principle, social capital should be a less useful asset where implementation strategies rely for their success on relatively institutionalized and routinized (or standardized) behaviors or transactions, and more useful where implementation activities are less so. For example, it is not clear that network-based strategies add much to regulatory mechanisms for inclusionary land use or fair housing enforcement. These mechanisms rarely offer us the leverage we would like, and beyond their political vulnerabilities, they are difficult to enforce well (see chapter 14). But procedures for reporting, investigating, and adjudicating are well defined and rely on the formal authority of law. There is a social context to reporting wrongdoing, to be sure, and to deciding on responsibility and remedies, but networks and other sources of social capital do not plausibly determine the success of housing rights enforcement.[11]

Affirmative marketing, on the other hand, that is, promoting residential locations to prospective in-movers on the basis of their race, income, or other status, is a much more relationship-driven and otherwise socially embedded business. Networks of referral, interpersonal encouragement (sales), mobilization of neighbors around welcoming and community improvement activities, and the influence of group attitudes and identity (felt obligations to one's own group or other groups) all play a part. Strategies conscious of social capital, of how it is made, deployed, and destroyed, are likely to fare better than alternatives that rely on "air war" marketing not embedded in social ties and inclusive norms. The best available evidence on what it takes for affirmative marketing to be successful corroborates this (Ellen 2000; Nyden, Maly and Lukehart 1997). But social capital may be "new wine in old casks," or at best new jargon for old wisdom, in this particular example.

Much less obvious is the power of the social capital concept to sharpen our thinking about what *brokers* or intermediary institutions do in this daunting segregation picture. From labor market ("job matching") intermediaries that directly affect access to economic mobility in metro markets (Harrison and Weiss 1998) to the even less appreciated (and much less studied) brokers of low-income housing markets, cultivating relationships with landlords and renters, improving information, facilitating transactions, often in the context of housing mobility programs (Turner 1998), brokers help break the link between place and prospects, or they help to mitigate the worst downsides in that association. Depending on how charter schools and other choice experiments in urban schooling evolve, brokers of information and referral may become important in public education as well (Nechyba 2001).

Likewise, social capital has been and will continue to be both a useful analytic lens and a deployable asset in the field of community development, which addresses spatial inequality by improving conditions in places starved for financial investments, political capital, and more. Recent analysis of "social capital as a development strategy" (Gittell and Vidal 1998), insightful as they are, leave on the agenda of future research a set of important questions about how to create much stronger, wider, and more useful bonding and bridging networks in the context of persistent conflicts of political interest and inequalities of political power.

Conclusion

As Camille Zubrinsky Charles (2001, 265) observes in a recent study of urban inequality in the United States: "As the Nation becomes increasingly diverse, the gap between haves and have-nots grows; this division is clearly color coded." Social capital is no panacea for residential segregation by race, attendant problems of political and economic inequality, or most other persistent social problems. Moreover, our stocks of social capital bear the imprint of a nation deeply divided by race and other differences since its early days. Spatial segregation, in particular, has shaped social connections by channeling interpersonal contact, creating an "American apartheid" in our political life (Massey and Denton 1993), and reproducing segregative institutions and attitudes—mediators of networks and their agendas. Prejudice and mutual ignorance will likely be with us for many years to come, no matter how fast our summary statistics reflect a "browning of America" and a steady decline in prejudicial attitudes (Charles 2001). Against this backdrop, we should worry, as Putnam (2000) has urged, not only about the overall decline in many useful forms of social capital over the past generation, but also about the particular dearth of bridging ties across race and class differences. Bridges are the ties that make multicultural democracy possible, particularly when social change is rapid and confusing (Briggs 2003a).

Even if social capital *is* part cure for segregation, our ability to engineer it in the right forms and direct it toward most of the right purposes is limited. When the question arises of how we should create more of this magic stuff and not simply analyze it or give thanks for the stocks of "good" social capital endowed us by history to date, social capital shows itself a slippery resource indeed. Still, strong, progressive community-based service providers and advocacy institutions, often creating synergies with both state and market, have developed and applied social capital for many years to both reduce segregation and mitigate its social costs.

In their assessment of social capital's value in the effort to alleviate poverty around the world, Michael Woolcock and Deepa Narayan offer a helpful three-part agenda for theorists, researchers, and policymakers:

. . . to identify the nature and extent of a community's social relationships and formal institutions and the interaction between them; to develop institutional strategies based on these social relations, particularly the extent of bonding and bridging social capital; and to determine how the positive manifestations of social capital—cooperation, trust, and institutional efficiency—can offset sectarianism, isolationism, and corruption. Put another way, the challenge is to transform situations where a community's social capital substitutes for weak, hostile, or indifferent formal institutions into ones in which both realms complement one another. (Woolcock and Narayan 2000, 239)

This paper has assessed both of the Woolcock-Narayan scenarios: social capital as a substitute for weak, hostile, *and* indifferent institutions that help structure inequality, and as a complement to these more formal structures, extending the reach of erstwhile efforts to connect people to quality jobs, housing, schooling, and to greater accountability by government, in spite of deep spatial inequalities. If the formal structures of government and the marketplace both constrain and enrich our lives on shared, contested metropolitan terrain, then social capital acts as a mostly nondirected buffer in some instances and a quite consciously applied instrument in others. This is particularly clear where local politics and local improvement strategies, from place-based community development to people-based "mobility" programs, are concerned.

Of particular importance is the under-appreciated role of intermediaries or brokering organizations in spanning the spatial and social divides so clear in metropolitan America. By spanning these divides, intermediaries help compensate for the uneven geography of opportunity that researchers from a variety of disciplines have outlined with increased precision and alarm over the past decade.

Closer to the forces that drive residential segregation rates, nothing about this analysis has suggested that America slow down an already lagging enforcement of fair housing laws or other efforts to fight discrimination in the marketplace. But the positive role of affirmative marketing groups and inclusive community institutions—collective action in a world of supposedly individualist consumers—becomes clearer in the light of social capital. Not only do such actors help shape cooperation to strengthen neighborhoods and make them more attractive to individual households, but they also affect the social context in which tough residential choices are made. Such agents of racial, class, or other integration do so, in part, by influencing movers and potential movers, as well as real estate professionals, lenders, and other market actors.

Would a nation of scaled-up, better equipped labor market brokers, affirmative marketers, and racially inclusive—not to mention relentless—community institutions be preferable to one in which the welfare state, public schooling, housing production and siting, and other systems are restructured to promote equality? No. It is hard to imagine that it would be. And some of our country's most important and influential civil society actors, for example, churches, synagogues, mosques, and other faith institutions, are, for the most part, stubbornly segregated by race or ethnicity (Putnam 2000). Nor is the thought of simply retrofitting a miswired world, thereby turning social capital into a shock absorber for deep spatial inequalities, adequate or just. These hypotheticals underline what is perhaps the most fundamental lesson of a social capital assessment of the problem of segregation. It is a lesson that echoes Woolcock and Narayan's point about substituting for effective public systems versus complementing them. There is nothing here to suggest that stockpiles of the right kinds of social capital *should* be made to substitute for the more just, more accountable government and market institutions that the core of the American experiment—opportunity for all—requires.

Notes

Celeste Benson provided superb research support for this work, and The Rocke-feller Foundation supported my research in the year when this project took shape, and MIT hosted me as the Martin Luther King, Jr. Visiting Fellow in Urban Studies and Planning. For helpful advice, I am grateful to the editors of this volume, partici-pants in the Lincoln Institute's International Seminar on Segregation and the City, and a number of colleagues, including Ingrid Gould Ellen, George C. Galster, John Goering, Douglas S. Massey, Robert D. Putnam, Thomas Sander, Robert J. Samp-son, June Manning Thomas, William Julius Wilson, Hal Wolman, and Michael Woolcock.

1. Though it is often attributed to him, Putnam (2000, 19) notes that the con-cept and phrase "social capital" have been "independently invented at least six times over the twentieth century": the first time (on record, in the En-glish language) by a local educator in West Virginia, not by a researcher; later by anthropologist Ulf Hannerz (1969) to describe benefits of net-works for residents of "ghetto" neighborhoods; then by economist Glenn Loury (1977) as a way of explaining racial inequality in economic out-comes; and still later, sociologist Pierre Bourdieu (1984), with a different emphasis, to help explain stratification and the reproduction of social classes. The late sociologist James S. Coleman's (1987, 1988) use of social capital to help explain the effects of private versus public schooling on children's educational attainment marks the beginning of the continuous and serious development of the concept in American social science. Putnam's own research, which has both popularized the concept enor-mously and advanced its intellectual content—rare for a social scientist on any topic—first turned to the concept for help in explaining the perfor-mance of regional governments in Italy (*Making Democracy Work: Civic Traditions in Modern Italy*, 1993). Soon after, Putnam used the social capi-tal concept to explore declines in certain long-standing forms of civic en-gagement and social trust in the United States. To capture the latter, he coined the widely traveled label "bowling alone," having found, as one of many such patterns of disconnectedness and lower associational involve-ment, that more Americans are bowling than ever, but fewer in leagues (Putnam 1996, 2000). For critiques of the concept, and of Putnam's pri-mary uses of the same, see Alejandro Portes (1998) and Robert J. Sampson, Stephen Raudenbush, and Felton Earls (1997).
2. For an encyclopedic review of the empirical evidence on social capital's ef-fects on social outcomes and institutional performance (e.g., by firms and governments), see Putnam (2000).
3. See www.worldbank.org/poverty/scapital and review and synthesis in Mi-chael Woolcock and Deepa Narayan (2000).

4. A recent case in point relevant to the themes of this book was an international conference focused on immigration, social capital, and public policy in wealthy nations, "The Opportunity and Challenge of Diversity: A Role for Social Capital?," organized by the Organization for Economic Cooperation and Development (OECD) and the Government of Canada, Montreal, Canada, November 24–25, 2003. See materials at www.oecd.org

5. Putnam's Saguaro Seminar on "Civic Engagement in America" grappled with these issues, yielding a summary report and a website for on-line exchange among those interested in taking action. See http://www.better together.org/.

6. These tests are all the more urgent in an era of globalization and globalized locales, with larger transnational flows of capital and labor increasing ethnic diversity and competitive pressures in many metropolitan regions; resurgent ethnic and religious group conflict over land and other prized assets, often where effective states and other coordinating and dispute-resolving structures have eroded or have yet to appear; larger and more capable civil society in the form of nongovernmental organizations and movements; and other trends (Briggs 2003b; Castells 1998).

7. "NIMBY" is the acronym conventionally applied in the United States to political resistance to "locally unwanted land uses" (LULUs), however, resisters may define the terms. Frequent targets of NIMBY-ism include affordable housing, municipal waste management facilities, highways, socially stigmatized retail businesses (such as exotic dance clubs), and commercial and industrial facilities perceived to represent public health hazards or a public nuisance (Popper 1981).

8. One can debate whether the full value of experience in integrated settings, especially for minority or "out" groups, is captured by *social* capital as Putnam, Coleman, Portes, and others have defined it. Pierre Bourdieu (1985) used the phrase *cultural capital* to refer to acquired or socially learned conceptions, dispositions, and habits that confer advantages in social life. His analytic interest was in the production and reproduction of social classes in France, but his penetrating insights have been applied to understand interracial and other cross-group contact and inequality patterns as well.

9. Larry Orr, Judith D. Feins, Robin Jacob, Erik Beecroft, Lisa Santonmatsu, Lawrence F. Katz, Jeffrey B. Liebman, and Jeffrey R. Kling (2003) remind us that the usual caveats of an experiment apply. For example, some "true impacts" large enough to be relevant for policy may not have been detected as *statistically* significant. Also, because some members of the experimental group moved again (after initial relocation), reported impacts may well understate the full benefits of prolonged exposure to low-poverty neighborhoods (see the Goering and Feins volume on the character of these areas and MTO participants' preferences).

10. Deconcentration aims to mix working and nonworking poor families in public housing complexes.
11. Social capital may offer much more where the successful implementation of *remedies* is concerned, since the latter depending on community problem-solving in the context of controversial ends (policy aims) and sometimes challenging means (operational requirements) as well.

Chapter 6

CAUSES AND CONSEQUENCES OF RAPID URBAN SPATIAL SEGREGATION

The New Towns of Tegucigalpa

Glenn Pearce-Oroz

Introduction

In Tegucigalpa, a quintessential case of urban spatial segregation, with its inherent positive and negative consequences, is currently underway. As noted in the operational definition suggested below, spatial segregation in this context focuses on accessibility to services. In the present case, thousands of families displaced by Hurricane Mitch, which devastated the nation of Honduras in October 1998, are being resettled in a valley twelve kilometers northwest of the capital on unpopulated rural land within the municipal jurisdiction of Tegucigalpa. The approximately thirty-six hundred families that will eventually be relocated to constitute the "new towns" of Tegucigalpa share similar socioeconomic characteristics. While the new residents will have access to basic infrastructure and social services (most will also possess legal title to their new properties), their connection to a large and diverse urban economy will be disrupted. Ironically, the majority of the population in the new towns will be living in inversely deficient conditions from which they came. Whereas prior to being displaced by the hurricane, most families lived within relatively easy access to established urban markets (e.g., labor and commercial) and common public areas facilitating social integration, they also lived predominantly in environmentally high-risk zones (those with excessive slopes on unstable land; predisposed to erosion and landslides) with either inadequate or incomplete basic services. Now, their access to basic services will be resolved, but their connection to the urban markets will be disrupted.

This case of spatial segregation is particularly compelling because of the extreme nature of the physical segregation (families are being resettled at a great distance from the capital) as well as the clarity of two sets of variables influencing the resettlement sites: land market forces and the political and social pressures that emerged in the aftermath of the hurricane. Analysis focuses on the extent to which land market imperfections and the political and social pressures have affected the resettlement of families to these new towns, and will be followed by recommended instruments for planning practitioners facing similar problems. First, however, the historical and spatial context of this phenomenon is addressed.

Explosive Urbanization in Tegucigalpa

Over the past thirty years, Tegucigalpa, presently home to a population of approximately nine hundred thousand or 15 percent of the country's estimated six million inhabitants, has been one of the most rapidly urbanizing cities in the hemisphere. According to the most recent projections by the *Centro Latinoamericano de Demografía* (CELADE 2000), Honduras will continue to register the highest average annual urbanization rates (4.0 percent) of the entire region for the period 2000–2005. The city's rapid rate of urbanization, however, contrasts sharply with the rural character of the country. The projected acceleration of urban growth provides clear evidence of a country in the midst of intense social and economic transition. In a region where 75 percent of the population is now urban, Honduras is one of three countries in Latin America that has remained predominantly rural with only 48 percent of Hondurans living in urban areas (CELADE 2000).

The urbanization of Tegucigalpa has followed the same trend, although perhaps more intensely, as that of many Latin American cities with informal settlements or marginal neighborhoods growing at the edges of the urban core on real estate, which is easily accessible to the urban poor due to its low value and undesirable topography. Similar to the *favelas* in Brazilian cities, *pueblos jóvenes* in Perú, and *callampas* in

Chile, the marginal neighborhoods in Tegucigalpa, which are often in areas with excessive slope or near the banks of the Choluteca River, are characterized by an improvised settlement pattern, a lack of integration with the rest of the city, and irregular land tenure. In addition, Tegucigalpa's mountainous terrain (altitude 1,200 meters) does not permit for natural urban expansion rendering certain low-lying areas more valuable and easier to service with public utilities than areas at higher elevations. As such, basic urban services, the extension of access roads, inclusion of green space and other community or social infrastructure (particularly schools and health clinics) tend to be lacking in these informal settlements, which in 1998 made up roughly 225 of Tegucigalpa's 340 neighborhoods accounting for a total population of 450,000 (PADCO 1998). According to these estimates, approximately half of the city is made up of informal settlements with varying degrees of consolidation.

The informal settlements that have proliferated throughout the city are driven in part by a deficient residential land market. Because access to the formal land market is not available to low-income sectors of the population, parallel or informal land markets have evolved to meet this unmet demand. The marginal neighborhoods of Tegucigalpa that have grown out of land invasions are one clear manifestation of the evolution of this parallel land market. The prevalence of distinct settlement patterns represented by the coexistence of formal and informal land markets has also been a driving force in establishing spatially segregated neighborhoods that in turn are the foundations for perpetuating an economically segregated urban population.

Even if Tegucigalpa's increasing urban population had settled in areas easily accessible for residential infrastructure, it is doubtful this infrastructure would have been forthcoming given the severe strain placed on already weak public services by the high rates of urban growth. The most recent data indicate that 89 percent of the urban population is connected to the public water supply network, 72 percent to the public sewer system, and 98 percent to public electricity (DGEC 2000). The high coverage rates of these public services, especially the water supply, belie the poor quality of service provided in certain marginal areas (e.g., service interrupted for days, low water pressure, poor maintenance, etc.).

Prior to Hurricane Mitch, spatial segregation was characterized by households having incomplete or deficient access to public networks or services, as well as by regular land tenure resulting from land invasions that later had to be submitted to a process of legal regularization. Despite these deficiencies, the populations of these marginal neighborhoods maintained relatively easy access to the urban economy, including jobs, consumer markets, financial and transportation services, and so forth. As will be discussed later, this characterization of spatial segregation is turned on its head for those families being resettled in the new towns of Tegucigalpa. There the nature of the segregation is based on the physical distance separating these residents from the urban economy. The fundamental element of access in each of these instances suggests an operational definition of urban spatial segregation: *unequal access to either public networks of services or private networks of the marketplace.* In Tegucigalpa, urban spatial segregation is, furthermore, a result of existing legal and institutional frameworks that are unable to prevent the proliferation of spatially segregated human settlements or effectively mitigate their negative consequences. In the absence of policy and legal reforms, these forces provide the context whereby spatial segregation will continue to occur and, under particular circumstances, become exacerbated as is demonstrated by the present case.

Unquestionably, there are a number of factors that have contributed to the most recent example of spatial segregation: income inequality, low levels of macroeconomic growth, the existence of a small construction industry, lack of diversity in financial services, poorly functioning public services, and so forth. Each of these factors should be considered accordingly. Nevertheless, the following analysis will focus on two particular sets of forces directly shaping the current scenario. First, the weaknesses of the land market will be discussed to understand its effects and conversely, its potential contributions to mitigating continued spatial segregation, and subsequently, the political and social forces that emerged in the aftermath of Hurricane Mitch.

Land Market Forces

The current imperfections in the land market in Honduras not only have direct consequences on the patterns of human settlement, but also have larger repercussions on the economy. Each year, an estimated 12 percent of GDP is foregone because potential investments are not completed due to delays produced by the land registry, a pivotal regulatory mechanism of the land market (Agüero 1998). These imperfections also impact the housing market and by extension the home building industry. In fairness, other factors, both structural and cyclical, affect the performance of the home building industry; however, the lack of available and accessible land as well as financing, another important obstacle for both supply and demand of housing, are all closely linked to the weak property rights regime.

The inefficiencies in the land market are caused primarily by an anachronistic land registry system that allows for numerous inconsistencies, combined with a land administration system involving multiple institutional actors and few control mechanisms. These inefficiencies lead to overlapping or disputed land tenure ultimately resulting in an unstable property rights regime. The final product is a system that is highly imperfect and provides few land tenure guarantees. Those able to navigate the multiple steps to register property transactions that lay claim to legal property titles may still have questionable ownership.

Given this context, few real estate transactions are conducted without the potential for disputed property rights. In practice, however, questionable land tenure is no longer an issue in many urbanized sectors of Tegucigalpa. In these areas, consolidated after years of development, outstanding property rights issues have most likely been resolved. In contrast to the more consolidated urban areas, marginal or recently urbanized areas of the city will most likely be subject to either disputes in property rights or occupation of land by nonowners and nonrenters. The successful real estate developer must, therefore, be able to identify potential land and absorb certain transactions or carry costs until the potential risks associated with ownership are resolved and its de jure ownership also becomes de facto. This type of practice obviously impedes the fluidity of real estate development and directly influences the timely purchasing and development of land for low-income housing immediately following Hurricane Mitch.

The extremely restrictive and exclusionary nature of the land market forces encouraged many families to look for alternatives outside the formal market. There are definite economic barriers impeding access to the housing market, even under optimal conditions. However, in addition to the economic limitations, in Tegucigalpa an estimated 49 percent of the population lives below the poverty line with average monthly incomes of

167 U.S. dollars (UNDP 2000), the structural barriers of the land market make the housing market even less accessible. Furthermore, few public programs are available to those families facing the greatest number of obstacles to the housing market, those that exist have not yet reached the dimension necessary to successfully address the problem, nor are they effective in targeting beneficiaries. With little to no real access to urban land and an equally difficult access to the rental market, alternative strategies for satisfying shelter needs, namely, land invasions, are adopted.

Faced with an enormous housing deficit, inadequate public sector responses, and a private sector without the necessary incentives to build affordable housing, the tolerance to land invasions by the municipality (especially invasions of municipal land) can be an expedient solution to sheltering the urban population. As demonstrated by the aftermath of Hurricane Mitch, the expedient short-term solution has led to human tragedy and more costly solutions in the long run. Not only are there long-term consequences for families being relocated to the new towns, but also there are long-term consequences for families who have remained in high-risk areas. For the families that have stayed behind, their need to access public and social services will either continue to be unmet, or will be addressed at a cost that is higher than the average per capita cost of service delivery (depending on location).

Political and Social Forces

The second set of forces influencing the latest example of urban spatial segregation involves the programmatic discussions and responses prompted by the aftermath of Hurricane Mitch. Immediately following the hurricane, displaced families began to occupy emergency shelters set up in churches, schools, and other public buildings. After three months, many families still lacked viable alternatives for permanent housing and remained in the emergency shelters, threatening to disrupt the school year beginning in February. To address these needs, macro-shelters were constructed both in the capital as well as in cities throughout the country to provide transitional solutions for displaced families until permanent solutions could be identified. In Tegucigalpa, four large macro-shelters were constructed with donor financing to house approximately twenty-five hundred families (11,500 people) on a transitional basis. More than three years after the hurricane, two shelters have been dismantled and two still remain under operation. Despite providing some complementary social services, such as childcare, health care, and vocational training, these shelters have become focal points for a number of social problems, principally drug abuse and gang related violence.

The existence of these social problems can be attributed in part to the prevalence of social ills that affect marginal neighborhoods. However, a number of new factors are introduced in the macro-shelters allowing for the intensification of these social problems. First and foremost, families from different marginal neighborhoods throughout the city were relocated to the cramped quarters of the shelters. The community networks that may have existed in the neighborhood of origin to help maintain a certain degree of stability and cohesiveness among neighbors were disrupted. Given the transient nature of the incoming and outgoing shelter residents, more opportunities existed for delinquency to take place unchecked by neighborhood controls. Not surprisingly, police presence in both the marginal neighborhoods of origin and the shelters is largely absent in all but the most serious of crimes.

In addition to this instability, families inhabited extremely cramped quarters (a family with up to five members was assigned a cubicle of ten square meters) and were obligated to use communal bathing areas and sanitary facilities. Living under these harsh conditions has also added its strain on the cohabitation of shelter families and has contributed to threats of violence, public health risks, and social stigmatization. Conversely, for the population at large, the prominence of the macro-shelters in Tegucigalpa is a constant visible reminder of the effectiveness of the reconstruction programs. The continuation of these shelters becomes a politically charged emblem of not only the disaster, but also of the government's response, whose policies and programs have focused overwhelmingly on national reconstruction.

Official government estimates (UPPV 2001) indicate that more than fifty-nine thousand housing units will have been built as part of the reconstruction efforts. Programs designed to contribute to the reconstruction, most of which were financed by sources external to Honduras, were immediately confronted by the inherent limitations of the housing market. Unable to utilize existing mechanisms to target beneficiaries, to channel subsidies, to identify potential sites, or to expand infrastructure, a virtually parallel housing market was mounted for the duration of reconstruction efforts. Similarly, in the absence of municipal capacity to enforce subdivision and construction regulations, many donors assumed a quasi-regulatory role by conditioning their financing of proposed developments to minimal technical standards.

In contrast to the development around Tegucigalpa, construction of new homes proceeded more rapidly outside the capital and the nine macro-shelters built in other cities were dismantled within twenty-six months of their construction. The availability of land was less of an obstruction in secondary cities than in Tegucigalpa where the initial process of identifying viable tracts of land for construction was extensive. Cities and towns outside the capital had available land reserves, with unquestioned land title (i.e., municipal land), which were quickly donated for the construction of new homes.

Initially, it was agreed that the municipality would take the lead in identifying sites. Because of weak municipal capacity, other donor-funded organizations eventually provided leadership in identifying potential sites for the construction of the homes. Ultimately, prospective areas were identified far from the urban core. Because land was perceived as the scarcest variable in determining construction sites, it quickly became the determinant factor. If land was available for acquisition, other considerations, such as the feasibility and costs of water and sanitation as well as mitigation measures such as storm drainage systems were quickly presumed to be resolvable. Of course this infrastructure can be built in most places, but issues of construction cost, cost recovery, maintenance, and operation have not been easily resolved in the new towns. In the absence of a water and sanitation authority able to provide for the rational extension of its systems, or of developers to recover the costs of these projects, donor agencies again stepped in to finance the construction of water and sanitation networks. Similar deficiencies have appeared with regard to health and education. Whereas according to the municipal zoning and subdivision law each settlement with five thousand inhabitants will be provided with a primary school, a health clinic, recreation facilities, and so forth, these measures have not been enforced and donors have once again filled the void and financed both temporary bridging measures as well as permanent structures.

Consequences of Spatial Segregation

The resulting spatial segregation of these new towns reveals both positive and negative consequences. Most of the positive consequences deal with the physical or built environment of the new towns which will eventually house an estimated eighteen thousand people. Scattered among six different neighborhoods within close proximity throughout the Amarateca Valley, the new inhabitants will eventually have access to a public network of services, including domestic connection to potable water, sanitation, and electricity. In addition, a number of initiatives are currently underway to fill unmet gaps in education, health, public safety, and garbage collection. The importance of these positive factors should not be downplayed, considering that they will provide for families' basic needs at higher standards than could have been reasonably expected in their previous situations. These families have been given a-once-in-a-lifetime opportunity to access a housing unit on a serviced lot in a low-risk area with appropriate community infrastructure. In many cases, they will also receive title to their new property for a fraction of its true construction cost and at half the monthly cost of competitive rental units in Tegucigalpa. These families have benefited from the reconstruction efforts that coalesced around this specific emergency and the extraordinary donor support that may not be repeated for many years (if ever). Without this type of heavy subsidization and unprecedented efforts in development of low-income housing, the ability of these families to access homes on their own would be difficult to imagine.

In addition to the built environment of the new towns, significant potential exists for the area to attract new industries that could provide much needed jobs to the local population. An estimated twenty medium to large factories already operate in the valley, which was zoned for industrial parks by the *Centro Urbano Nueva Amarateca* Plan of 1976. But one of the most limiting factors to future economic, as well as residential development, will be the availability of water. For Amarateca to become a new outlet for the capital's growth, improved access to water and provision of other public infrastructure is necessary. Unfortunately, at this time capital improvement projects are targeted towards resolving existing deficits rather than providing incentives for future growth. Therefore, the prospects for introducing the necessary public works in the valley remain slim.

In contrast to the positive attributes these new towns offer, there are numerous negative elements, which, if left unmitigated, will undermine the consolidation of the new towns and determine the extent to which their residents will experience spatial segregation. First and foremost, the element of distance from the urban core and the requisite transportation to and from the capital must be addressed. Most of the settlements are between twelve and twenty-six kilometers from the outskirts of Tegucigalpa and its areas of economic activity. Travel can take up to forty-five minutes to arrive at the city's outskirts. The resettled population is one which is closely tied to the diverse urban economy and prior to Hurricane Mitch had been employed as informal workers, petty merchants, street vendors, mechanics, domestic servants, and so forth (AMDC 1999). Whereas in their previous locations (both before the hurricane and in the shelters), they maintained a reliable connection to prospective places of employment, there are now additional hurdles in their access to an already difficult job market. For example, a worker commuting six days a week from the new towns to Tegucigalpa would spend $5.16, 10 to 16 percent of a median weekly household income estimated between $33 and $50 (IOM 2001). The employed population of the new towns must therefore either absorb the transportation costs (time and money) to remain active participants in the Tegucigalpa economy or retool to become more competitive in the local job market. Preliminary studies indicate that unemployment has increased for these new inhabitants from 20 percent when they lived in Tegucigalpa to 28 percent after moving to the new towns (IOM 2001).

The lack of reasonable access to consumer markets is another negative consequence of the locations of these new towns. Residents needing to travel to buy consumer goods, therefore, also incur transportation costs. In the new towns, where the population is much more homogeneous at lower income levels, the consumer market can be expected to be more limited and even more costly due to reduced competition and increased transportation costs. Based on preliminary data, shopping trips are more common (60 percent of all trips initiated) than commuting for employment (40 percent of all trips initiated) (IOM 2001).

Other factors that will also influence the level of spatial segregation can be attributed to the absence of traditional mechanisms of interaction among urban dwellers (public schools, public health clinics, recreational and cultural spaces, and trade union halls). While these services may be replicated in the new towns, the level of integration they may offer will be completely different due to the spatial distance of new town inhabitants from a larger, more heterogeneous population and diversified economy. Therefore, the opportunity to interact with different sectors of the population afforded by public spaces in an urban center will not be readily available to the new inhabitants. The importance of having equal access to public spaces and mechanisms where different socioeconomic classes are equal consumers of space rests in the need for promoting democratic practices at the local level. These traditional mechanisms for integration loosely reflect access to political power inasmuch as they provide opportunities for association and organization. When certain groups are excluded from these mechanisms and the opportunity for association that they represent, because of spatial segregation for example, the groups are excluded from one potential opportunity to collectively advocate for their interests.

Finally, the issue of sustainable water and sanitation will be a factor affecting the future course of development of the new towns. Unlike the larger public systems found in the urban core, the new towns will have independent networks servicing their neighborhoods. Despite the positive impact of having household connections to water and sanitation systems, the independent networks represent economic and operational risks. In terms of the financial sustainability of this system, operational costs (e.g., employment of a small maintenance crew, provision of electricity for pumping stations) will require establishing and maintaining an effective cost recovery and accounting system. Likewise, the maintenance of such an expansive water and sanitation system (1,071 domestic connections in one town, and 1,200 in another) will require some minimum training for the work crews. When these families lived in Tegucigalpa, they were connected to water networks as consumers and clients, and would not have had the experience of serving on a water commission. Continued technical assistance will be necessary to develop the nascent water commissions until they become administratively self-sustaining. The lack of sustainable water and sanitation systems may become a powerful disincentive for families to remain in the new towns and may eventually promote return migration to the city.

Instruments to Mitigate Negative Effects

Given the present context and functioning of the land and housing markets, the replication of spatially segregated human settlements in Tegucigalpa is likely to continue. Any long-term improvement in the production
of affordable housing in a spatially integrated context will require legal
reforms to remove structural impediments and inefficiencies that limit accessibility for a significant sector of the population to the land and housing markets. Currently, legislative proposals being discussed by the Honduran Congress to reform the land administration system as well as to
create a new legal framework regulating the housing market. These reforms will by no means alleviate the entire problem of spatial segregation, but will have the potential of providing an enabling context within
which more effective, and hopefully efficient, programs and mechanisms
can be implemented. Notwithstanding the imminent legal reforms, local
urban planners, in order to mitigate negative consequences, resulting
from the urban spatial segregation of the new towns, can apply a series of
instruments. Although equitable living conditions across income groups
will not be achieved, certain measures can and should be taken in order
to provide greater equality to access services provided by both public and
private sectors.

Identifying the Issue and Targeting the Population

Spatial segregation is difficult to objectively define because of its qualitative nature and the unconventional measurements that should be used in
its identification. As demonstrated, segregated populations in Tegucigalpa are not always entirely deficient in their living conditions or in
their access to certain basic and social services. Instead, often times they
have access to shelter, some form of basic service, education or health,
and can be quantified by targeted sectoral indicators as part of a population with satisfied needs. Policies and programs that are organized secto-
rally may be able to mitigate certain facets manifested by segregation but
are often times unable to address crosscutting issues of access. Housing
programs may resolve the shelter issue, but may also place populations

at a disadvantage, as the present case demonstrates, in accessing the private networks of the marketplace. Similarly, vocational programs may provide job training, but may have difficulty reaching target populations if segregated groups have limited access either to information or vocational centers. Finally, water supply programs may be successful in constructing a distribution network, but may be limited in their usefulness because of poor operation and maintenance.

As a point of departure, more effective ways for recognizing the needs of the spatially segregated populations need to be introduced and applied. A more effective approach would differ from traditional methodologies for problem identification by focusing on the concept of "access deficiency," as suggested in the operational definition for spatially segregated populations in Tegucigalpa presented earlier (unequal access to either public networks of services or private networks of the marketplace). Once the issue of segregation and specific problems of access deficiency are defined, appropriate mitigation measures, some of which may be sectoral in nature, can be more easily identified. Five instruments are particularly important for mitigating the negative consequences of segregation; they are access to (1) jobs, (2) safe and effective transportation, (3) financial services, (4) health care and educational services, and (5) consumer markets.

Preventative Measures

Preventative measures available to local planning practitioners relate largely to the normative provisions that can be introduced in identifying design and development of new human settlements or alternatively in promoting increased urban density and subsequent uses of existing infrastructure. In Tegucigalpa, the regulations summarized in the municipal zoning, subdivision, and construction ordinance are necessary for ensuring the observance of a minimal standard that can contribute to the access of safe living conditions for both occupants of the new developments and the public at large. However, many of the most common instruments (subdivision, community infrastructure, construction, and basic services standards) are focused on the internal integrity of the development without addressing the integration of the settlement with its larger context. In Tegucigalpa, the ability to prevent many of the negative effects of spatial segregation is severely limited by both the structural limitations of the land and housing market as well as by the municipality's own institutional limitations in enforcing existing norms and regulations.

Corrective Instruments

Once certain problems are detected, such as those in the new towns, corrective instruments should be identified and applied. In terms of improved access to consumer and job markets, corrective measures to mitigate this deficiency are related in part to the availability and access to transportation. In this area, norms regulating public transportation can be utilized along with incentives for private or public companies (permits, leases, and concessions) to provide for the transportation needs of the segregated population. In addition, low-cost improvements can be made to the improvised bus stops that now dot the highway at the entrance to each new town. In terms of matching potential employers with the potential labor force, the municipality can serve as an effective information conduit to identify both supply (through business licenses and cadastre data) and demand (through demographic data including education levels and vocational skills). Similarly, with regards to accessing consumer markets, the municipality can facilitate access to existing markets and can create new local markets. Through the regulation of public transportation, it can target increased transport to commercial districts while at the same time constructing a local marketplace and offering a concession for its operation.

Ultimately, however, the ability of local planners to avoid these negative consequences (preventative measures) or mitigate their effects (corrective instruments) is dependent on the regulatory effectiveness and institutional capacity of the municipality. In this respect, the reduction of segregation is directly linked to the institutional capacity of the local government. A weak local authority with little management or programmatic capacity will not be an effective agent for preventing or correcting the negative consequences of spatial segregation. Corrective instruments, operating either through the coercive capacity of the state or through the implementation capacity of local government, have been extremely uncommon scenarios in the Honduran context due to both lack of enforcement ability and fiscal limitations. Budgetary constraints faced by the municipality perpetuate the endemic cycle of incapacity; the municipality is ineffective because of budgetary constraints—a product of its inability to enforce ordinances and capture revenues.

Conclusions

The origin and growth of the new towns of Tegucigalpa provide a clear example of the potential consequences of a poorly functioning formal land market. The deficient land market, combined with other important factors such as economic stagnation, prohibitively expensive housing finance, explosive urbanization, and unresponsive governmental policies, have contributed to the proliferation of informal settlements in the capital as well as to the chain of events leading to the construction of the new towns after the hurricane. Land market inefficiency has also been one of the principal factors affecting the response of housing reconstruction for Tegucigalpa's displaced families. In addition, because of the weak institutional capacity to enforce adequately its own zoning and construction regulations, the municipality has become an accomplice to the uncontrolled urbanization of the last forty years and the construction of the precarious settlements which were devastated by the effects of the hurricane.

Even with a functioning land market, powerful market forces will continue to limit accessibility to land by certain sectors of the population. But access is made even more difficult by a poorly functioning land administration system and an insecure property rights regime skewed against the poorer sectors of the population. Faced with ever fewer alternatives in the formal market, these families have been offered an opportunity of a lifetime—a house in one of the new towns. Despite the distance separating them from the urban economy, they will benefit from housing standards and a built environment that, under normal circumstances, would have been inaccessible.

Given the current situation, the capacity of local government to facilitate low-income residential development, or conversely to mitigate the negative effects of spatial segregation, becomes even more important. One of the first steps required for the Municipality of Tegucigalpa, or any municipal government, to become an effective actor in this area, is to improve its financial administration system and establish the necessary control mechanisms to increase its revenue capture. Municipal initiatives will invariably be limited by budget availability. While municipal budget is not the only factor—technical and policymaking capacity will also be important elements—it is indispensable.

Two potential scenarios are evolving regarding the future of these new towns. The first scenario contemplates the part-time or full-time return migration of resettled families to the city, occupying once again land in environmentally vulnerable areas. It would be understandable for these families to adopt this survival strategy (part-time migration) whereby the principal income earner spends most of their time in Tegucigalpa while the rest of the family remains in the new towns. This approach would imply the maintenance of two residences during periods of active employment. Alternatively, the families may opt for full-time migration, where the home they own in the new town is traded, sold, or rented out to a third party, while the family returns to the city to resume its urban life. In the future, both part-time and full-time migration may result from the lack of nearby employment opportunities or onerous daily commutes (both time and expense) combined with unsustainable basic services and little improvement in access to the private networks of the marketplace. There have already been some preliminary indications that a few families have already opted to return to Tegucigalpa because of incomplete permanent sanitary services combined with the difficulty of finding employment.

The second potential scenario is related to the successful completion and consolidation of the new towns. This scenario will require the completed construction of all outstanding services as well as their successful operation and maintenance over the medium- and long-term. As for the private networks of the marketplace, sufficient attention will have to be placed on the issues of access and employment. However, consideration of access and employment would need to take a radically different approach from the current strategy being pursued by the municipality and the central government. To date, the national and local governments have been unwilling to address the issues of segregation proactively but instead have deferred to international organizations for assistance. This passivity is misguided. In all likelihood, the causal relationship between limited land access and spatial segregation will continue as a general trend. As such, it would be in the best interests of central and local government authorities to mitigate problems caused by current population flows and to ensure the long-term sustainability of the new towns. A successful consolidation of the new towns would provide an important precedent in demonstrating the viability of integrated residential development.

Part II

Housing Markets, Public Policies, and Land Use

Chapter 7

EXPERIENCING RESIDENTIAL SEGREGATION

A Contemporary Study of Washington, D.C.

Gregory D. Squires, Samantha Friedman, and Catherine E. Saidat

Introduction

Racial segregation is as taken for granted as any feature of urban life in the United States. Whites, on average, live in neighborhoods that are nearly 83 percent white, Blacks live in neighborhoods that are 56 percent black, while Hispanics, on average, reside in communities that are 42 percent Hispanic (Lewis Mumford Center 2001a). The fact of severe and persistent racial segregation of housing patterns in metropolitan areas is not contested, though the causes of segregation are hotly debated.

Unexamined in most of this literature is the experience of segregation and racial discrimination in housing. This chapter explores the types of neighborhood amenities and characteristics (including their racial composition) families seek out, the ways different racial groups pursue housing opportunities, the outcomes of those processes in terms of the housing that is ultimately secured, how racial minorities respond if they believe they have encountered discrimination, attitudes on the extent to which race and racial discrimination affect housing opportunities, and generally the extent to which race affects housing and neighborhood related preferences and practices. Understanding the experiences of various actors in urban housing markets can help explain the phenomenon of segregation and inform current policy debates.

This study focuses on Washington, D.C., which is an ideal setting for exploring racial segregation. Greater Washington typifies metropolitan areas in the United States in terms of the extent of racial segregation. Like other communities it has become increasingly diverse as Asians and Hispanics are among the fastest growing groups in the local population. And policy debates over the causes and consequences of racial segregation persist among community organizations, public officials, and academic researchers.

Perspectives on Segregation

Explanations of racial segregation have centered around three hypotheses. One perspective focuses on individual choice, arguing that most households prefer to live in culturally homogeneous neighborhoods. The housing market, from this perspective, reflects the freely chosen preferences of millions of buyers and thousands of housing providers who make voluntary decisions in a free market (Glazer 1975; Thernstrom and Thernstrom 1997).

A second explanation focuses on economics arguing that the spatial concentration of racial groups basically reflects the relative financial status of those groups. Since Whites in general have higher incomes and control more wealth than racial minorities, Whites have more (and non-whites have fewer) choices in the housing market (Becker 1957; Clark 1986). If Whites are hesitant to move into nonwhite neighborhoods, it is argued, this reflects race-based neighborhood stereotyping (e.g. concerns about presumed correlations between racial composition and property values as well as other neighborhood characteristics) rather than discrimination per se (Ellen 2000). Therefore, from this perspective, housing segregation, primarily reflects impersonal market forces.

A third perspective points to a range of discriminatory private practices and public policies that restrict housing opportunities for nonwhites and serve to create and perpetuate segregated housing. It is argued that these policies and practices, and the individual-level prejudices and stereotypes upon which they are based, are primarily responsible for the formation of racial and ethnic ghettos and for the persistence of segregation to this day in urban housing markets (Massey 2001; Massey and Denton 1993; Yinger 1995).

While each of these three sets of factors contributes to the segregation of metropolitan areas, the weight of social science evidence points to the latter set as the primary cause (see below). Income and preferences do count and for some households may be the overriding consideration, but they are clearly secondary to discrimination. Specific private industry practices include racial steering, blockbusting, and the provision of different levels of service to Whites and nonwhites by real estate agents (Fix and Struyk 1992). Redlining and racially discriminatory practices by mortgage lenders (Goering and Wienk 1996; Munnell et al. 1996) and property insurers (Squires 1997), including the refusal to serve and the provision of inferior products and services to minority markets, undercut property values and trap minorities in segregated neighborhoods. Racially discriminatory appraisal practices result in the undervaluation of properties in minority neighborhoods causing lenders to deny mortgages even when willing buyers and sellers agree to the price, thus further isolating minorities in segregated communities (Pittenger 1996; Schwemm 1996). When all else fails, violence and intimidation have been utilized to maintain the color line (Massey and Denton 1993).

Public policies include the Federal Housing Administration (FHA) discriminatory lending practices. Take, for example, this statement from the agency's early underwriting manual: "If a neighborhood is to retain stability, it is necessary that properties shall continue to be occupied by the same social and racial classes" (U.S. Federal Housing Administration 1938, para. 937). Enforcement of racially restrictive covenants, exclusionary zoning ordinances, the concentration of public housing in central city neighborhoods, and the construction of a federal highway system that facilitated suburban development are among a range of public policies that have nurtured and reinforced racial segregation (Jackson 1985; Rusk 1999).

In 1989, the Department of Housing and Urban Development (HUD) and the Urban Institute conducted one of the most comprehensive analyses of the housing market. Utilizing paired testing (where comparably qualified white and nonwhite "testers" posing as homebuyers approach housing providers to rent or purchase advertised, vacant units) researchers found that Blacks and Hispanics encountered some form of unlawful discrimination in almost half their encounters with real estate agents (Fix, Galster, and Struyk 1992, 22).

In addition, available evidence tends to undercut the "preference" and "economic" explanations as primary causal factors. Public opinion surveys demonstrate that racial minorities prefer integrated to segregated neighborhoods (Schuman et al. 1997). And among those minority households who do choose homogeneous minority communities, the motivation is often to avoid the harassment and intimidation they fear may occur in predominantly white areas (Feagin and Sikes 1994). Whites express preferences for predominantly white communities, which limits the choices that Blacks have within the housing market, but Whites' realization of their residential preferences is not the result of white preference alone. Instead, discrimination in the housing market allows Whites to avoid coresidence with Blacks (Massey and Denton 1993, 97). Discriminatory practices keep Blacks out of most white neighborhoods and in turn, allow Whites to move to predominantly white neighborhoods.

The fact that, in the case of Blacks, indices of racial segregation vary little with socioeconomic status undercuts the economic perspective from being a viable explanation of the persistence of residential segregation (Massey 2001). Higher status African Americans may reside in neighborhoods with more Whites than do those with less income and education. But middle-class African Americans live in less affluent and desirable neighborhoods than do middle-class Whites. Race, in other words, still affects residential options available to middle-class Blacks (Alba, Logan and Stults 2001).

Race and racial discrimination appear to continue to play a critical role in shaping the experiences of individuals in the segregated housing market that exists in urban America. But most of the housing segregation literature has focused on residential preferences (e.g., Clark 1991, 1992; Farley et al. 1994) and the geographic mobility of individuals that underlies segregation (e.g., Massey, Gross, and Shibuya 1994; South and Crowder 1997, 1998). What is missing from this earlier research is any systematic exploration of the experience of segregation, particularly as felt by the participants and how its victims feel about these processes. How successful are racial minorities, compared to Whites, in efforts to secure the home of their choice? How do they respond when they have been subject to racial discrimination? How do Whites and nonwhites assess available opportunities for racial minorities in the housing market?

Such questions are among those addressed in this chapter. This study explores the salience of race by examining differences between Blacks and Whites in the significance they attach to racial composition and other neighborhood characteristics in the selection of homes and communities, the home-seeking tactics of Blacks and Whites, initial outcomes of that process, the frequency with which home-seekers believe they or their friends have experienced discrimination in the housing market, what actions (if any) they have taken when they believed they were victims of unlawful discrimination, and general attitudes about the extent to which equal opportunity prevails in the housing market.

The preceding discussion of the perspectives explaining segregation lends itself to the development of a few key hypotheses. The racial discrimination perspective predicts that race will be significant in explaining the variation in the outcomes discussed above, even after controlling for differences that exist between Whites and Blacks in socioeconomic and demographic characteristics. Indeed, if race is significant with respect to the outcomes related to the home search process, experience with discrimination, and attitudes about the extent to which equal opportunity exists in the housing market, the racial discrimination perspective will be reinforced. If race is insignificant in the analyses, the choice and economic perspectives will be supported.

Among the policy implications of the controversy over the causes of housing segregation are debates over the extent to which race-specific approaches (e.g. affirmative marketing, subsidized mortgages for "pro-integrative" moves) as opposed to more universalistic remedies (e.g. subsidies for more affordable housing development) should be pursued and whether those policies should be "pro people" or "pro place." (Wilson 1996, 1999; Massey and Denton 1993). Presumably, more informed policy decisions might be made as more is learned about the dynamics of segregation and the role of racial discrimination. Informing those policy debates is a primary objective of this chapter.

Methodology

The data for this study are derived from a telephone survey of 921 adults, 480 from the District of Columbia, and 441 from the nearby suburbs of

Maryland and Virginia, which was conducted in the spring of 2001 by the George Washington University Center for Survey Research. [Editor's note: Interested readers should contact the primary author for a more detailed discussion of the survey methodology.]

Washington, D.C. is fairly typical of metropolitan areas in terms of the segregated nature of its housing patterns. The index of dissimilarity (ID) in Washington has mirrored that of the nation's major urban centers for at least thirty years, reaching the mid-60s even among households with incomes greater than $50,000 (Massey and Denton 1993, 86). The D.C. area has a slightly larger black population than most major metropolitan areas. The 2000 census data show that Blacks comprise 26.0 percent of the population in the Washington, D.C.–Maryland–Virginia–West Virginia Primary Metropolitan Statistical Area (PMSA), while in the Detroit, Chicago, New York, and Philadelphia PMSAs, they comprise 22.9 percent, 18.9 percent, 24.6 percent, and 20.1 percent of the populations, respectively (U.S. Bureau of the Census 2001a). Like many other large cities, Washington and the surrounding suburbs have become more diverse. In 2000, Asians comprised 7 percent of the metropolitan area's population, up from 5 percent in 1990 (U.S. Bureau of the Census 2001a) and has also become a magnet for immigration (Singer et al. 2001). In 1998, one in six persons in the area was born outside of the United States (Bureau of the Census 2000), a striking contrast from 1970 when 1 in 22 persons were foreign born. Blacks, however, remain the dominant minority group.

Despite the large presence of Blacks in the area and the increasing racial and ethnic diversity of the metropolitan area's population, the black/white ID remained virtually unchanged throughout the 1990s, going from 65.7 in 1990 to 63.1 in 2000 (Lewis Mumford Center 2001b). Moreover, the area's current level of segregation dropped only 6.9 percent from the 1980 black/white ID of 70.0 (Massey and Denton 1993, 76). The persistence of segregation in the area is illustrated by the fact that in 2000, approximately two-thirds of the black population in the metropolitan area lived in the District of Columbia and Prince George's County, areas where at least 60 percent of the population was black (Bureau of the Census 2001b, 2001c, 2001d). Thus, only one-third of the black population in Greater Washington lived in counties that were not predominantly black.

As is the case nationwide, racial discrimination appears to be a major contributor to the segregation that exists in the Washington, D.C. metropolitan area. In 1997, the Fair Housing Council of Greater Washington (now part of the Equal Rights Center) utilized paired-testing to investigate the home purchase, rental, and mortgage-lending marketplace throughout the metropolitan area. Investigators found that Blacks were discriminated against 33 percent of the time in their efforts to buy homes, 44 percent of the time when they attempted to rent, and 37 percent of the times they applied for mortgage loans. Discriminatory practices included racial steering, misrepresentation about the availability of homes, differences in rental rates for the same units and the number of units that were shown, disparities in mortgage interest rates, differential application of particular standards, and others (The Fair Housing Council of Greater Washington 1997a, 1997b, 1998).

Because the focus of this study is on the Washington, D.C. metropolitan area, the data collected during the 2001 telephone survey are weighted in order to more accurately represent the area's population. Without weights, the data are an over-sample of the District of Columbia. The weights, when applied to each individual in the sample, make each individual represent the number of persons within the metropolitan area's population, so that the 921 individuals in the sample are representative of the 2.7 million people, aged eighteen and older, within the Washington, D.C. metropolitan area defined here.

After applying the weights to the data, which are scaled down to maintain unweighted sample frequencies, 53.0 percent of the sample is white and 29.8 percent is African American. The remaining 17.2 percent are Hispanics, Asians, and those of other races. The weighted sample is quite representative of the racial composition of the Washington, D.C. metropolitan area, as defined in this study. Of the 2.7 million residents, aged eighteen or older, within the metropolitan area, 50.4 percent are white, 29.2 percent are African American, and 20.4 percent are Hispanic, Asian, and those of other races (Bureau of the Census 2001b, 2001c, 2001d). This analysis focuses on white and black respondents because discrimination has been particularly salient in race relations between Blacks and Whites.

The 2001 survey elicited responses from individuals about the circumstances surrounding the search for their current home, their neighborhood satisfaction, experience with discrimination, and their attitudes about racial equality. Descriptive statistics were developed to indicate what differences, if any, were associated with race in each of these areas. Multivariate analyses were then conducted to determine the extent to which these differences were associated with race independent of age, socioeconomic status, measured in terms of income and educational level, housing tenure, length of stay in the current neighborhood, and geographic location (e.g., city or suburb). The primary objectives were to assess the extent to which selected preferences and behaviors as well as outcomes vary by race, the salience of race and racial discrimination in shaping the taken for granted segregated patterns of most urban housing markets, how attitudes about inequality are influenced by race, and finally what, if anything, can be accomplished via public policy to ameliorate racial inequality.

Findings

Blacks neither have the same housing search experiences, nor do they enjoy the same outcomes in the home search processes, as do Whites. Even after controlling on a range of demographic characteristics in the Washington, D.C. area, racial disparities persist as salient features of the local housing market. [Editor's note: Tables supporting conclusions are available from the primary author.]

Blacks and Whites differed significantly on most of the characteristics that they rated as very important when they were selecting their current neighborhood of residence. For example, more than half of black respondents (i.e., 58 percent) rated proximity to public transportation as very important as compared to about one-third of Whites (i.e., 34 percent). Blacks were also significantly more likely than Whites to rate level of crime, neighborhood racial composition, taxes, and public services as being very important in the selection of their current neighborhood of residence.

Housing affordability, school quality, and proximity to work were equally important to Blacks and Whites. The fact that Blacks were more likely than Whites to rate neighborhood characteristics, like the proximity to public transportation and public services, as very important in the selection of their current neighborhood may reflect the fewer private resources Blacks have to draw from to obtain these services. Whites have more resources to provide for transportation (e.g., automobiles), security guards (e.g., gated communities), recreation (e.g., country clubs), and other amenities. Although the median household income of Blacks is almost 70 percent of that of Whites, Blacks control less than one-tenth the wealth of white households nationwide (Oliver and Shapiro 1995, 85–86). Therefore, Blacks may believe they have to be much more selective in terms of the neighborhoods in which they decide to live.

Respondents were asked: "If you could find your ideal neighborhood in the two or three blocks around your home, how many of the families would be black?" As expected, about 50 percent of Whites, compared to 77 percent of Blacks, would prefer a neighborhood that is racially mixed or where Blacks comprise the majority of residents. The pattern of results for this question is consistent with the pattern of results found in other studies on residential preferences (Charles 2001; Farley et al. 1994), despite the fact that differences in the wording of the questions exist.

Interestingly, about 1 in 4 Whites, as compared to 1 in 10 Blacks, claim that in deciding upon an ideal neighborhood in which to live, the number of Blacks present in the neighborhood did not matter to them. Whether these are Whites' honest answers to this question is somewhat questionable. Previous research has demonstrated that Whites' answers to questions regarding racial issues are more liberal when they are engaged in a telephone or face-to-face interview as compared to when they have more privacy to respond to such questions as in a mail-back survey (Schuman et al. 1997).

We also asked respondents about the most important source of information they used when they bought or rented their homes. Although Blacks were less likely than Whites to use real estate agents in their search, the difference is not statistically significant. Indeed, the results reveal that Whites and Blacks are no different, statistically, with respect to the sources of information that they found to be most helpful in searching for their current housing units.

Another set of questions focused on the outcome of the search. Respondents were asked if they were able to get their first choice of available housing units when they were searching for the home in which they currently live. If they were unable to get their first choice, they were asked why this was the case. Blacks were significantly less likely than Whites to obtain their first choice. Approximately 33 percent of Blacks were not able to move into their first choice, as compared to 20 percent of their white counterparts. Contrary to what might be expected according to the economic perspective, Blacks who did not get their first choice were no more or less likely than Whites in the same situation to report that they were unable to meet the financial requirements involved with obtaining their first choice. However, Blacks were significantly more likely than Whites to report some "other" reason for their inability to obtain their preference. ("Other" could include discriminatory housing practices by housing providers.) Taken together, these results suggest that Blacks continue to experience discrimination in the housing market.

Since Blacks were significantly less likely than Whites to obtain their first choice of housing units, it is probably not surprising that Blacks were significantly less likely to be satisfied with their neighborhood than Whites (72 percent versus 82 percent). Furthermore, Blacks were significantly more likely than Whites to want to live somewhere else in the Washington, D.C. area (16 percent versus 7 percent). Considering that Blacks were unable to get their first choice of housing units during the search for their current unit, it is likely they will have difficulty again if they try to move in order to find a more satisfactory home and neighborhood.

A separate set of questions spoke directly to the issue of discrimination. Respondents were asked if they, or anyone they knew, encountered any form of racial discrimination within the past three years in their efforts to obtain housing or mortgage loans. Those who reported that they faced discrimination in the housing market were asked how they responded (e.g., filed a lawsuit or complaint, looked for another home). Consistent with the racial discrimination perspective, Blacks were significantly more likely than Whites to either experience discrimination themselves, or know of someone who experienced discrimination in their efforts to obtain housing or secure financing for housing. Black respondents were about five times as likely as white ones to report that they had experienced discrimination themselves (11 percent versus 2 percent), and they were nearly three times as Whites to report that they knew someone who experienced discrimination (25 percent versus 9 percent). These results are consistent with the testing evidence described earlier.

Few respondents, black or white, did anything if they experienced discrimination. Just over 95 percent of Blacks neither filed a complaint with a civil rights or fair housing organization nor filed a lawsuit. About 62 percent of Blacks talked with family members, friends, and neighbors about their encounter with discrimination, but decided to take no legal action. The results for Whites are similar to those for Blacks, even though fewer Whites said they experienced racial discrimination in their efforts to obtain a home or secure financing.

Why did the majority of Blacks fail to take legal action even though they experienced discrimination? About 30 percent reported that they did not have the time, 20 percent stated that they did not have the funds, and 17 percent said that they did not know where to file a complaint. Approximately 50 percent of Blacks reported that they did not think anything would come of filing a complaint or a lawsuit. Fifty percent of Whites felt the same way. This clearly suggests a lack of confidence in the administrative and legal systems that are in place to protect those subject to racial discrimination. Such a lack of confidence could be grounded, in part, in the fact that between 1989 and 1997 less than 6 percent of complaints filed with HUD, that were not settled, resulted in a charge of discrimination against the respondent (Schill and Friedman 1999, 66).

A final set of questions focused on respondents' views on whether Whites and nonwhites with similar incomes experience equal opportunity in the housing market and their opinions regarding the extent to which racial disparities generally reflect unequal opportunities, or different levels of effort on the part of various racial groups. While about 58 percent of Whites believed that Whites and Blacks have the same choices and opportunities in the local housing market, only 16 percent of Blacks felt the same way. A similar disparity exists between Whites and Blacks in their beliefs about the housing opportunities available to Hispanics as compared to Whites. These findings are consistent with previous research (Blauner 1989; Kluegel and Smith 1986; Sigelman and Welch 1994).

Consistent with expectations derived under the racial discrimination perspective, Blacks were significantly more likely than Whites to agree with the opinion that generations of slavery and discrimination have created conditions that make it difficult for Blacks to experience upward mobility. Whites, however, were neither more nor less likely than Blacks to believe that the reason racial inequality exists is because Blacks do not try hard enough to be as well off as Whites.

A number of key findings emerge from our descriptive analysis of respondents' experience with residential segregation in the Washington,

D.C. metropolitan area. Blacks and Whites differ with respect to a number of aspects of the housing search. Blacks are significantly less likely than Whites to obtain their first choice of housing units they visited and are, consequently, significantly less likely than Whites to be satisfied with their neighborhoods. Blacks were significantly more likely than Whites to encounter discrimination and know others who have experienced it. Interestingly, however, out of the 11 percent of Blacks who reported that they experienced discrimination within the housing market, more than 90 percent did not take legal action, and one of the key reasons for not doing so was because they thought that nothing would come of it. Finally, Whites are significantly more likely than Blacks to believe that there is equal opportunity within the housing market for Whites and minorities. Such attitudes make it more difficult to combat the discrimination that exists against minorities within the housing market.

Although the results up to this point are quite informative with respect to Whites' and Blacks' experiences within the racially segregated housing market in Washington and nearby suburbs, the descriptive analyses do not control for the socioeconomic and demographic differences that exist between the two groups, for example, that Blacks are significantly less likely than Whites to own their homes, to have a household income above $75,000, to have a college or graduate degree, and to live in the suburbs. A question that arises is whether, after taking into account the differences that exist between Whites and Blacks on these socioeconomic variables, race continues to play an important role in the experiences of residents within the area's housing market.

A series of logistic regression analyses (results not included here) were conducted to test for the impact of race, controlling for the impact of other background variables. The results showed race continuing to be salient with respect to respondents' abilities to obtain their first choice housing unit when they were searching for their current home. Blacks were three-fifths as likely as Whites to obtain their first choice housing unit, even after controlling for differences in income, education, housing tenure, length of stay in the current neighborhood, age, and their place of residence. These results suggest that discriminatory forces are at work in limiting the ability of Blacks to realize their mobility expectations and plans, consistent with the racial discrimination perspective. However, Blacks and Whites did not differ in terms of the information sources they used to conduct their housing search and there were also no significant differences by race in neighborhood satisfaction. The latter result is consistent with the economic argument.

Several other logistic regression results support the racial discrimination perspective. Blacks were significantly more likely than Whites to report that they, or someone they know, have experienced discrimination in their efforts to obtain housing or mortgage financing. In addition, Blacks were significantly less likely than Whites to believe that Blacks and Whites have the same opportunities within the housing market. The survey findings, combined with the findings of the audit studies conducted by the Fair Housing Council of Greater Washington suggest a number of directions for policy initiatives to ameliorate discrimination and segregation in urban housing markets.

Policy and Research Implications

Enforcement

These findings clearly reinforce calls for more effective enforcement of fair housing laws. One important step would be to increase the use of paired testing along the lines carried out by the local Fair Housing Council. There is some evidence that where testing is employed, enforcement agencies secure larger settlements for complainants (Fix and Turner 1999). Most, but not all, fair housing and fair lending agencies utilize this investigative technique.

A second step would be for HUD to make greater utilization of secretary initiated systemic investigations. By law, HUD is required to investigate each complaint it receives. But the processing of even large numbers of individual complaints is not necessarily responsive to the broader institutionalized practices of discrimination. Those practices could be more effectively targeted by carefully developed secretary initiated complaints.

Education

At the same time, HUD and private housing providers could more effectively educate the public about its rights under the law. Many protected class members may not realize that HUD is obligated to investigate each complaint it receives, or that the agency will provide complainants representation if the case is taken before an administrative law judge. In other words, processing such complaints would not cost plaintiffs anything. HUD already works with several state and local agencies and private housing providers on a range of initiatives. But the message is not getting through as effectively as it should. Perhaps public and private authorities should work more closely with faith-based organizations to deliver this message. The church has long been a vital part of civil rights initiatives in the black community. Today churches are increasingly active on a range of community development initiatives. No doubt, their congregants could benefit from such efforts.

Enforcement and education can be mutually reinforcing. High visibility cases not only provide remedies for the immediate victims, but also others hear and read about them. As residents become more informed about and confident in available law enforcement agencies and remedies, the more they will utilize those tools. As more people in more communities become informed about the prevalence of discriminatory housing practices, disparities between Blacks and Whites in their perceptions of the extent to which equal opportunity prevails will likely ameliorate. This, in turn, would lead to broader support for stronger enforcement efforts. Education and enforcement clearly go hand in hand.

Mobility Programs

Another response to racial segregation has been a small number of programs designed to help low-income residents of central city neighborhoods, often in public housing complexes, move to outlying urban and suburban areas. Perhaps the best known is the Gautreaux program in Chicago, which helped 7,100 families relocate between the late 1970s and 1990s (Rubinowitz and Rosenbaum 2000). This led to HUD's Moving to Opportunity initiative, which has assisted 4,610 low-income families relocate in Baltimore, Boston, Chicago, Los Angeles, and New York (Johnson, Ladd, and Ludwig 2001).

The numbers of participants in these programs are quite small. Given the politically feasible level at which they are likely to be supported, they will not substantially change indices of segregation. Another concern is that the neighborhoods left behind may lose key community leaders. But these programs appear to make a positive difference in the lives of program participants and they appear to demonstrate that, under the right conditions, low-income black residents can thrive, along with their new neighbors, in middle-income white neighborhoods.

Fair Share

In order to maximize housing choice, some communities have taken steps to increase the availability of affordable housing in suburban jurisdictions where housing, in general, has been more expensive. One of the challenges confronting fair housing and affordable housing advocates has been the exclusionary zoning laws of most suburban municipalities. Restrictions on the number of multifamily housing units, minimum lot size and maximum density requirements, and front and rear setback requirements are just some of the rules that increase the cost and exclusionary nature of much suburban housing, and have disproportionately limited housing options for racial minorities (Jackson 1985; Orfield 1997; Rusk 1999). A number of approaches have been taken to increase affordable housing choices and disproportionately benefit minorities in metropolitan regions throughout the nation.

After more than twenty years of litigation, legislation, and other political battles, the Mt. Laurel case in New Jersey resulted in the state requiring each municipality to develop a plan for housing their "fair share" of their community's low-income households (Kirp, Dwyer and Rosenthal 1995). The fair share concept has driven other initiatives. In Montgomery County, a Maryland suburb bordering Washington, D.C.'s northwest side, new subdivisions must set aside 15 percent of housing units for moderate-income households (Rusk 1999).

Such regional approaches offer the possibilities for some unique political alliances. Traditionally, fair housing and affordable housing community organizations have been lonely voices calling for elimination of exclusionary zoning laws and development of affordable housing throughout metropolitan areas. But in recent years, many suburban employers, unable to recruit the workers they need (in part because those workers cannot afford the housing near those suburban work sites), have become involved in affordable housing fights. Some suburban developers who would like to develop such housing and local lenders who would

like to finance these units are also beginning to see how exclusionary suburban zoning laws undercut their financial interests. At least some members of these various groups have begun to work together to change local
and state zoning laws in order to provide for more units of affordable
suburban housing (Squires et al. 1999).

Community Reinvestment

The greater importance Blacks place on such neighborhood amenities as
proximity to public transportation and public services in general reinforces
the importance of public investment in basic services. Such investment improves the quality of life for all residents, increases the attractiveness of local
communities to private business aiding economic development efforts, and
helps ameliorate racial disparities on several quality of life measures. Some
progress has been made along these lines as indicated by the "New Urbanism" and "smart growth" experiments to improve public transportation
and encourage job growth on mass transit lines and the growing population
in recent years of many cities that had been losing population for decades
(Bullard 2001; Glaeser and Shapiro 2001; Grogan and Proscio 2000).

At the same time, public investment must be complemented by private
investment (Goldsmith and Blakely 1992; Squires 1994). The federal
Community Reinvestment Act (CRA), passed in 1977, prohibits redlining and requires federally chartered depository institutions to affirma-
tively ascertain and be responsive to the credit needs of their entire service
areas, including low- and moderate-income areas. According to the National Community Reinvestment Coalition, this statute has led to more
than $1 trillion in new private investment for community development
(Silver 2001). But the CRA applies only to depository institutions (e.g.,
banks. savings and loans), and these account for less than half of all
mortgage loans in today's market. Independent mortgage banks, insurance companies, and other financial service providers account for an increasing share of housing finance and are not covered by the CRA. Enactment of the Community Reinvestment Modernization Act (HR 865),
introduced by Congressmen Tom Barrett (D-WI) and Luis Gutierrez (D-
IL) in 2001, would expand the CRA to independent mortgage banks and
create comparable community reinvestment obligations for insurance
companies, securities firms, and other financial service providers.

Such "place-based" approaches can ameliorate segregation in two general ways. First, by reinvesting in distressed neighborhoods those areas become more desirable places to live and property values increase. This increases the chances for residents (or at least home owners) in these neighborhoods to move, if they should so desire. Second, revitalizing previously distressed neighborhoods would encourage greater socioeconomic diversity, particularly if those communities offered amenities like proximity to downtown offices, cultural attractions, and other traditionally appealing aspects of city life, even though ameliorating segregation may not be a priority of many community development organizations.

Conclusions — Making Race Matter Less

Matters of race and practices of racial discrimination continue to be salient elements of the housing market and of neighborhood life in Washington, D.C. generally and in other urban communities around the nation. Preferences and economic circumstances play a role. But if voluntary self-segregation and economics play a role in the racial segregation of urban communities, the context in which these choices and circumstances are grounded must be considered (Krysan and Farley 2002). It is difficult to disentangle the choices people make and the circumstances they find themselves in from attitudes and practices that have long been, and continue to be, grounded in the dynamics of race. Consequently, current research and policy debates often take on a rather polarizing character. Should the focus be on race specific or universalistic policies? Should the target be people or places? In fact, it is not as easy (as much current debate suggests) to separate policy choices along these dimensions. And where specific policies appear to fit one label more closely than another, it also appears that each approach may be necessary. A few examples will illustrate these complexities.

Urban revitalization strategies are, arguably, universalistic. Improving schools, hiring police, repairing the roads should benefit entire communities, assuming these improvements are not explicitly racially gerrymandered, as has often been the case historically. But in the minds of many, "urban" means black. And even when such stereotypes do not hold, given the reality of racial segregation, these "universalistic" strategies clearly disproportionately benefit nonwhites. Affirmative action, arguably a race specific strategy, can benefit an entire community by enabling it to draw from the entire stock of human capital and not just those who have been privileged in the past.

Place-based strategies (e.g., creation of empowerment zones, implementation of community reinvestment agreements) obviously benefit those households that live in the target area receiving the resources—households that are usually considered the appropriate beneficiaries of public policy. Mobility programs that are directed to specific types of families (i.e., pro-people strategies) can benefit entire metropolitan areas by reducing the concentration of poverty and the many metropolitan-wide social costs associated with uneven development (e.g., policing and security costs, political unrest, declining social capital). Each of these tools, and more, has a place in what Christopher Edley Jr. has referred to as "the opportunity agenda" (Edley, Jr. 1996, 46). And each has a role in expanding housing opportunities specifically as well as in enhancing the overall quality of neighborhood life for racial minorities in urban communities.

One of the researchers who participated in Russell Sage's recent multicity study of urban inequality concluded that, "Race is woven into the fabric of residential and industrial location choices, of hiring and wage determination, and of the human perceptions that underlie all these processes" (O'Connor 2001, 28). If this is the reality today, it is a reflection of policy choices that have been made. And this fabric can be unraveled with different policies. Racial segregation is not inevitable. It is clearly a fact of urban life, but it is not a healthy feature of cities and metropolitan areas. And it is not something a willing community must tolerate in perpetuity.

Note

Chapter 7 draws from an article of the same name published in *Urban Affairs Review* 38, no. 2 (November 2002): 155–183.

Chapter 8

INEQUALITY, SEGREGATION, AND HOUSING MARKETS

The U.S. Case

N. Ariel Espino

Theoretical Underpinnings: Inequality, Segregation and Planning Policy

One of the most fruitful ways of dealing with the topic of segregation is through the detour of the analysis of inequality, for segregation is generally understood in the policy debate as nothing else but a spatialization of power differentials between social groups or classes. We are usually concerned with segregation because we see it as both an expression and a cause of social inequality. Inequality and segregation, however, need not coexist, and in fact diverge frequently in the historical and anthropological record. Historically, many societies with dramatic degrees of social inequality have allowed fairly unsegregated urban structures where mingling and residential closeness of rich and poor was the rule more than the exception. As generally understood in social theory, this is so because space is just one of many means available for managing the interaction between classes and for sending appropriate signals of social identity and status. In terms of behavior, the relation between classes was managed through strict codes of deference so that the daily and visible homage paid by the powerless to the powerful left no doubt of who was in command and allowed for stress free and predictable interaction. In terms of patterns of consumption, strict rules regulating the types of clothing (and other consumer goods) of different classes, generally known as sumptuary laws, had the similar effect of visually sorting out power groups in the absence of spatial segregation. Both of these mechanisms were used in many European societies (and in many other parts of the world) through the nineteenth century.

In many cases, the urban social mix took the form of multistory buildings with floors differentiated across class lines. This "vertical segregation" was common in European cities well into the nineteenth century (Kostoff 1992, 117 ff.) In this case, of course, it would be inaccurate to assume that space had no role in assigning social status. The floor occupied within the building was frequently an important status indicator, for example, the higher up one lived the better, but sometimes the other way around. The Italian *piano nobile* and the proverbial Parisian garret of the starving artist are examples of these socially marked internal spatial areas. (In the suburban United States today, the much-regulated accessory apartment would be another example of a potentially lower-income unit integrated spatially within a more expensive residential structure.)

If certain nonspatial mechanisms, like sumptuary laws, facilitated social mixing in premodern cities, other factors made social mixing necessary. Prior to the development of modern transportation technologies, urban elites, needing the services of the poor (either as laborers or domestic servants), had no alternative than to tolerate them as neighbors. The mutual influences between the evolution of modern transportation systems and residential segregation are very clear in the history of both British and U.S. suburbanization (Fishman 1987). Changes in labor relations and house chore technologies also had an effect, as Donald J. Olsen argues in his history of three European capitals:

Socially mixed neighborhoods remained so [in the eighteenth and nineteenth centuries] because the middle classes required the services of their less affluent neighbors. . . . It is precisely because today's middle classes are less able to exploit the working classes that our cities have become more segregated than they were. It was only when the servantless, do-it-yourself household became the norm, with the large refrigerator, deep freeze, and the family car permitting once-a-week shopping at a distant supermarket, that the cluster of mews, back courts, and mean streets ceased to be the necessary adjunct to any middle class neighborhood. (Olsen 1986, 133)

Robert Fishman argues that suburbanization in Britain, beginning in the eighteenth century, provided the basis for the modern idea that "social distinctions require physical segregation" (1987, 32). In England, the rise of this ideology accounted for a process of estrangement between business elites and their masses of workers who flocked to urban centers, to cities such as London, Manchester, and Birmingham, to work in the new factories. The old personal relationships, daily contacts, close living quarters, and mutual trust that existed between the shop owner and his handful of workers and apprentices, was transformed into a more impersonal relationship based on notions of class division when workers became an anonymous mass who labored under the capitalist factory regime. The elite's response was suburbanization, that is, residential segregation, to escape from the disease, filth, and overcrowding in cities, and took on the aesthetic and ideology of antiurbanism, domesticity, and privacy. Historically, suburbanization in the United States, which started in the mid-nineteenth century, can be seen as a reaction to similar fears: fear of disease, Blacks and immigrants, crime and poverty (Jackson 1985).

It is now generally assumed that in most contemporary, industrial societies, location in physical space has become an indicator of location in social space (Rapoport 1990, 71). With no stable consumption patterns for sorting people out, space has become a critical indicator of social standing. The loss or absence of interclass behavioral codes encourages people to pursue daily interaction only with those who have comparable levels of income, education, and culture, that is, social power. This not only means that modern cities have a tendency to be residentially segregated, but it also implies that contact between classes in public spaces is more problematic, because it affords none of the historic status-reinforcing interactions and, in fact, may confuse the identity of the participants. Nowadays, one needs not only to live in the right place, but also to shop and recreate in the right places, too. Public settings have, therefore, become group-specific (Rapoport 1990, 185). In some cases, the workplace is the only setting where people from different classes (e.g., a CEO and a janitor) can still interact (Rapoport 1980/81).

Not all modern societies place the same importance on residential space as a demonstration of status, however, and the degree and manner in which this takes place is a matter for empirical research (J. Duncan 1982). In terms of Pierre Bourdieu's (1984, 1990) theory of social stratification, households can deploy different forms of capital, symbolic or economic, available to them in a particular society to define social standing:

social capital—social prestige, as indicated, for example, by well-known family names, or cultural capital—education or taste, or economic capital—material resources usually expressed through conspicuous consumption. Forms of symbolic capital (social or cultural) are generally weak in the United States, especially for the middle- and working-classes, and this has transformed space, in the form of widespread concerns about residential address and neighborhood character, into a veritable battleground for the negotiation of social standing (Perin 1977 and response by Rapoport 1979; Cullingworth 1993, 103 ff. for comments on the general concern with neighborhood character" in U.S. urban planning). For Bourdieu, the U.S. middle-class is precisely characterized by its "low degree of institutionalization of symbolic capital," "low degree of mutual acquaintance," and "multiple," "fluid," and "blurred" hierarchies, all of which leads to the pervasiveness of "pretention" and "bluffing strategies" (Bourdieu 1990, 139, 304 n. 5; Knox 1992).

In the United States, however, there is a highly popular middle-class housing model whose stability across time and space cannot be accounted for simply by the view that the residential landscape is the product of pure material competition. This model—the owner-occupied, single-family home in a standardized suburban subdivision, which has served as the society's model for good residential environment—has for decades received the backing of government policies and planning regulations, often times at the expense of the renting poor. In her classic anthropological work, Constance Perin (1977) argues that the social symbolism of this residential environment is based on the notion of a "ladder of life" where families start as (urban) apartment renters and work their way up to full home ownership with a house in a suburb, perhaps to return to an apartment at retirement age. The detached, privately owned, single-family house functions as the common symbol of one's arrival to middle-class status, or to the American Dream, complete with its associations of credit worthiness (obtained through determinations made by mortgage lenders), independence, and a family-centered life. The distinction between renters and multifamily apartment dwellers on the one hand, and home owners and single-family house dwellers on the other, seems to mark a crucial symbolic watershed in the United States, though most home owning families do not keep their first house, but trade up for a better and larger one as soon as feasible. There is, thus, competition, but within a stable framework, that distinguishes the highly valued middle-class from others that are seen to be beneath it.

Segregation is problematic when it produces and reinforces social inequality and when it impedes the access of poorer households to urban goods and services that are considered essential or worthy of universal provision. These may include good schools, parks, cultural facilities, or jobs (as measured, for example, in comparable commuting times across income groups). The main issue is, therefore, one of "equality of access" (Lynch 1981, 228 ff.) and its relation to segregation. How do we guarantee an urban mix that affords different groups and classes a reasonably equal access to urban services and amenities? What is critical is not social heterogeneity at the neighborhood level, but rather at the community or municipal level (Gans 1961).

In the United States, this form of segregation tends to exclude whole groups and classes from localities through the use of exclusionary and fiscal zoning—the highly fragmented nature of urban governance and finance, the workings of a highly commodified land market, and the deployment of houses as investments by home owners. The next section discusses these issues as they relate to land and housing markets and planning policy.

U.S. Land Markets, Urban Planning, and Segregation

In the United States today, as in other countries, the workings of land markets contribute to the production of social segregation. It would be a mistake, however, to assume that land markets conform to the idea of free bidding for residential land by multiple buyers with disparate incomes. Each society has different land markets (i.e. forms of distributing residential land to different people) constituted by particular rules and practices, and responding to its particular social dynamics. A productive way of investigating and understanding these markets is by exploring the ideas, rules, and conventions that underlie the daily practices of buyers and sellers of land and housing, and that are reflected in laws and regulations.

This discussion draws on qualitative research of U.S. urban development practices and my own ethnographic research among developers, neighborhood activists, real estate agents, and home owner association managers in the city of Houston. As is usual in this approach, emphasis will be on practices, perceptions, and beliefs, rather than on statistical data. And, while it is acknowledged that racial and income segregation usually follow and reinforce each other, the focus will be mainly on segregation by income. This focus will also be narrowed to middle-class, single-family housing (suburban) neighborhoods built for fee simple ownership, which constitutes the predominant form of housing development in the United States.

Social segregation is one of the main objectives and organizing principles of the U.S. land development system. Segregation is sought in the production of the urban landscape and guaranteed in its long-term management. Anthony Downs (1993, 1999, 2000) argues that U.S. land markets are not really free markets, but are rather highly regulated ones. Zoning and other controls place all kinds of restrictions on the way land can be developed and transformed. One can visualize a free land market as a landscape of plots and parcels any of which can be sold and bought for whatever purposes the buyer deems appropriate. But as Downs observes, the U.S. city is not a city of plots; it is rather a city of neighborhoods. The city is built as a patchwork of subdivisions, each of which is targeted to a narrow range of house prices (and, therefore, income groups).

The U.S. land development system has had two mechanisms for building and preserving segregated residential neighborhoods: private restrictive covenants (or deed restrictions) and zoning. Borrowed originally from England, restrictive covenants function legally as private contracts between sellers and buyers of land, and allow residential developers to impose a series of common restrictions to all the lots of a subdivision. Used in the U.S. for the first time during the suburban expansions of the late nineteenth century, restrictive covenants resulted in the exclusion of lower-income families, racial and/or ethnic minorities, and the exclusion of businesses. Discrimination based on race is now unconstitutional. Deed restrictions are currently used to guarantee a middle-income level for the subdivision, a common architectural vision, and adequate levels of property maintenance. When a neighborhood contains serviced lots for sale, deed restrictions guarantee that all the houses built on them will be of a minimum size (by regulating minimum square footage) and quality (by regulating materials), thus precluding cheaper units being built at any time in the future. Deed restrictions thus indirectly establish the income of a neighborhood's home buyers by regulating the price of homes and by incorporating amenities and aesthetic standards that only certain households can afford. In this sense, deed restrictions segregate by establishing a socioeconomic floor for every neighborhood.

The use of exclusionary and fiscal zoning play a crucial role in keeping low-income housing out of whole municipalities and regions by zoning vacant areas for costly, large lot residential development. Because these tools segregate before the fact, they represent planned segregation. As Perin (1977) points out, the U.S. zoning system reflects the ideal of a politically influential middle-class urban order enforced at the level of the autonomous local municipality (see also Krueckeberg 1999). This order consists of a hierarchy of land uses, with the owner-occupied, single-family housing neighborhood occupying the apex. Commercial uses and more dense residential developments are zoned away from single-family residential areas in an increasing gradient of density and intensity of land use. Home owners in low-density subdivisions consider their neighborhoods to be spoiled by the presence of nearby apartments for rent or lower-income developments. Fear of lower-class crime is also a factor. All these social and aesthetic valuations are translated into a concern about property values, which serves as an important banner of neighborhood mobilization in relation to the control of development.

This emphasis on housing investments is the other great force influencing the production of segregation in the United States. The concern of home owners with property values is well known (Agnew 1982; Babcock 1966), and the market practices described above, that is, the production and maintenance of neighborhood homogeneity and the use of hierarchical zoning, can be, and frequently, are justified simply as a means to preserve the property values of the homes and prevent economic losses to home owners.

The investment potential of homes is related to two important expectations: the uses of the house as a direct source of equity and as a steppingstone to higher-income housing. The former refers to the possibilities the home offers as a storage and generator of capital through home equity, in which case any increase in the value of the property is a potential net gain in available cash or credit for the household. The second factor relates to the association of upward social mobility with geographical mobility. Increases in household income are typically linked to moves to a higher-income subdivision. Improvements on the spot are discouraged through regulations and are considered irrational from an economic standpoint. [Editor's note: In tight housing markets, home owners do improve their homes substantially in order to move up the housing ladder without moving on. See Brozan 2004.] Improving without moving can lead to overinvestment in the house, that is, the idea that one should not improve one's house so its value surpasses the neighborhood's average. Properties tend to be appraised in relation to the neighborhood they belong. This means one may not be able to "get the money out," that is, recover the investment linked to property improvements. One could say that neighborhoods tend to be built as static, finished products for a particular social group (Franck 1987). Once all units in a neighborhood are sold and all amenities built, further change of any significance is generally discouraged. This link between social and geographical mobility reflects a highly structured housing industry, which offers products differentiated in accordance with an imagined trajectory of home buying: there is entry-level production, starter homes, move-up homes, and second move-up homes. An appreciating property is essential for this process of trading up; see Hazel A. Morrow-Jones' (1998) analyses of the impacts of repeat home buying at the metropolitan scale.

Residential mobility (as a function of career and/or social advancement) is, therefore, an important variable fueling the speculative use of houses and its associated spatial management practices. The United States has one of the highest residential mobility rates in the industrialized world (Long 1991). And while three-fourths of moves are by renters, mobility among home owners can also be relatively high. In Houston, a high mobility city, between 12 and 15 percent of home owners were moving every year in the early 1980s, before the real estate market crashed (Long 1988, 217). The numbers are, however, less important than the expectations. As a Houston home owner association manager put it, "everyone knows they're going to sell someday." Real or expected mobility is expected; the fact that the U.S. home is no longer thought of as a family patrimony, that key inheritance for the children that so obsesses other societies (especially in the developing world), but only as a temporary possession of the parents (or, in their place, the childless couple), who can convert it, if necessary, into pure equity as part of their own retirement plans (Varenne 1996). At the level of public discourse, the character of residential property as a source of wealth is continuously claimed and emphasized: from the chairman of the Federal Reserve, who argues that residential properties, more than stocks, are still the most important source of wealth for U.S. families (Greenspan 1999), to economists who propose forms of insuring this form of wealth (Shiller and Weiss 1999), to poverty analysts who argue that the problems minority households (especially Blacks) have, due to discrimination, in obtaining residential property in areas where its value can appreciate over time, is one of the main reasons why the wealth and income gap between white and minority households persists in the United States (Conley 1999).

Pervasive use of houses as investments, or the future expectations thereof, and the popular discourses that foment such a mentality have a great influence on the regulatory climate of U.S. cities and promote segregation. The most significant impacts occur when zoning controls new development. Perin (1977) has described how zoning functions as a risk management tool when seen in light of neighborhood concerns with property values. It might not always be the case that apartments for rent reduce the property values of adjacent home owners, but because this is the popular belief and the economic stakes are perceived as so high, it is a risk worth avoiding through exclusionary zoning. Middle-class home owners can impose zoning through their strong influence on municipal policies. In an already built landscape, property values may be influenced by factors other than tenure type, for example, the quality of services or the level of property upkeep. This, however, does not deter the use of zoning for exclusionary purposes.

Municipalities comply readily with this exclusionary logic to please their more powerful constituencies and because the quality of services depend to a large extent on real estate taxes. The higher the property values the more taxes are generated (see Wassmer, chapter 9). The taxed value is conceptually identical to the value that concerns the home owner, that is, the hypothetical (speculative) price that the house could command if it were sold in an open market. Cities, thus, zone out housing developments that are seen as unable, due to their low cost, of paying for the municipal services they would have to receive.

Policy Solutions

Anthony Downs (1999) has proposed three strategies to deal with urban concentrations of poverty and income segregation: (1) a system of regional land use planning that can prevent the use of exclusionary zoning; (2) a system of regional tax-base sharing that can reduce the fiscal incentive to use exclusionary zoning; and (3) programs for affordable housing projects, vouchers, subsidies, or quotas (imposed on developers) that can guarantee availability of affordable housing throughout metropolitan regions. There is little more that one can add to this list. Some control over exclusionary and fiscal zoning is obviously necessary, but this is clearly not enough. Even without zoning, the way housing prices are set by neighborhoods, the highly dynamic character of U.S. housing markets, and the incentives that U.S. legislation offers home owners to speculate with their property (such as the tax exemptions on capital gains from housing sales), almost guarantee inflationary housing markets and affordable housing crises in times of urban growth, especially when accompanied by widespread waves of gentrification. Houston, a large unzoned city, is a case in point. The city has seen annual increases up to almost 20 percent in housing prices in the more central areas during years of economic growth, as in the early 1980s and since 1997 (Bivins 1999). While the lack of zoning historically has allowed the construction of a large number of apartment units and other more affordable housing types throughout the city, these options have not been exempt from inflationary pressures either.

Thus, America's high home ownership rate contributes to economic segregation and inequality. Home owners' ability to speculate with their houses widens the wealth gap with renters, especially in times of housing inflation (Case and Cook 1989). In addition, during times of rising housing costs, when home owners are protected behind fixed monthly mortgage payments, renters suffer rising rents (which may force them to move), and potential first-time buyers are shut out of the market. To address these problems, some affordable housing programs come in the form of nonequity or limited-equity, owner-occupied housing, usually managed by local governments, nonprofit agencies, or cooperatives. The Moderately Priced Dwelling Unit (MPDU) program of Montgomery County, Maryland, described by David Rusk (1999), is an example. A county agency builds affordable townhouses in wealthier neighborhoods and sells the units to qualifying families. Capital gains from the sale of the townhouses by the home owners are controlled for the first ten years, and split with the housing agency after that, with the funds being used for the financing of more units. (A similar example is Santa Barbara's La Colina housing project, reviewed by Michael Pagano and Ann O'M. Bowman [1995, 133–134]). The virtue of these types of programs is that they allow for the conservation over time of an affordable housing stock in areas subject to dramatic housing price increases, which is an advantage over housing vouchers, subsidies, or quotas that have no such control over inflationary pressures over time.

There is a more radical scenario: to decommodify housing in the United States (Achtenberg and Marcuse 1983). This would eliminate the use of houses as investments for all owners by regulating housing transactions or taxing housing profits. In theory, this might curb speculation and possibly housing discrimination, since there would be no economic incentive to avoid racial diversity. Owner-occupied homes would have a use value, but not an exchange value (Logan and Molotch 1987; Gottdiener 1994); this would presumably ameliorate the anxieties of home owners over property values. Decommodification could also address a potential problem with nonequity or limited-equity affordable housing programs: they can worsen the inequity already characteristic of the U.S. home ownership system. Under such a dual housing system, higher-income owners enjoy their houses as both living spaces and investments, while lower-income households are limited to only the former use value. Short of generalized government-sponsored nonequity housing production, a general decommodification could be obtained on a massive scale and with less government intervention through land-value taxation and land-value capture policies, for, as we know, housing cost inflation is generally little else than land-cost inflation. Land-value taxation and capture policies try to capture (through taxation) the increases in property values that take place as a result of urban land price inflation. A steep tax on capital gains from housing sales could be used to eliminate housing reselling profits as a trade-off for lower housing costs in general. Unfortunately, the political will needed to try these types of tax policies remains elusive (Case 1992).

Conclusions: Perspectives for International Comparative Research

This chapter has reviewed some of the social forces behind the modern processes of urban segregation and the particular characteristics of the United States' case. The most serious problems caused by segregation are those that involve exclusion of low-income housing from entire localities, thus reducing access to good jobs, good schools, and so forth. While a general reduction of wealth disparities and the promotion of mixed-income neighborhoods are worthy goals of urban policy, an intermediate and more modest initiative should concentrate, at the very minimum, on the elimination of exclusionary zoning and other planning practices that impede the construction of affordable housing developments more uniformly across urban regions. The incentive to zone out affordable housing developments in the United States has social, economic, political, and fiscal dimensions and is a response to the way social identities are constructed through housing consumption, the way housing is deployed as an economic resource, how political jurisdictions are defined, and how municipalities obtain their revenues. In addition, the U.S. land use philosophy is characterized by the preferential treatment given to the middle-class, single-family housing neighborhood and a corresponding hierarchical scheme of land use relations that puts affordable housing developments at a disadvantage. These factors account, at least in part, for what Perin (1977, 197) described as the "extraordinary sensitiveness of property to its surroundings" in the United States.

This sensitivity is precisely what one might study using the United States as an example. This would be particularly appropriate for societies with highly commodified, free land and housing markets, which is the model used and promoted increasingly around the world. What degree of sensitiveness do people (home owners or their equivalents) in other societies have in relation to the type of housing developed adjacent to their neighborhoods? What are the sources of opposition or concern, social (e.g., status, crime), fiscal, or economic? What are the meanings of housing in play? Is housing a status marker, an investment, a fiscal resource, or a family patrimony (i.e., an inalienable, intergenerational property)? And, what are the implications of all of this for land use planning and management styles?

The meanings and motives behind segregation may vary, for segregation is always a means to something else, not an end in itself. Segregation may be used to control social interaction, may help establish social identities, or may have economic effects for low-income people. Understanding the meanings of segregation, and the particular sociospatial order in which it takes place, would be a fruitful area for future research.

Chapter 9

AN ECONOMIC VIEW OF THE CAUSES AS WELL AS THE COSTS AND SOME OF THE BENEFITS OF URBAN SPATIAL SEGREGATION

Robert W. Wassmer

Introduction

Spatial segregation by income, class, race, and ethnicity exists in urban areas throughout the United States and the world. Such segregation occurs across local governmental jurisdictions and neighborhoods in metropolitan areas. Spatial segregation, therefore, is a public policy concern because of the severe limitations it places on quality of life and upward mobility for those who would benefit from a more nonsegregated distribution of people in urban areas (powell 2002). Paul A. Jargowsky (2002) describes how a neighborhood's class composition influences individual outcomes, independent of one's class status, through a number of mechanisms. These include an emulation of the negative behavior of neighbors, a lack of role models, and an absence of neighborhood institutions that buffer against deprivation.

Policy efforts to induce greater income, class, racial, and ethnic diversity in inner cities and urban neighborhoods focus on the removal of those institutional factors that foster segregation. Exclusionary zoning, redlining by lenders and insurers, racial steering by real estate brokers, and discrimination by property owners are rightfully pointed to as important causes of urban spatial segregation.

This chapter demonstrates that even if racial prejudice disappeared and discriminatory institutional practices were eliminated, natural market-based factors would still drive some forms of spatial segregation in metropolitan areas. Urban planners and policymakers need to understand this fact if they want to develop effective policies to promote greater levels of racial and economic integration. Besides neoclassical microeconomics, there are many other rich and relevant ways of explaining the persistence of spatial segregation in metropolitan areas. But if the economic approach described here is ignored, a key causal reason for urban spatial segregation has been overlooked.

The chapter is divided into four sections: (1) a review of the economic forces that promote spatial segregation in a metropolitan area beginning with the seminal work of Charles Tiebout (1956) and continuing with a relevant theoretical extension by Kerry D. Vandell (1995); (2) a summary of the empirical evidence in support of expected relationships using Tiebout's model of metropolitan residential location choice, and the subsequent segregation it generates, as it applies to the real world; (3) a description of the costs and benefits arising from metropolitan governmental fragmentation; and (4) economic policies that might alleviate the problems resulting from segregation.

Economic Causes of Urban Spatial Segregation

Voting with One's Feet

Tiebout set out to describe a theoretical construct in which a public good (or service) could be efficiently provided by local governments in a metropolitan area through a decentralized pricing system. Once public goods are produced for an area, it is extremely difficult to exclude residents living in the area from consuming them. Before Tiebout, most public economists believed that this "non-excludability" prohibited the efficient provision of a public good through decentralized pricing.

By using a system of decentralized pricing to provide a public good, consumers reveal their true preference for different amounts of the public good in the form of their own personal demand curve. In other words, they can tell a government producer the maximum prices they would be willing to pay for all possible quantities of the public good. By under-standing the non-excludable nature of public goods, economists believe that the natural response of consumers is to reveal a lower preference (de-mand) for the good than is truly desired in an attempt to "free ride" off the larger amount desired and paid for by others. Of course, everyone faces this incentive to free ride and the aggregate result under this form of decentralized pricing is an under provision of the public good.

As a way to resolve this problem, Tiebout envisioned an urban area with many local governments, each providing a different level of the local public good, and charging a tax price (in his model a per person tax) for a consumer to live in the community equivalent to the average cost to provide the good to them. Tiebout asserted that this simple mechanism could effectively eliminate the free-rider problem by forcing consumers to reveal their true preference for a local public good by "voting with one's feet." If a person truly desires the level of the public good provided and is willing to pay the appropriate tax price to cover its production cost, then the only way to consume the good is by residing in the community pro-viding it. The choice of alternative communities or the competition gen-erated among local governments, keeps local providers of public goods from charging more than their average cost to add another resident. As Tiebout (1956, 422) describes: "Spatial mobility provides the local pub-lic goods counterpart to the private market's shopping trip."

At the extreme of Tiebout's theoretical urban area, a separate local government would be required for each level of local public good provi-sion desired by citizens in an area. In reality, however, the high average cost of providing a certain level of a public good, if only a few consumers demand it, forces a less-than-perfect sorting of like-minded individuals into separate communities. Nevertheless, Tiebout's thinking points to a clustering effect in which people with very similar demands for the local public good naturally choose to live in the same community. Since indi-vidual demand for a local public good (such as primary and secondary public education) is often related to both the household's ability to pay (income) and the household's "taste" or desire for the good, which is often tied to social class, Tiebout's mechanism results in urban spatial segregation by income and class when local public goods are provided in a decentralized manner. Since income and class are correlated with race and ethnicity (i.e., in the United States high-income people are less likely to be racial or ethnic minorities), voting with one's feet can also result in spatial segregation by race and ethnicity.

If independent local governments within a metropolitan area provide local public goods and services, then the mechanism described by Tiebout produces urban spatial segregation by income, class, and even race/ethnicity. The important point is that this spatial segregation is independent of the racial and ethnic segregation that arises through the bigoted desires of some people not wanting to live near others of a certain race or ethnicity. The purpose here is not to downplay the importance of these bigoted views or the discriminatory institutions that support them, but to describe a separate economic mechanism that results in segregated communities in a metropolitan area.

In reality, Tiebout's original model is simplistic in its assumptions. Tiebout considers only one type of public good, which is provided at different levels of quantity and quality by different local governments in a metropolitan area and is paid for with a direct fee. Consumers knowledgeable about local levels of provisions and prices would be able to move to the community that satisfies their preference for a local public good. In addition, Tiebout assumes no spillovers of local public good provision across community boundaries. Spillovers refer to the benefits (or costs) of a local government's provision of a good or service being enjoyed (or suffered) by surrounding communities without them paying for the benefit (being compensated for the cost). Even given this simplicity, Tiebout's archetype has become the basis for economic deliberation on just how households sort themselves into communities in a metropolitan area (O'Sullivan 2002).

In the more than forty years since its publication, economists have attempted to fill in real life bits and pieces left out of Tiebout's original eight-and-a-half page article. These gaps include consideration of the fact that local governments provide more than one public good, how local public goods are paid for, how the necessary supply of communities in a metropolitan area arises, and how business location and consumer's choice of housing/neighborhood are factored in (Ross and Yinger 1999).

Since the degree of urban spatial segregation is further affected by the metropolitan consumer's choice of house type and type of neighborhood that the house is in, a brief review of economic thinking on these issues is covered next.

Choice of House and Neighborhood

When deciding upon a community of residence, people pay close attention to differences in local public good provision in prospective communities and differences in the local tax prices they need to pay to consume those goods. Most real estate agents are asked about the quality of local public schools and the amount of local public taxes on a home. As originally discussed by Tiebout, this typically causes a sorting of individuals by income and class across communities in a metropolitan area. But when choosing where to live in an urban area, people are also concerned about the type of housing and the attributes of the neighborhood that come along with a local public goods/tax package. As discussed by Vandell (1995), these concerns usually work to further the degree of spatial segregation across an urban area.

Vandell defines a "heterogeneous neighborhood" as a contiguous region of an urban area in which all residents and housing units vary with respect to: (1) housing and lot characteristics, (2) neighborhood amenities, (3) accessibility characteristics, and (4) resident attributes. Resident attributes include race, income, wealth, education, family composition, and occupation. By modeling metropolitan housing demand and supply, Vandell shows that market forces are likely to generate neighborhoods distinguished by a limited variety in the attributes of residents living in them.

In the Vandell model, utility (happiness) maximizing households in a metropolitan area demand housing of all types; the housing is supplied by profit maximizing builders. When exhibiting their demand for a certain type of housing, consumers act on their preferences and ability to pay for a home, structural, site, and neighborhood characteristics (including the race and ethnicity of residents); and the accessibility of a particular house at a particular location. When considering whether to supply a particular type of housing, a builder considers the profit to be gained from the sale of a particular type of housing unit and the cost to produce it at a given site. Suppliers of a type of housing can face different costs depending on their market niche and the attributes of the site the house is located on.

Local public service provision, access, and naturally occurring amenities vary by space in a metropolitan area. If preferences for one or more of these attributes differ by residents' characteristics, then residents with a given characteristic (i.e., race, ethnicity, income, wealth, education, family composition, occupation, etc.) are likely to outbid others for a neighborhood that possesses the desired attribute(s). Even if preferences for one or more of these characteristics are constant across all homebuyers, households with higher incomes are able to pay more for housing sites with the desired characteristic. The result is a clustering of high-income households closer to spatially based amenities.

Vandell concludes that the forces of supply and demand in a metropolitan area's housing market work to create spatially distinct concentrations of similar income residents and housing units in urban neighborhoods. If racial and ethnic minorities possess lower household incomes, the observed result can be greater spatial segregation by race/ethnicity.

In addition, many people consider neighborhood racial composition in choosing where to live. As discussed in John F. Kain (1985) and William A. V. Clark (1991), evidence from the United States indicates that Blacks are more likely to desire residence in a racially integrated neighborhood (defined as 50 percent black), while Whites on average find it desirable to have a much higher proportion (80 percent or more) of their own race in their neighborhood. On average, a black household with the same level of income as a white household would be willing to pay more for a home in an integrated neighborhood and, therefore, be more likely to live in one. These preferences, which can differ by race/ethnicity, help to reduce the long-term stability of integrated neighborhoods or cities. This is because the type of integrated neighborhood preferred by Blacks (half white and half black) is different from the integrated neighborhood preferred by Whites (i.e., mostly white).

One way to alter the economic processes that work against integrated neighborhoods, just described, would be appropriately used subsidies. For example, a high-income household, desiring a greater amount of a local amenity than is available in a neighborhood with a majority of lower-income residents, may be willing to accept the lower amount of the amenity if the subsidized price of housing is low enough to compensate. Alternatively, high-income people could be attracted to a majority low-income community through a metropolitan-wide or a state provided subsidy of a locally provided goods or service that is particularly desired by high-income residents. Subsidy schemes such as these are discussed later in the chapter. Affirmative marketing is another approach to integrated neighborhoods (Galster 1990a).

*Heterogeneity in Population Characteristics and the Number of Local
Governments*

Tiebout's model indicates that urban residents sort themselves into different communities based in part on similar desires for the levels of local
public goods provided in these different communities. If the appropriate
number of communities in a metropolitan area is too small to meet the
varied desires of residents in the area, Tiebout argues that more are eventually created through the incorporation of new local governments. If the
number of local governments in a metropolitan area is greater than appropriate, they are eventually reduced through annexation and consolidation.

Tiebout's method of sorting helps to solve the problem of how to efficiently provide local public goods in a decentralized fashion. Regretfully,
it can also generate spatial segregation by income, class, and even race
and ethnicity. An indirect test of whether this is actually happening is to
assess whether the degree of variation in the socioeconomic characteristics of residents living in a metropolitan area exerts a positive influence,
holding other causal factors constant, on the number of local governments in the area.

The following six empirical studies show that increasing variation
within a metropolitan area leads to an increase in the number of local jurisdictions in that area.

- Michael A. Nelson (1990), using 1982 data from 296 Standard Metropolitan Statistical Areas in the United States found that the number
  of jurisdictions in a metropolitan area is in part positively related to
  greater variation in variables that likely measure greater variation in
  individual preferences for locally provided public goods.
- Jorge Martinez-Vazquez, Mark Rider, and Mary Beth Walker (1997),
  utilizing data on the number of school districts in all U.S. metropolitan areas for 1972, 1982, and 1992, found that racial heterogeneity
  and age heterogeneity exerted a significant positive influence on
  school district number, while income heterogeneity did not.
- Ronald C. Fisher and Robert W. Wassmer (1998) found that the coefficients of income and age variation in a metropolitan area exerted
  positive influences on both the number of general-purpose governments and the number of school districts. They found that racial

variation in a metropolitan area exerts no statistically significant influence on the number of school districts but contrary to what might be expected, have a significant negative influence on the number of municipalities and townships.

- Alberto Alesina, Reza Baqir, and Caroline Hoxby (2000) found that greater racial diversity in a U.S. county is at least as important a driver of the number of local governments in a county as greater income diversity.
- David M. Brasington (2000), using Ohio school district data observed that greater diversity in race and income in a school district's boundaries leads to greater school district fragmentation; age diversity, on the other hand, leads to greater school district consolidation.
- Robert W. Wassmer and Ronald C. Fisher (2000) provide strong evidence that increasing income variation within large metropolitan areas contributes to an increased number of school districts, special districts, and special districts with property taxing power.

In one form or another, each of the six different empirical studies described above offer support for the hypothesis that increasing variation in a metropolitan area in the socioeconomic characteristics thought to influence the demand for local government services leads to an increase in the number of local jurisdictions in that area. These results are consistent with the operation of a Tiebout-type process in which individuals seek local governments that provide a set of local services most closely aligned with their demand. If the desired local governmental structure does not exist, there is some evidence that the process of creating it begins in as short a period as a decade. Based upon these findings, we cannot dismiss Tiebout's assertion that individuals seek similar individuals to reside with and if possible, create a local government structure that allows it. The strongest sorting factor to come out of these studies is income. In only the Martinez-Vazquez, Rider, and Walker (1997) study was income heterogeneity not found to exert a significant influence on the number of local governments in a metropolitan area. Greater variation in race and age exerted significant positive influences on the number of local governments in U.S. metropolitan areas in about half of the studies examined.

Thus, the empirical studies of economists offer evidence that residential sorting driven by economic considerations motivates some forms of spatial segregation by income, class, and race/ethnicity in U.S. metropolitan areas; though it is important to note that economists have also discovered that purely economic processes do not fully explain the degree of race/ethnic sorting actually observed in the United States. For instance, Stuart A. Gabriel and Stuart S. Rosenthal (1989) have found that a Black in the United States, with many of the same attributes, including household income, as a White, is more likely to live in a central city. Furthermore, John F. Kain's (1985) analysis showed that if intrametropolitan location decisions were only based on household attributes like income, family size, age of head, and so forth, and not race, about twice as many Blacks would have resided in U.S. suburbs than actually did at the time of his study.

In the next section, the benefits and costs that flow from Tiebout's process of sorting people by income and other characteristics into cities and neighborhoods in an urban area are described. This is offered as background to the policy suggestions made in the last section.

Benefits and Costs of Spatial Segregation

Benefits of Tiebout Sorting

Because people of comparable desires for local government services are more likely to be located in the same community within a metropolitan area, Tiebout's sorting mechanism reduces, but is unlikely to eliminate, variation in a citizen's desire for the quality and quantity of local government services within a jurisdiction in a metropolitan area. Variation is not eliminated because a local government cannot be created for each type of household demand for local public goods. This reduction in variation within a jurisdiction in citizen demand reduces the inherent dissatisfaction produced through a voting process to determine the levels of local public goods provided in a community. In addition, the usual reliance on local property taxes to pay for local public goods produced in a competitive structure by many local governments in a metropolitan area can often yield close to a benefit structure of finance for them. The benefit structure arises because the consumption of a high (low) level or quality of a local public good is paid by local residents in the form of higher (lower) prices for homes or higher taxes in the local jurisdiction producing it (Fischer 1996).

Economists also point to the competitive efficiencies associated with a system of choice and mobility as a valuable benefit generated from having a large number of local jurisdictions in a metropolitan area in which each is nearly homogenous in terms of income and social class. Just as it is good to have a large number of dealerships to choose from when you wish to purchase an automobile, so is it good to have a large number of local governments.

From a purely parochial perspective, people who have high levels of demand for a local public good benefit from joining with others with similarly high levels. If financed by a local property tax, the local price paid to provide this high level of public good is distributed equitably among high demanding residents. A lower-level demander of the public good is prevented from free riding off the demands and payments of the high level demanders in the community because the only way he/she can get the high levels of service is to pay the appropriate higher taxes and/or higher local home prices for them. Moreover, in an urban area with many local governments, government providers of high-level local public goods are less likely to charge more than what is reasonable for a high level of provision because if they do, high-level demanders will migrate to a jurisdiction in the metropolitan area providing the next most suitable level of provision.

Costs of Tiebout Sorting

The efficiency benefits of Tiebout sorting must be considered in light of the social costs that arise from urban spatial segregation. Just as the Tiebout mechanism produces more homogeneously higher income, higher class, and higher public good providing communities, it also generates more homogeneously lower-income, lower class, and lower public good providing communities. The existence and isolation of these two types of communities from each other is the prime source of the equity costs of Tiebout sorting.

One of the important social costs of concentrating poverty in a few communities in an urban area is the concentrated violence and crime that it can generate in those communities. This not only lowers the quality of life for residents in the communities with the higher rates of violence, but it can also spill over the boundaries of these communities and affects the quality of life in surrounding jurisdictions. Even Tiebout recognized this limitation of his model and for simplicity sake assumed that these forms of spillovers did not exist. Recognizing that such spillovers do exist in the real world, economists that study local government finance have called for an appropriate level of intergovernmental revenue sharing to support local public service provision (e.g., police protection) when such sharing benefits neighboring communities. Unfortunately, it is not always easy to gain political support for such socially beneficial revenue sharing schemes.

In addition, the less income diversity that exists in a community the fewer opportunities exist to undertake any form of redistribution within the community between rich and poor. In fact, when many local governments exist in a metropolitan area, a locally based redistribution scheme in a mixed-income community will often be self defeating because it serves to drive the wealthy out of the locality pursuing it and to attract the poor to it.

Perhaps the greatest equity concern generated by Tiebout sorting is the limited life opportunities it generates for some individuals (Jargowsky 2002; powell 2002). This occurs for at least two reasons. The first is through the intrametropolitan labor market occurrence of "spatial mismatch." This happens when low-skilled workers are concentrated in one location (usually in the central city or inner-ring suburbs) and many low-skilled job opportunities occur elsewhere. Economists have shown that this results in the spatially concentrated low-skilled workers earning less than they would if residing closer to where the potential low-skilled jobs are. As Harry J. Holzer (1991) notes however, empirical research provides mixed support for the spatial mismatch hypothesis.

Urban spatial segregation also leads to inequities in public education within a state. For public primary and secondary education, and many other locally produced public goods, the level and quality of service produced depends not only on the amount of dollars spent on it, but also on the environment and characteristics of the local population it is produced for. As documented in many studies like those contained in Gary Burtless' (1996) edited volume, a student's achievement not only depends on books, classrooms, and teachers, but also to a great deal on the characteristics of the student's classmates and their families. If the presence of higher-income and higher-class students at a school site improves the performance of lower-income and lower-class students, then the education provided students on the lower end of the income and class spectrum in a Tiebout sorted school district is necessarily lower than it would be in a more heterogeneous one. However, this line of reasoning works in the other direction as well. The presence of lower-income and lower-class students may bring down the quality of the education experience offered higher-income students. The decline would provide yet another reason for parents of higher-income students to try and sort themselves into distinct school districts.

Public Policies to Reduce Urban Spatial Segregation

Even if all bigoted views and discriminatory practices were eliminated, strong economic forces would still exist that must be addressed if the degree of spatial segregation in a metropolitan area is to significantly decrease. The relevant policy question is: What is the best way to reduce the private and social costs of urban spatial segregation, while still preserving as many of the benefits of Tiebout-type sorting as possible?

Increased Resources or Physical Mixing?

To determine the appropriate policy tool to best moderate the costs of urban spatial segregation it first must be determined whether the costs arise primarily from a lack of local resources in some communities or from the physical separation of different types of people from each other. In other words, does the policy solution entail the redistribution of resources from high-income communities to low-income communities (or neighborhoods)? Or does it require the more drastic step of physically moving types of people between communities in a metropolitan area (or neighborhoods in a city)?

From an economic perspective, the unequal distribution of local monetary resources that naturally results from Tiebout sorting in a metropolitan area is best moderated through a system of progressive income taxation that is applied equally throughout a metropolitan area (or a state). Ideally, the proceeds of the tax are then distributed back to low-income communities within the metropolitan area (or state) in the form of grants.

Most states within the United States pursue this process to one extent or another. This is justifiable from both the standpoint of equity and economic efficiency. Equity is invoked if society has deemed that all are entitled to a minimum level of provision of local public goods and this level is not being provided in poor communities. Intrametropolitan redistribution is economically efficient if it is done as a subsidy to poor communities for locally provided public goods that exhibit large positive externalities in consumption (i.e., the benefits of someone consuming a local public good extend beyond the person to benefit others as well). Local public goods that are likely to exhibit large externalities and hence qualify for intrametropolitan redistribution schemes include public safety, sanitation, and public education.

The degree that this form of redistribution should be pursued in a given situation is open to debate; however, the greater the spatial segregation by income in the urban area, the greater the economic justification for such redistribution schemes. Additionally, this form of redistribution is commendable, because it does nothing to change the motivation for efficient Tiebout sorting within an urban area because high-income people face the same taxes anywhere they choose to reside within the region (or state). However, if one state pursues such forms of progressive taxation and redistribution greater than others it encourages its wealthy citizens to go elsewhere. This is especially the case when a metropolitan area straddles two states and one state exercises a higher degree of income redistribution than the other. Wealthy people can still work at the same job but reside in the state pursuing the less aggressive policy of income redistribution.

Regrettably, the simple redistribution of resources from spatially segregated high-income communities to low-income communities is unlikely to fully alleviate all of the costs of spatial segregation in a metropolitan area. Even if redistribution generates equal monetary resources for all communities, spatial segregation will still yield unequal levels and quality of local public good provision across communities. The reason is that the levels of most local public goods are significantly affected by characteristics of the environment and the people they are produced for. This is particularly true for the two local public goods, public safety and public primary and secondary education, which generate the greatest costs and benefits to residents other than those who consume them, and generate the greatest agreement that there is a minimum level of acceptable provision for all.

For this reason, and because of the economic costs arising from spatial mismatch, as well as the other social costs stemming from segregation, it is may be appropriate to encourage moves leading to greater population heterogeneity. How can this be accomplished?

Consider a community in an urban area that decides to provide a high level of local public education by collecting a high per-student level of local property taxes from households in the community. In scenario one, local zoning allows only high quality homes on large plots of land. These units sell for a high price and generate a high level of property tax revenue. As an example, consider a community whose residential zoning requirements limit the locality's housing stock to homes valued at $500,000 or more. Assume that one child resides in each home and each year the school district taxes each home at 2 percent of the property's market value and raise $10,000 a year to fund each child's public education. In a second scenario, the community contains a housing stock mixed with respect to acreage and quality. The natural forces of the metropolitan wide housing market would raise the value of the small and/or low quality homes and would lower the value of the large and/or high quality ones.

The reason why a small or low quality home sells for more in a community that also contains large or high-quality homes is the positive capitalization of the underpayments in local property taxes that a small or low-quality home in this situation makes over its lifetime. To understand why this occurs, think about a community that contains all $500,000 homes and one home that would cost $100,000 if it were built in a community of all homes just like it. This mixed-house community can tax property at two percent of its value and still raise nearly $10,000 a year for the public education of each home's child. Every household, except the one living in the $100,000 home, is paying its fair share of taxes. If the small home sold for $100,000 in this mixed-house community, it would only pay $2,000 in property taxes and receive nearly $10,000 in public school services. This amounts to an $8,000 a year windfall for this property. People who like to live in small homes and consume large quantities of public schooling will observe this occurrence and express their desire to live in this home by bidding its price up until the net present value of the yearly $8,000 windfall is perfectly capitalized into a price higher than the $100,000 it would sell for in a community of all small homes. Alternatively, for a large or high-quality home that exists in a community that also contains small or low-quality homes, negative capitalization or a reduction in value occurs because of the overpayments in local property taxes made for the local services received.

In both of these situations (where the community decides to provide a high level of local K-12 education by collecting a high per-student level of local property taxes) few, if any, low-income households would be attracted. Scenario one does not allow homes of a size and quality that the poor can afford and the second scenario demonstrates that the natural operation of housing markets prices low-income households out of even small or inferior quality homes.

From a purely economic perspective, households in this homogenously high-income community are very reluctant to accept low-income housing into their community because such housing would not pay its "fair" share of local property taxes. That is, the low assessed value of such property taxed at the city's high rate of property taxation would not cover the costs of providing city services and public school education at that location. In addition, because of "peer" effects, the presence of lower-income households is likely to diminish the quality of the locally provided public services. A solution could be a cash payment to residents of the high-income community, paid for by the entire metropolitan area or state, to encourage its acceptance of lower-income households. Alternatively, encouragement either could come in the form of a noncash supplement, again paid for by the entire metropolitan area or state, of a locally provided goods or service that high-income households value (e.g., more public parks), or mitigate the consequences of low-income households in the community (e.g., enrichment programs for low-performing students).

Subsidies to High-Income Households

To many, the idea of offering subsidies to higher-income households so that they will accept the poor as neighbors is unethical and therefore unacceptable. But before such a scheme is dismissed outright, consider a policy alternative that is now more likely to be pursued; under an inclusionary zoning plan, a locality forces developers to include a certain percentage of lower-income homes in new developments even if these developments are in high-income areas. Similarly, a higher-income school district might be forced to take a certain number of low-income children into its class-rooms. Typically these policies are carried out by higher government fiat or as a result of decisions by activist judges without compensation to lo-calities for the negative impacts they can impose (an underpayment of taxes for the additional locally provided goods or services, a decline in property values, a reduction in the quality of local public services through peer effects, etc.).

Forced income integration, in the form of inclusionary zoning require-ments or busing across school district boundaries may result in a more heterogeneous community (or more heterogeneous schools) for a while, but if other higher-income communities exist that are not subject to such integration directives, affluent people are very likely to vote with their feet and to move to these other locations. Alternatively, higher-income people may attempt to create new municipalities (or other types of local government) in formerly unincorporated areas. This creation almost al-ways occurs at the urban fringe of a metropolitan area and can be consid-ered to be a generator of urban sprawl. This propensity to create new governments could be reduced if all existing and future communities and public school sites in a metropolitan area were required to accept lower-income housing or students, but this extensive requirement is unlikely to happen throughout all residential locations in most American metropoli-tan areas. Even so, the imposition of such an extensive requirement will generate ill will and an economic cost upon those who it is imposed upon.

Conclusion: Economic Lessons for Crafting Policy to Deal with Urban Spatial Segregation

This chapter set out to describe the powerful economic forces that pub-lic policies designed to break down urban spatial segregation must over-come in order to fully succeed. When crafting policy instruments in such situations, economists concur that it best to not work against the mar-ket. Instead, policy makers should recognize that urban communities that are nearly homogenous in income or class structure offer benefits to their residents that would be lost if the community is forced to integrate. At the same time, most people recognize that society would benefit from more income and class integrated communities. So to create integrated communities where they do not arise naturally, and to guarantee their long-term stability, "carrots" for the wealthy to accept more poor within their community, or to get the wealthy to move to poorer communities, may need to be given.

Economists generally agree on this policy course. Many would go further and suggest that a market method, currently used to reduce air pollution in the United States, should be considered. Such an approach would recognize that the high-income communities most unwilling to accept the poor that have the most to gain from keeping them out and hence are the ones that should be willing to pay the most for this privilege. The following policy prescription begins with inclusionary zoning requirements equally distributed throughout all communities in an urban area. This means that a certain percentage of a community's housing must be affordable to all. This type of requirement is not new in the United States. The proposed twist on this requirement is the allowance that the inclusionary zoning requirement for one high-income community be tradable in a free market between other high-income communities in the metropolitan area. So if residents in one high-income community wish to exclude low-income housing they can purchase the right to do so by paying another high-income community in a metropolitan area to accept greater than its fair share. The result would be that more low-income people would be moving into some previously exclusive high-income enclaves. The difference is that no high-income enclave could claim that it had no alternative but to allow low-income housing into its borders. If the private benefit of preserving exclusive high-income status is so important under this scheme, they have the ability to buy this right from another high-income community.

Though no doubt controversial, the above contains policy lessons that flow from an economic perspective on the causes, costs, and consequences of urban spatial segregation. The merits and concerns that are present and the policy lessons derived from it deserve further discussion in the broad context of all the interdisciplinary arguments surrounding urban spatial segregation included in this volume.

Chapter 10

DOES DENSITY EXACERBATE INCOME SEGREGATION? EVIDENCE FROM U.S. METROPOLITAN AREAS, 1980–1990

Rolf Pendall

Introduction

In recent years, urban sprawl has captured increased attention and calls for new policy interventions. By many definitions, sprawl has been shown fairly consistently to degrade wildlife habitat, threaten agricultural productivity, and raise the cost of public services at all levels of government (Alberti 1999; Ewing 1997). The magnitude of these costs, and whether they outweigh the benefits that sprawl provides, remains an issue of intense debate (Ewing 1997; Gordon and Richardson 1997). Many observers also assume that urban sprawl also exacerbates inner-city distress, since sprawl and urban decline have happened simultaneously, but systematic research on this question is both sparse and inconclusive (Burchell et al. 2001; Downs 1999). Distress often associates with segregation, whether by race or by income. Metropolitan areas that are more segregated by income embody conditions of concentrated affluence and poverty that may have negative effects for all residents (Galster 1992; Massey 1996).

This chapter examines the relationship between one measure of urban sprawl (low density) and one indicator of distress (spatial segregation of households by income level). It tests how and whether the recently observed increase in segregation by income (Jargowsky 1996) can be explained in part by recently observed declines in population density (Fulton et al. 2001). The chapter begins with a review of "smart growth," density, and income segregation; next, it provides a review of the literature on measuring sprawl and a discussion of studies that link density and sprawl with social problems. Next, I discuss the data sources and methods used to identify the links between sprawl and segregation and present my results. These results suggest that if any changes in the spatial pattern associates with increased income segregation within metropolitan areas, it is density increase, not sprawl. To the extent that density increase associates with income segregation, it becomes even more important to enact measures that guarantee a mix of housing types and incomes as a fundamental component of local and regional land use planning.

Income Segregation, "Smart Growth," and Density

Metropolitan areas in the United States have recently become substantially more segregated by income, even as racial segregation has declined. Douglas S. Massey and Mitchell L. Eggers (1990) found that interclass segregation intensified for Blacks in the 1970s, whereas that of Hispanics and Whites decreased in fifty-two and forty-one (respectively) of the sixty areas analyzed. Using a different index and a more complete dataset, Paul A. Jargowsky (1996) found increasing income segregation not only for Blacks, but also for Whites and Hispanics in both of the decades between 1970 and 1990, intensifying in the 1980s. In a parallel trend, many researchers have found increases in the concentration of poverty and the number of high-poverty tracts between 1970 and 1990 (Jargowsky 1997; Kasarda 1993). Analysis of income segregation during the 1990s has still not commenced as of this writing. (*Editor's note:* See the Preface for more up-to-date results dealing with income segregation.)

There has been much speculation, but little recent systematic research, about the connections between various dimensions of sprawl and various unwanted social outcomes, including segregation by race and income. There is a very rich literature documenting that Whites move away from areas where Blacks are concentrated (Clotfelter 2001; Crowder 2000; Frey 1979; Galster 1990b; Jonas 1998; Marshall 1979; Thompson 1999). Such "white flight" often entails moves to suburbs, school districts, or neighborhoods that sprawl on one or another dimension, but only in an indirect sense do these studies link white flight and sprawl; segregated regions can occur at high or low density, with high- or low-degrees of mixed use, and with varying levels of urban clustering.

Empirical literature on how sprawl associates with segregation is sparse. Yet many organizations that seek to curb sprawl contend that their policy solutions will reduce segregation, in particular segregation by income. The Smart Growth Network Subgroup on Affordable Housing, a coalition of organizations and government agencies, defines smart growth as "that which invests time, attention, and resources in restoring community and vitality to center cities and older, inner suburbs. Smart growth in new developments is more town centered, transit and pedestrian oriented, and has a greater mix of housing, commercial, and retail uses" (Arigoni 2001, 9). One outcome of such development, they contend, will be income integration:

Smart growth promotes mixed-income communities and connects the development of affordable housing to jobs, services, commerce, transportation, and recreation. When housing, particularly affordable housing, is dispersed throughout a region and connected to other land uses, the need for long commutes to work or shopping can be reduced. Pockets of poverty and disinvestment are less likely to occur as a result. (Arigoni 2001, 20)

Some advocates of smart growth downplay the importance of density, stressing instead the need to mix uses and housing types. Even though the advocates do not emphasize density, however, smart growth may require higher density development. Mass transit and pedestrian orientation require higher densities than those typically attained by new development. New construction in old neighborhoods, furthermore, will naturally result in higher population density in established urban areas and less new development at lower densities.

The effects of higher density on income integration are unclear. Although high-density housing is more affordable than low-density housing, housing types often sort out across neighborhoods. Hence, even relatively high-density metropolitan areas might be composed of neighborhoods of very distinct densities, housing types, and affordability levels. As density increases, sorting may intensify rather than abate for several reasons. First, competition for infill sites may intensify as people and businesses with more resources outbid those with fewer resources. Many neighborhoods may shift from a mix of very low and low-income people to a more uniform low-income character, as the poor outbid the very poor, and as very low-income people unite in larger (and more crowded) households to pay for higher housing costs. These neighborhood shifts are sometimes dramatic enough to qualify as gentrification—the wholesale transformation of low-income neighborhoods to upper-income enclaves.

Until the late 1900s, most social researchers were more concerned about the negative social effects of density than the negative effects of sprawl. Starting around 1900, Ebenezer Howard (1898), a pioneer of modern city planning, advocated the creation of a network of moderate-density "garden cities" as an alternative to the high density of English industrial cities. Clarence S. Stein (1957), a planner active in the United States throughout the first half of the twentieth century, advocated the demolition of high-density central city neighborhoods and their replacement with moderate-density superblocks. Such sociologists as Louis Wirth (1938) reinforced the prevailing antidensity mood.

Since mid-century, efforts to connect density (either high or low) and pathology have been mostly unsuccessful (Hawley 1972). Stephanie A. Huie and W. Parker Frisbie (2000), testing whether density is associated with racial residential segregation, found that densely populated regions have less, not more, black-white segregation. Another study, by Anthony Downs (1999), reports few links between any of nine sprawl indicators and measures of either central city decline (population change) or distress (a battery of indicators of population change, crime, poverty and income, education levels, unemployment, and old housing stock; see also Burchell et al. 2001, 397). Both of these studies have limitations, however, partly because their measures of density and sprawl are either inadequate or inaccurate. Important questions still remain, then, about connections between density, sprawl, and unwanted outcomes. The remainder of this chapter considers only one of these questions: does high density, or growth in density, either aggravate or reduce the economic segregation many researchers have observed in metropolitan America?

How Density Shapes Income Segregation

This section begins with a more explicit discussion of the hypotheses that will be tested in a series of multivariate regression analyses. This is followed by a discussion of the formal model, the data and their limitations, and the results of the analysis.

Hypotheses

My main interest is the relationship between density and segregation. It is important, however, to control for other regional characteristics. I am particularly interested in income distribution and level; racial and ethnic composition; foreign-born composition of the population; age composition of the population; manufacturing and deindustrialization; and neighborhood size.

Density. I expect high-density regions to be more segregated by income, all else being equal, than low-density regions. I expect economic segregation to be more pronounced in regions with high-density neighborhoods for a variety of reasons. First, people in high-density regions live closer to one another than do people in low-density regions. Upper-income people often prefer to avoid residential proximity to low-income people; if high-density neighborhoods are also high-proximity neighborhoods, then high-density neighborhoods are less likely to contain a mix of upper- and lower-income residents than low-density neighborhoods. Second, competition over space will tend to be higher in high-density regions, producing the spatial sorting described in the previous section. Third, although high-density housing is more affordable than low-density housing, density is often achieved and maintained through the construction of neighborhoods consisting entirely of one housing type. Since many single-family residential neighborhoods in the United States have large lot sizes, it is possible to maintain or increase density even in single-family neighborhoods without mixing attached housing with detached houses. I expect these relationships also to persist through time, for regions that become denser to become more segregated, and for regions that lose density to become less segregated.

Neighborhood size. Most studies that compare segregation across metropolitan areas use census tracts as their base. Yet the size of census tracts both differs across metropolitan areas and changes through time.[1] In general, indices of segregation are lower for large areas than for small ones; I therefore expect segregation levels to be higher in regions with small tracts.

Metropolitan area population and population growth rate. I expect larger metropolitan areas to be more segregated by income than small ones. Large regions tend to have more internal differentiation than small ones. Population growth rates are also likely to have an effect on income segregation levels; fast-growth metropolitan areas tend to integrate by race more rapidly than slow-growth regions, but the direction of effect in the case of income segregation is less clear. Since the general trend nationwide is toward segregation by income, it is possible that fast-growth regions could be moving more rapidly in that direction. Conversely, fast-growth regions have many new neighborhoods that are not "marked" according to their socioeconomic status and that may therefore be more permeable to those of many different income levels.

Income distribution and level. Income distribution both differs across metropolitan areas and changes through time. Income inequality increased dramatically in the United States starting in the late 1960s. The Gini index of income distribution, which varies from 0 to 100 with 100 indicating complete inequality, rose from a record low 38.8 in 1968 to a high of 45.9 by 1997 (U.S. Census Bureau 2001). In the 1980s alone, for example, income inequality among households rose by almost 11 percent (Madden 2000, 1). Income inequality across households has also been rising within metropolitan areas, more extremely in some regions than in others (Madden 2000). In metropolitan areas with more unequal household incomes (either compared to one another or through time), poor households are likely to be more segregated from nonpoor households. In these areas, disproportionately low numbers of middle-income households are more likely to share neighborhoods with poor households than are upper-income households. Furthermore, because income inequality is growing, we might expect income-based segregation to grow even in the absence of any household mobility (Jargowsky 1996). By holding constant the level of income inequality, I control for variations in income segregation that are a mere byproduct of income distribution. Mean income, also, is likely to associate directly with income segregation; in regions with higher mean incomes, poor families are likely to be less "like" other families, and therefore to live in separate neighborhoods.

Racial/ethnic composition. Income and racial segregation are intimately linked. Blacks, in particular, are highly segregated from Whites in U.S. metropolitan areas, especially in the Northeast and Midwest, and although black-white segregation has fallen gradually in the past thirty years, segregation of Hispanics is increasing in many metropolitan areas (Lewis Mumford Center 2001a). In the past, this segregation has kept poor and nonpoor Blacks in the same neighborhoods (Massey and Denton 1993); that is, there has been less intraracial economic segregation, at least among Blacks. But since Blacks tend to earn less than Whites, regardless of educational level, regions with higher percentages of Blacks in the population are likely also to have higher overall levels of income segregation, all else being equal. Moreover, in recent years nonpoor Blacks have been able to move out of ghettos and into nonpoor neighborhoods (Wilson 1987), even though those neighborhoods may not be mixed by race (Quillian 1999; Pattillo-McCoy 2000). Income differentiation is more likely within the black population in metropolitan areas with large black populations; such regions are also likely to have a larger number of nonpoor neighborhoods with some, and sometimes many, black residents. For all these reasons, I expect income segregation to be higher in regions with higher shares of black residents. Since upper-income Whites are more likely to avoid and discriminate against low-income Blacks than against low-income Whites (Farley, Fielding, and Krysan 1997), I also expect that regions in which Blacks constitute a disproportionate share of the poor population will have higher levels of income segregation than those in which Blacks are no more likely to be poor than other residents.

Hispanics are less segregated from Whites than are Blacks (Lewis Mumford Center 2001a); therefore, I expect the relationships outlined between Blacks and Whites to be less pronounced, but still direct. That is, regions with more Hispanics and in which Hispanics constitute a greater share of the poor population are expected to have higher levels of economic segregation.

Foreign-born population. Regions with high shares of foreign-born residents are likely to have enclaves of foreign-born people who gather together for mutual support and advancement. These enclaves tend to have strong income mixing (Alba, Logan, and Stults 2000). I, therefore, expect metropolitan areas with large shares of foreign-born residents to have lower levels of income segregation, all else being equal. Because the percentage of Hispanics and the percentage of foreign born are highly correlated, I test the effects on income segregation of the percentage of Hispanics who were foreign born, a variable that is not as strongly correlated with the percent Hispanic as is the percent of the entire population born abroad.

Age composition of the population. Elderly people generally have lower incomes than non-elderly people, because labor force participation is lower among the elderly. Yet elderly people may have accumulated significant wealth, at least in the form of houses they own, and may, even if poor, be more acceptable as neighbors of wealthy people. Hence, I expect that regions with larger shares of elderly residents will have lower levels of income segregation.

Household size. Since I am measuring household income segregation, it is important to hold household size constant. Regions with small households are likely to have more income-based segregation because such households (especially those without children) are likely to sort into different kinds of neighborhoods based largely on income, socioeconomic status, and preferences. Larger households, by contrast, may have common needs and preferences for schools and other services for children that encourage them to locate in similar neighborhoods despite income differences.

Deindustrialization and manufacturing employment. Since the late 1960s, the United States has undergone a dramatic economic transformation. Some observers contend that this deindustrialization process has exacerbated the spatial mismatch between low-income workers, especially Blacks, and low-wage jobs (Jargowsky 1996; Wilson 1991). Manufacturing plant closures have been disproportionately concentrated in and nearby black-occupied neighborhoods, at least through the 1980s (Galster, Mincy, and Tobin 1997). Recent studies tend to support the spatial mismatch hypothesis, although its underlying causes are still imprecisely understood (Ihlanfeldt and Sjoquist 1998). [Editor's note: Holzer (1991), cited in chapter 9 by Wassmer, mentions that empirical research provides mixed support for the spatial mismatch hypothesis.] By reducing the number of middle-wage jobs, deindustrialization can also affect the distribution of wages among households, regardless of any changes in the location of jobs and workers. There may, therefore, be some correlation between growth in income inequality and declines in the percent of workers employed in manufacturing. If deindustrialization is expected to associate with growing income segregation, then high levels of manufacturing employment in any one year should be expected to associate with lower levels of income segregation.

The Models

I rely on two main econometric models to explain differences in the level of economic segregation across metropolitan areas. The first is a model of segregation at one point in time (1980 or 1990), represented by this equation:

$$\text{Segregation}_{i,t} = a + b\text{DENSITY}_{i,t} + c\text{TRACTSIZE}_{i,t} + d\text{MSAPOP}_{i,t} + e\text{INCSPLIT}_{i,t}$$
$$+ f\text{MEANINC}_{i,t} + g\text{PCTBLACK}_{i,t} + h\text{PCTHISP}_{i,t} + j\text{BLACKPOOR}_{i,t} +$$
$$k\text{HISPPOOR}_{i,t} + m\text{PCTHSPFOR}_{i,t} + n\text{PCT65UP}_{i,t} + p\text{POPHH}_{i,t} +$$
$$q\text{PCTEMPMFG}_{i,t}$$

Where Segregation is the dissimilarity or isolation index for poor households, DENSITY is the number of households per acre of urbanized land, TRACTSIZE is the area of the seventy-fifth percentile tract (see explanation below), MSAPOP is the population of the metropolitan area, INCSPLIT is the ratio of the eightieth to the twentieth percentile household income, MEANINC is the mean income, PCTBLACK is the percent of households whose head is black, PCTHISP is the percent of households whose head is Hispanic, BLACKPOOR is the concentration of black households in the "very low income" bracket (less than 50 percent of area median), HISPPOOR is the concentration of Hispanic households in the very low income bracket, PCTHSPFOR is the percent of the Hispanic population born abroad, PCT65UP is the percent of the population over age sixty-five, POPHH is the average number of persons per household, and PCTEMPMFG is the percent of workers in manufacturing industries. The subscripts stand for metropolitan area i and time t.

The second is a model of change through time, represented by this equation:

Segregation$_{i,t+1}$ = a + bSegregation$_{i,t}$ + cDENSCHG$_i$ + dTRACTSIZECHG$_i$ + eMSAPOPCHG$_i$ + fINCSPCHG$_i$ + gMEANINCCHG$_i$ + hPCTBLACKCHG$_i$ + jPCTHISPCHG$_i$ + kBLACKPOORCHG$_i$ + mHISPPOORCHG$_i$ + PCTHSPFORCHG$_i$ + pPCT65UPCHG$_i$ + qPOPHHCHG$_i$ + rPCTEMPMFGCHG$_i$

Where Segregation$_{i,t+1}$ is segregation in 1990, Segregation$_{i,t}$ is segregation in 1980, and all the variables ending with "CHG" represent either percent change (density, tract size, population, income split, mean income, poor black concentration index, poor Hispanic concentration index, persons per household) or change in percent (percent black, percent Hispanic, percent of Hispanics foreign born, percent over sixty-five, percent employed in manufacturing) in the variables tested in cross section in the first model. This model is a change model because of the inclusion of segregation in 1980 as one of the control variables.[2]

Unit of Analysis and Period of Measurement

This analysis uses the Census Bureau's smallest metropolitan-area definition, the metropolitan statistical area (MSA) or Primary Metropolitan Statistical Area (PMSA), as its unit of analysis, testing whether aggregate metropolitan indicators of sprawl influence aggregate metropolitan indicators of segregation, holding other factors constant. The MSA or PMSA is an appropriate unit of analysis for the study of both sprawl and segregation; it is an area that encompasses both commuting patterns and housing markets. The Consolidated Metropolitan Statistical Area (CMSA) tends to include numerous economic subregions and housing markets. Since consistent national land use data are not available below the county level, I use New England County Metropolitan Areas (NECMAs) instead of the town-based MSAs and PMSAs in the six New England states. Metropolitan areas change through time. This analysis uses data from 1980, 1982, 1990, and 1992. I therefore use 1990 PMSA, MSA, and NECMA definitions to compute all variables.

Measuring Segregation by Income

Thus far, most analyses of income segregation have used the national poverty line as a standard, and have computed segregation indices based on the concentration of families or persons living below the poverty line. Some analyses have suggested that the official poverty line is no longer an appropriate reflection of minimum living standards (Short 2001). A national poverty line also obscures important regional differences in cost of living, especially in housing costs (U.S. General Accounting Office 1995). Few analyses of income segregation use a relative regional standard to estimate income segregation levels. Paul A. Jargowsky (1996, 1997) is an exception to this rule; he computed a Neighborhood Sorting Index (NSI) as the ratio between the standard deviation of the neighborhood income distribution and the standard deviation of the regional income distribution. Although this measure has some advantages, it hinders evaluation of the extent to which shifts in the regional income distribution contribute to income-based segregation. Instead of the NSI, I therefore use the dissimilarity and isolation indices[3] to measure the segregation of very low-income households, that is, those earning less than half their metropolitan area's median income, from other households. I use very low income rather than lower income (all those earning less than 80 percent of the area median) because segregation is more likely to be observed at the very low-income level, and because the lower-income population constitutes a much larger share of the total metropolitan population. Consistent with common practice in studies using indices of segregation with limited ranges (Jargowsky 1996; Massey and Denton 1988), I use the log-odds transformation to convert the D indices to continuous variables with theoretically infinite range.[4] This transformation makes the dependent variable more appropriate for OLS regression, but hinders interpretation somewhat.

Measuring Sprawl/Density

I use two sources to compute urban density. The first is a national survey that measures the actual use of land, rather than population density. That survey, the National Resources Inventory (NRI), is conducted every five years by the U.S. Department of Agriculture. The most recently available NRI was conducted in 1997 and released at the county level in spring 2001. This survey estimates the amount of built up/urban land in every county in the United States in 1982, 1987, 1992, and 1997. The second data source needed to compute urban density is an estimate of the number of households for each county in the United States. I estimated the number of households for 1982 by converting the Census Bureau's county-level population estimates to households based on the observed persons per household and household population in 1980 and 1990. For 1992, I interpolated county-level population from 1990 and 2000 census results. Having estimated the number of households in each year, I computed the estimated density of households per urbanized acre in 1982 and 1992 and the percent change in household density between 1982 and 1992.

Other Variables

Most of the other variables are taken or computed from the decennial U.S. census in 1980 and 1990. Population, persons per household, percent of households with black and Hispanic householders, and the percent of population over age sixty-five are from STF1. I used household income distribution data from STF3 to compute the 20th and 80th percentile incomes; I use the 80:20 household income ratio as my indicator of income inequality. Based on STF3, I computed the percent of very low-income households (in 1990) or families (in 1980) with a black or Hispanic householder. I divided this by the percent of all households or families in the very low-income category to yield a concentration index of black and Hispanic households or families in the very low-income range.[5] The percent of workers in manufacturing is from the U.S. Department of Commerce's Regional Economic Information Service (REIS) and is based on place of employment rather than place of work. I obtained a special tabulation from the Census Bureau of the Hispanic population according to their foreign-born status. To control for the effect of different tract sizes, I used the 75th percentile tract size, because I wanted a measure that was most sensitive to the existence of a substantial component of very large census tracts, where income mixing is most likely. The 75th percentile tract size is also less correlated with my measure of residential density than the other measures.

Results: Sprawl, Income Segregation, and Their Relationship

According to the USDA's NRI, the average density in 1982 was 1.65 households per acre in the 319 PMSAs and MSAS for which data were available[6]; the median density was only 1.47 households per acre, and the

95th percentile was 2.83 households per acre. (Because of space limitations, the tables have not been included in this chapter; they are available from the author). The New York, Jersey City, and San Francisco PMSAs, and the Honolulu MSA were outliers, all with over four households per acre of urbanized land in 1982. Pueblo, Colorado, and Las Cruces, New Mexico, were unexpected outliers and probably reflect data errors in 1982; the USDA may have missed urbanized land in these two MSAs, because in both cases their density dropped by 1987 to levels that were consistent with similar MSAs. By 1992, the average density dropped to 1.51 households per acre, the median to 1.36, and the 95th percentile to 2.58. By the density definition, sprawl therefore clearly accelerated in the 1980s in these metropolitan areas; while their population grew about 12 percent and the number of households by 16 percent, the amount of urbanized land grew 24 percent. Population density fell 9.5 percent, from 5.0 to 4.5 persons per urbanized acre, while household density declined by a more modest 6.3 percent.

As metropolitan America sprawled during the 1980s, the poorest households and families in U.S. metropolitan areas grew more residentially segregated from wealthier households and families. The unweighted mean dissimilarity index for households rose from 25.3 in 1980 to 26.7 in 1990. The mean isolation index also grew. In 1980, in the average metropolitan area, the average very low-income household lived in a neighborhood in which 29.2 percent of residents also earned very low incomes (i.e., the average metropolitan area had an isolation index of 29.2), even though only 23.2 percent of households earned very low incomes. By 1990, the average isolation index had increased to 30.2 while the mean percent very low income remained at 23.4 percent. Across the distribution from the minimum, through the 25th percentile, median, 75th percentile, and the maximum, these indices rose uniformly for households and families except the minimum isolation of very low-income households. These findings are consistent with Jargowsky's (1996) findings, using his NSI, that poor and rich households became more segregated in the 1980s.

At first glance, the comparatively low segregation level for very low-income households and families may seem surprising. It is explicable on several fronts, however. First, income does not translate directly to social status; people with high social status can earn low incomes when they are in college or at the beginning of their careers, after they retire or when they are temporarily between jobs. Second, reporting of income to the Bureau of Census is not always accurate and is likely to be understated, rather than overstated. Third, very low-income households may be sharing neighborhoods with large numbers of households earning between 50 percent and 80 percent of the area median; the assignment of households into discrete categories according to their income levels tends to overstate the real (social) difference between the categories.

The fact that accelerating sprawl was linked to increased income segregation might lead to the conclusion that sprawl led to income segregation in the 1980s. But as discussed earlier, many other forces also contribute to income segregation. First, income distribution shifted in the United States in the 1980s. In the average metropolitan area in 1980, 23.2 percent of households earned less than half of the metropolitan median household income, while 40.0 percent earned more than 1.2 times the area median. By 1990, the split had shifted to 23.4 percent and 40.5 percent, respectively; the middle had shrunk. Another measure of income division, the ratio between the 80th and the 20th percentile household income, also grew, from 3.95 to 4.15 at the mean.

In addition, the foreign-born population grew substantially in some metropolitan areas, and manufacturing employment shrank in most metropolitan areas; both of these forces have been hypothesized to influence income segregation, but in opposite directions. In the next section, I use regression analysis to identify the unique contributions of these patterns and trends to metropolitan segregation levels and changes in the 1980s.

Sprawl and Income Segregation, 1980–1990: All Metropolitan Areas

As mentioned earlier, four metropolitan areas had extraordinarily high household density in 1982 and 1992, well above four standard deviations above the mean. Because of this outlier status, I omit these metropolitan areas from the regression analysis reported here, but I briefly mention below the results obtained when they were included. I also omit both Las Cruces and Pueblo, because they had suspiciously high densities in 1982 probably indicating unreliable data. This leaves 313 metropolitan areas in the analysis.

Between 1980 and 1990 household density for these 313 metropolitan areas fell from 1.54 to 1.45 households per urban acre, with a mean density decline of 5.6 percent. The average region had declining household size, large tract size, growing population, and growing income inequality. The concentration of poverty among both Blacks and Hispanics appears to have dropped, on average, although the changing unit of analysis between the 1980 and 1990 versions of STF3 (from families to households) reduces the strength of this comparison. Whereas black families in the average region were 2.0 times more concentrated in the very low income bracket in 1980 than their share of the population would predict, black households were only 1.7 times as concentrated in that bracket in 1990. The Hispanic concentration also fell, from 1.64 (families) to 1.28 (households), between 1980 and 1990. Meanwhile, the share of Hispanics born abroad also increased, from 18 to 22 percent mean, while the average percent Hispanic headed households also grew from about 4 percent to 5 percent. Elderly residents and households headed by Blacks also grew at the average.

The regression results showed no significant relationship between density and income segregation, by either the dissimilarity or the isolation index, in 1980. In both cases, the coefficients are positive (though miniscule in the analysis of isolation), but the levels of significance are low to very low. (We cannot, therefore, rule out an inverse relationship between density and income segregation in 1980.) In 1990, by contrast, higher-density regions were significantly ($p < 0.001$) more segregated by income than lower-density regions; very low-income households were more unevenly distributed and more isolated from other households in metropolitan areas whose density levels were high than in areas where density was low. This result provides evidence in support of the initial hypothesis. In the analysis of change during the 1980s, density change had a significant relationship to the change in dissimilarity, but not to the change in isolation. Even for dissimilarity, the significance level is marginal ($p < 0.10$ in a one-tailed text, $p = 0.10$ in a two-tailed test). The effect of density may have been swamped by the inclusion as a control variable of the 1980 segregation level. When I did not exclude New York, San Francisco, Honolulu, and Jersey City from the analysis, density had no significant relationship with income segregation in any of the analyses. Further research on the extent and nature of income segregation in these four high-density regions might reveal interesting lessons for the rest of the nation.

Therefore, high density does appear to have some direct relationship with income segregation. It is plausible to suggest that high density leads to income segregation, for the reasons explored above. Competition over urban land is more intense when density is higher; in such competitions, people with lower incomes lose, and end up living in a more limited set of less desirable neighborhoods as higher-income people outbid them in the housing market. Is it reasonable to propose that income segregation produces high density, rather than the other way around? At most, one might make the argument that income segregation can facilitate density, but it is hard to make the argument that segregation produces density. If nonpoor people prefer not to live near poor people, and if poor people are segregated in their own neighborhoods, then nonpoor people can relax about density because they know that their nearby neighbors will probably not be poor. If their neighbors are not quite so close by (i.e., if the density is lower), then perhaps they will not mind sharing their neighborhoods with low-income people. I do not test econometrically whether there is a feedback relationship here, but the possibility should be kept in mind as a caution, especially when interpreting the coefficients. Further research on segregation-density dynamics would be useful.

These results for density hold even when the size of the 75th percentile tract is held constant. Regions whose biggest tracts were very large had lower dissimilarity and isolation indices in 1980 and 1990, suggesting that larger neighborhoods can accommodate more internal diversity, irrespective of density level. Furthermore, dissimilarity levels rose more rapidly in metropolitan areas where the largest tracts were shrinking faster (i.e., as large tracts were subdivided into small ones). Changes in tract size were not significantly correlated with changing isolation indices. Smaller tract size and shrinking tracts may themselves be a byproduct of higher density, as discussed earlier, though correlations between these measures and the density measures are generally fairly low. If anything, these results suggest that density may exacerbate income segregation more than indicated by the density measurement alone.

Many other variables have more important and consistent effects on segregation than density. Income associates with segregation levels as expected; income segregation is higher in MSAs with higher mean incomes and greater income inequality, as measured by the 80:20 ratio, in both 1980 and 1990. Faster rates of growth in income inequality also correlated with faster rates of growth in income segregation, as expected, but change in mean income did not have a significant relationship to change in income segregation.

Population had the expected result; larger metropolitan areas had higher levels of income-related segregation by both indices in 1980 and 1990, probably because large metropolitan areas provide more variety in neighborhood type, allowing households to sort out more effectively by income when they prefer to do so. Population change did not correlate significantly with segregation change over the 1980s, however. This result contrasts with findings about race-related segregation. Many studies have found that fast-growth regions become integrated more rapidly, perhaps because new neighborhoods can reflect changes in social norms, regulations, and penalties about racial discrimination. Since the United States generally became more divided by income over the past thirty years, it should come as little surprise that fast growth does not erase income sorting. Perhaps the real surprise is that fast growth did not significantly exacerbate income segregation.

Ethnicity and race also had many of the expected effects on income segregation. Metropolitan areas in which larger shares of householders were Black and Hispanic had higher income dissimilarity than those with fewer such householders; income-related isolation was higher in regions with high shares of black householders, but the Hispanic share did not have a significant effect. Income dissimilarity grew more rapidly in regions where the share of householders who were black grew more rapidly in the 1980s, but the shift in the black share of householders had no significant effect on income isolation. Hispanic householders had the opposite effect; regions in which the Hispanic share of householders grew rapidly became more integrated by income by both indices. This result must be interpreted within the context of the foreign-born status of the Hispanic population. As expected, both indices of segregation were lower in 1980 and 1990 in metropolitan areas where larger shares of the Hispanic population were born abroad, and the dissimilarity index fell significantly in the 1980s in regions where the share of Hispanic householders grew rapidly. As hypothesized earlier, this may be a result of the formation of immigrant enclaves, which tend to have high levels of income mixing.

Native-born Hispanics tend to live in class-stratified neighborhoods rather than in ethnic enclaves because middle- and upper-income Hispanic households tend to assimilate, leading to greater income segregation in regions where native-born residents dominate the Hispanic population than in those with large proportions of immigrants. The ethnic composition of low-income families and households had a more limited independent relationship to income segregation. Metropolitan areas where Blacks were highly concentrated in the very low-income category had more income segregation by both measures in 1990, but not in 1980; the reverse was true for Hispanics.

These results on race and ethnicity provide support for both Douglas S. Massey and William Julius Wilson. Massey contends that race constitutes an essential category for understanding the sorting of American metropolitan areas by class (Massey and Fischer 2000); my results show clearly that regions with larger black populations experience higher levels of segregation, even holding constant the share of very low income families or households who are black. Moreover, I found some evidence that very low-income households were more segregated at the metropolitan level when Blacks headed relatively high shares of these households. Wilson argues that race is losing significance while class is gaining (Wilson 1987, 1991). Other studies have shown that Blacks in many regions are sorting out by class (Quillian 1999). I found that metropolitan areas with large and growing concentrations of Blacks both are, and are becoming, more segregated than areas with smaller black concentrations. This suggests that regions with larger black populations have greater internal diversity of black residents and, therefore, a greater range of neighborhoods in which nonpoor black households will live. The consequence for poor black households, however, is greater income segregation from all nonpoor households.

As expected, metropolitan areas with high proportions of elderly residents, and those with large households, again as expected, had lower-income segregation in both 1980 and 1990. This result was both strong and significant for both indices of segregation for the senior population, while it was significant except for the relationship between household size and isolation in 1980. Segregation levels fell more rapidly when the share of senior citizens grew more rapidly; change in household size did not have a significant effect on either index.

Industrial structure, as expected, had a significant independent relationship with income segregation, most consistently and significantly as measured by the dissimilarity index. In both 1980 and 1990, metropolitan areas with high shares of workers in manufacturing had lower income segregation levels than those with more limited manufacturing bases. Furthermore, income dissimilarity grew more rapidly in regions where the share of jobs in manufacturing fell more rapidly, at more marginal significance levels. Manufacturing had the same relationship to the isolation index, but it was significant only in 1980 and then only at marginal significance levels ($p < 0.10$). This finding, while consistent with Jargowsky's (1996), also holds constant the level of metropolitan income inequality.

How might deindustrialization directly reinforce income segregation? In the 1980s, plant closings in deindustrializing regions tended to concentrate in and around predominantly minority (and presumably low-income) neighborhoods (Galster, Mincy, and Tobin 1997). As these plants closed, workers would move to new jobs, and possibly even migrate to other regions, if they had the opportunity to do so; those left behind would tend to be poorer than average for the neighborhood, and the entire region would become more segregated by income and probably more "spatially mismatched," that is, with a higher degree of separation between low-income and minority workers and low-wage jobs.

These results are fairly robust. They explain about 53 percent of the variation in metropolitan dissimilarity levels in 1980 and 1990, 60 percent of isolation in 1980, and 71 percent of isolation in 1990. The change models are very strong, with R-squares exceeding 0.80, but this is a reflection of the model structure, which included 1980 segregation levels as a control variable. Additional analysis, perhaps including the incorporation of additional variables to represent other dimensions of urban form, might help reduce the unexplained portion of the variation in the 1980 and 1990 models. They suggest that pro-density efforts should proceed with caution and safeguards if we wish to avoid income segregation. Since such policies will take different forms in different regions, I examine in the next section the relationships between density and segregation in low-density, fast-growth metropolitan areas, where the pursuit of pro-density policies would seem most urgent.

Do Density and Income Segregation also Coincide in Sprawling, Fast Growth MSAs?

Policies can affect density levels. Infrastructure investments encourage higher density, for example; exclusionary zoning tends to reduce density (Fulton et al. 2001; Pendall 1999). But these policies will have different effects and varying levels of appeal in different kinds of regions. Slow-growth regions will take a long time to change, whereas fast-growth regions can change in dramatically different directions in a matter of a decade or two depending on the policies that are in place to shape that growth. The most logical target for pro-density policies are therefore fast-growth, low-density regions; in these areas, the environmental, social, and fiscal costs of growth are likely to be high (Burchell et al. 2001), and residents and decision makers at all levels are likely to look for new policies to reduce sprawl. If they seek to promote density, however, can they expect and possibly counteract higher levels of income segregation?

To answer this question, I selected all the metropolitan areas whose growth rates exceeded the metropolitan average in the 1980s and whose density levels were below average in 1982. (Atlanta, Charlotte, Dallas, and Tucson were a few of the metro areas on this list.) When I compared their mean values to those of the complete set, these seventy-six MSAs had lower mean dissimilarity and isolation indices in both 1980 and 1990 than the complete set of MSAs. They also had lower mean population, lower concentrations of Hispanics, higher shares of their Hispanic population born abroad, and fewer workers in manufacturing. Their 80:20 income ratio was equal to that in the complete set of MSAs in 1980, but was lower in 1990 (average of 4.01, compared to 4.14). Otherwise there were few differences between the subset and the entire group.

Density and change in density correlated much more strongly with income dissimilarity in these fast-growth, low-density MSAs than in all 314 MSAs. The coefficients are larger than in the complete dataset, and they are significant at conventional levels ($p < 0.05$) for 1980, 1990, and change over the 1980s. Isolation of very low-income households, by contrast, is more weakly related to density and attains significance at exactly $p = 0.10$ only in 1990. Once again, these results hold true even while the 75th percentile tract size is held constant. (The effects of tract size are not as consistently significant in this analysis as in the previous one, but where they are significant, MSAs with larger tracts are still significantly less segregated by income.) Where significant, the other variables are also consistent with the earlier regressions, with one exception. In 1990, very low-income households were more isolated in MSAs with high shares of workers in manufacturing, opposite both the expected result and the result obtained in 1980 and for change in percent in manufacturing between 1980 and 1990. This contradiction and the weak level of significance suggest that this result be taken with due caution.

Summing Up: Density and Segregation

The results discussed here suggest that both density at a single point in time and increasing density over time can exacerbate income-related segregation. High density is both a cause and a consequence of high land values. Poor people tend to lose bidding wars over urban space; such bidding wars intensify in regions where density is high and increasing. As a consequence, poor people are often relegated to a limited number of low-quality neighborhoods that often combine very high population density with low quality of life. Falling density, on the other hand, means that fewer people are bidding for every urban acre. Less competition may make it easier for low-income households to maintain a place in mixed income neighborhoods.

In addition, new developments in fast-growing and high-density regions typically have few new neighborhoods with mixed housing types; instead, new development occurs as a sea of large single-family homes on small lots or massive two- to three- story apartment complexes surrounded by seas of parking. Local zoning laws, builder characteristics, and banking practices all contribute to this spatial fragmentation of dwelling types. Local governments designate most residential areas exclusively for single-family housing, and even high-density regions have vast areas zoned exclusively for single-family dwellings at densities not to exceed eight units per acre (Pendall 1995). Although mixed housing types are often permitted in multifamily zones, in most markets one housing type is usually clearly more profitable than another, especially over a short period of time, and so builders gravitate to that building type. Furthermore, most builders do not have expertise in both single and multifamily development, and bankers tend to be conservative about financing more than one housing type at a time.

Even where mixed-use neighborhoods with many housing types do exist, rising metropolitan density and competition over land will tend to make them too expensive for low-income households. Such neighborhoods have in recent years become more fashionable; when situated in convenient locations, they can command a high premium, potentially leading to substantial displacement over the course of a decade (the time period evaluated in this study). Many advocates for smart growth already acknowledge that compact growth can lead to gentrification; PolicyLink, an organization based in the San Francisco Bay Area, has even developed an antigentrification toolkit to help avoid this unwanted side effect of compact growth (PolicyLink 2001).

The effects of density on income segregation are strongest in the fastest-growing and lowest-density regions of the United States. These regions are exactly those in which decision makers are most likely to pursue pro-density policies, because growth has created the impetus for new land use policies; pro-density policies are also likely to be effective because these regions have low density to begin with, suggesting an abundance of infill and intensification opportunities.

Portland, Oregon, offers a telling example of the conflicts between density and affordability. Metropolitan Portland is renowned for its urban growth boundary; the region also has been subject for over twenty years to the Metropolitan Housing Rule, which requires that at least half of each jurisdiction's zoned residential development capacity must be multifamily and that all its jurisdictions' zoning ordinance meet minimum density targets of six, eight, or ten dwellings per acre (Abbott 1997). For at least a decade, these rules helped boost the density of single family and apartment developments, improving housing supply and reducing upward pressure on prices. Housing affordability has deteriorated in the 1990s, however, as the regional economy has improved and land has become scarce. Now the regional government is struggling to identify politically feasible measures to promote long-term housing affordability, but real estate interests have foreclosed several important options by working with conservative state legislators to pass legislation prohibiting inclusionary zoning and real estate transfer taxes (Martin 2001).

How should policy makers respond to these findings? I certainly do not suggest that state and local governments should pursue exclusionary zoning and reduce funds for centralized infrastructure so that density drops even faster as a strategy for income integration. The low density that would result is likely to have many other ill effects on the environment, fiscal health, and society; furthermore, low density may still associate with other social injustices, for instance, more separation from employment for low-income households, that are not captured by the income segregation measures I used here.

Pro-density policies, then, are still critically necessary; the most careful research to date has shown that low-density development costs more to serve with private and public infrastructure, has more harmful effects on air and water quality, and requires more driving than high-density development. But density alone is not enough. As the literature review suggested, density is only one aspect of sprawl. Another dimension of sprawl, the lack of land use mix, may have a much stronger direct relationship with levels of segregation than does density. Future research is needed to test whether regions with mixed land uses and neighborhoods with varying housing types have less economic segregation than those with less mixing of use and housing type. Scatteration of development may also influence economic segregation; two metropolitan areas with equal density but different degrees of residential clustering may differ in their economic segregation. Smart growth strategies emphasize not only density, but also, and perhaps more importantly, mixed uses, compact (contiguous, nonscattered) development patterns, and more choice in housing type within neighborhoods as well as among them.

Even with a full range of such smart land use policies, however, the fundamentals of land economics are likely to induce income sorting because of higher density. If decision makers want mixed-income neighborhoods, therefore, they are likely to need more explicit policy tools to get them. Inclusionary housing policies, for example, encourage not only a mix of housing types but also guarantee long-term affordability for a specified share of dwellings. Montgomery County, Maryland, part of Metropolitan Washington, D.C. has had an inclusionary housing program since 1973; the program has produced over ten thousand affordable housing units simply by requiring builders of large housing developments to make between 10 percent and 20 percent of the dwellings affordable to low-income families (K. Brown 2001). In exchange, builders receive a substantial density bonus; this element of the program has also helped satisfy demand for market-rate units and thereby mitigate price pressures in a very high-cost region. As a consequence of these and other policies, Montgomery County both ranks among the highest-density suburban counties in the Northeast and has a substantial portion of permanently protected open space and agricultural land. Other programs that can guarantee both affordability and income mixing include redevelopment set-asides for affordable housing, community land trusts, and real estate transfer taxes earmarked for affordable housing.

At a broader level, of course, these results show that density is much less important than some other factors in sorting out American cities by income. In particular, income inequality is among the most powerful forces propelling income segregation. Policies to produce a more even distribution of income, for example, amendments to make income taxes more progressive, would likely have a much more substantial effect on income segregation than any policy on land development. Development policy tends to have a direct effect only on the new increment of growth and only indirect effects on established neighborhoods; income policy should affect everyone. Conversely, land use policies that might exacerbate income segregation will probably have modest effects; land use regulations have some effects, but modest ones, on density (Pendall 1999), and density has some effects, but modest ones, on income segregation. Therefore, pro-density policies should not be avoided simply because they may modestly and indirectly exacerbate income segregation. Rather, if decision makers wish to produce regions with better air and water quality, more transportation choices, more efficient public services, and neighborhoods that are mixed by income, they should supplement pro-density policies with many other policies, both land use related and otherwise, that shape metropolitan areas that are sustainable by economic, environmental, and equity criteria.

Notes

1. Local committees draw up tract boundaries. In 2000, the Bureau of Census established a minimum of fifteen hundred persons per tract for noninstitutional tracts and one thousand persons for institutional ("special place") tracts (U.S. Census Bureau 1997). The optimal population per tract is four thousand persons. Local committees often prefer to keep old boundaries, however, to maintain geographic consistency through time; while they frequently split fast-growth tracts, they are often reluctant to combine tracts

that have lost population and are, in fact, granted exceptions to the Census Bureau's minimum tract threshold to avoid unwanted boundary changes. Exceptions are granted, however, for tracts whose boundaries have changed slightly or not at all.

2. I used this model form rather than a model of percent change because the logit transformation of the dissimilarity and isolation indices, which range between 0 and 1, yields a negative number between –2 and 0. Consequently, segregation indices that increased in the 1980s (by either the transformed or untransformed measure) would show a percentage decrease in the transformed index.

3. The dissimilarity index is represented as $D = 0.5 * (\Sigma \mid x_i / X - y_i / Y \mid)$, where x_i and y_i are the number of households in categories x (very low income) and y (not very low income) in tract i and X and Y are the number of households in categories x and y in the metropolitan area. The isolation index is represented as $xP^*x = \Sigma \{ (x_i /X)*(x_i / t_i) \}$, where x_i and t_i are the number of very low-income households and the total number of households in the tract, respectively, and X is the number of very low-income households in the metropolitan area.

4. The log-odds transformation for the D index, for example, is computed as $\ln(D/(1-D))$.

5. STF3A reports family income but not household income by race in 1980; this measure is therefore imperfect for 1980 and as an indicator of change between 1980 and 1990.

6. Anchorage is not included because the NRI does not include Alaska.

Chapter 11

SPRAWL AND SEGREGATION
Another Side of the Los Angeles Debate
Tridib Banerjee and Niraj Verma

Introduction

If Atlanta is the poster child for urban sprawl, Los Angeles is the most controversial example. Proponents of the compact city and new urbanism consider Los Angeles the epitome of sprawl, of unplanned, unchecked, profligate, profit-driven urban growth (Calthorpe 1993, 142–168; 2000). Historians see the influence of planners in the dispersed and polycentric urban form of Los Angeles tracing it to an aristocratic dream of transforming a Latino land into an Anglo city (Starr 1991) or to industrial location decisions in the early twentieth century (Hise 1998). Some economists see Los Angeles' polycentric form as the product of market choices representing economic vitality, individual liberty, freedom, and the preeminence of property rights (Gordon and Richardson 1997, 2000). Yet others, notably postmodernists (Davis 1992, 1998; Scott and Soja 1996), take a much wider view seeing Los Angeles and its style of land use as the dystopia that awaits other cities. Postmodernist literature is impressive in drawing on the perspectives of different disciplines from both inside and outside academia. Much of this discussion is highly charged and deeply polarized, generating at least as much heat as light.

This discourse, however, remains curiously limited to physical and land use issues. It is common to read claims and counterclaims about density, loss of farmland, congestion and average travel times, loss of environmental quality, as well as other such issues. Conspicuously absent is the question of segregation as an issue of civil rights and the consequences of communities divided along racial and ethnic lines, with the notable exception of research by Robert D. Bullard, Glenn S. Johnson, and Angela D. Torres (2000a, 2000b). Although there are several studies of segregation in Los Angeles (Bobo et al. 2000; Ethington, Frey, and Myers 2001; Myers and Park 2001), there is little in the literature that discusses whether segregation may be linked to urban sprawl with the exception of Rolf Pendall's chapter 10 in this volume.

Adding concerns of equity to a discourse that is otherwise characterized by a debate between market choice, on one hand, and environmental quality, on the other, requires a political economy perspective. Relevant to this approach is Charles Tiebout's (1956) much-cited public choice thesis. In the case of locally occurring, nonrival goods, that is, goods for which the market cannot sort between different categories of consumers, Tiebout argues that a de facto sorting happens when people "vote with their feet," when they choose localities that offer different bundles of these nonrival goods. The fragmented metropolitan space, thus, represents a political marketplace where efficiency is obtained in the allocation of resources to deliver public goods and services (see Wassmer, chapter 9).

Tiebout's perspective provides a theoretical understanding of sprawl that simultaneously incorporates concerns of efficiency and metropolitan management. We find, however, Tiebout's positivist standpoint and lack of normative discussion limiting. Our discussion of segregation and distribution goes beyond this paradigm. We use empirical analysis of the land use characteristics of the eighty-eight cities of Los Angeles County to make our arguments.

Our main thesis is that the problem of segregation in contemporary metropolitan areas is inextricably linked to the phenomenon of urban sprawl, the fragmentation of the political space, and the land use configurations of the cities that constitute that political space. Thus, we must understand the political economy of metropolitan governance in order to derive policies related to issues of segregation.

The extensive and growing literature on urban sprawl has been evaluated in several recent articles (Burchell 1998; Galster, Hanson, and Wolman 2001; Squires 2002). The literature offers very little insight into the social implications of sprawl. On the one hand, writings on sprawl that are empirically grounded have failed to consider the social implications in terms of segregation or equity. On the other hand, writings that are clearly normative and have seemingly championed environmental, libertarian, or efficiency values have been totally remiss, or at best indifferent, to the social implications of urban space and form.

In general, the literature is mute or inconclusive on two questions. Does sprawl cause or exacerbate segregation? To what extent does sprawl contribute to social inequity and/or environmental injustice in Los Angeles?

Recent Literature on Ethnic Diversity in Los Angeles

While the general literature on sprawl is not particularly enlightening, two recent studies have focused on segregation, inequality, and injustice in Los Angeles (Bobo et al. 2000; Dear 2001). Using a 1993–1994 survey of more than four thousand L.A. County residents, Lawrence D. Bobo, Melvin L. Oliver, James H. Johnson, Jr., and Abel Valenzuela conclude that in the last two decades racial diversity in the metropolitan area increased mainly due to the growth of nonwhite immigrant populations. An examination of the results makes clear, however, that the increased diversity is attributable to the mixing of various population groups other than non-Hispanic Whites, that is, Asians, Blacks, and Hispanics, rather than a mixing of all racial groups. Thus, the majority of the non-Hispanic white population seems to have retreated to the periphery of the metropolitan area, to the coast, valleys, edge cities, or exurbia, while Hispanics and nonwhites have remained in the center city and its immediate vicinity. Additionally, the authors find that interethnic tensions and negative attitudes have reinforced the preference of Whites to live in all white neighborhoods.

Results based on the 2000 census, however, appear somewhat contradictory. The overall results are highly dependent on the spatial unit of analysis and overall methodology used, for example, census tracts versus incorporated cities. The Philip J. Ethington, William H. Frey, and Dowell Myers (2001) report on the "resegregation" of the Los Angeles area, which uses historical census tract level data from 1940–2000, finds that segregation has been rising faster than integration. But another study by Dowell Myers and Julie Park (2001, 1) that focuses on city-level ethnicity dynamics between 1980–2000, concludes that while there is more balance, this balance has been achieved because of the greater mixing of minority groups, mainly Asians and Hispanics, but not necessarily because of white and nonwhite integration.

Systematic efforts are currently underway to document the social and environmental injustices that result from patterns of racial concentration and segregation. Studies show that as Whites and upper-class nonwhites relocate to the periphery, lower-income nonwhite racial groups remain ensconced in central areas and, consequently, are subjected to greater concentrations of air pollution, toxic hot spots, and related health hazards (Pulido 2000, *Sprawl Hits the Wall* 2001). These reports point to the metropolitan social ecology of inequality in housing, mobility, amenities, and health risks. These studies, however, fail to explain how this pattern emerged and what the political implications might be for metropolitan governance.

Tiebout Sorting and the Los Angeles Sprawl

Charles Tiebout sorting (Musso 1999) is a well-known concept based on his original 1956 journal article (Tiebout 1956). Tiebout argues that a fragmented metropolitan region might be seen as a political marketplace where residents make location choices to consume a particular bundle of public goods offered by a municipality. Interestingly, Tiebout and his colleagues based their case on the political fragmentation of Los Angeles (Ostrom, Tiebout, and Warren 1961). Since Tiebout's "public choice" argument essentially rationalized metropolitan fragmentation as an efficient outcome for nonrival public goods, it is understandable that they failed to anticipate racial segregation and environmental injustice, but it is also curious, because by the 1960s significant political activism against the practice of exclusionary or "snob" zoning was already under way.

Today, the Tieboutian world is an established reality and remains a major challenge for metropolitan governance. Los Angeles is truly a "fragmented metropolis" (Fogelson 1993) because it includes, but is not limited to, Los Angeles County, and has the largest number of incorporated cities of any region in the United States. Here local communities compete with each other in attracting revenue-generating businesses, which further contributes to the sprawl. The communities exploit California's tax increment financing provision in order to increase revenue-generating development, while depriving the counties of property tax revenue sorely needed for various social and human services. More specifically, the localities use tax increment financing provisions to redevelop blighted areas, because when an area is declared blighted, it is designated as a redevelopment area and the existing property tax base is frozen. The incremental tax revenue generated from future improvements is then used to finance infrastructure improvements, land assembly, and other capital costs associated with redevelopment. Property tax revenue limitations imposed by the taxpayer revolt of the 1970s, however, have exacerbated such local tendencies. Indeed, as localities now rely on sales tax revenue, there is a growing tendency toward what is called "fiscalization of land use," or development decisions that favor land use, such as retail, and particularly "big box" retail, that generate more tax revenue (Lewis and Barbour 1999).

As cities compete for tax revenues, redevelopment dollars, and investment capital, they become entrepreneurs, and are often in partnership with private developers (Frieden and Sagalyn 1989; Loukaitou-Sideris and Banerjee 1998). Such dogged pursuit of local economic goals has often produced negative externalities, that is, increased traffic and pollution for neighboring cities and the denial of collective welfare for the entire region. The classic scenario of the "tragedy of the commons" (Hardin and Baden 1977) gradually but inexorably unfolds. Fair share issues related to affordable housing, social services, and health care become more critical. These issues are not just limited to the Los Angeles area only; they are becoming major concerns for all metropolitan regions experiencing sprawl and suburbanization (Guhathakurta and Wichert 1998; Sellers 1999).

To confirm that municipalities function as Tieboutian clubs, Eric Heikkila (1996) undertook a three-stage multivariate analysis of L.A. County's 1990 census data. Using factor analysis followed by analysis of variance, he demonstrated that "municipal boundaries reinforce club distinctions along four dimensions: urban scale, ethnicity, household type, and economic class" (Heikkila 1996, 204). Subsequent cluster analysis failed to produce meaningful clusters, which suggests that these municipalities do indeed function as Tieboutian clubs in a highly fragmented metropolitan area.

None of the above-mentioned research, however, discusses segregation or inequality. Confirmation of a public-choice-oriented Tieboutian world does not say whether all municipalities are clubs of the same status. Furthermore, the research does not indicate, for example, whether all are equally exclusive or whether we might call them "country clubs;" some of them might be more like "union halls" or "soup kitchens." The following section investigates these issues within the Los Angeles metropolitan area context.

Community Land Use Portfolios in Los Angeles

Whereas Heikkila emphasizes socioeconomic data, we focus on urban form variables and land use configurations of various municipalities. We reason that the land use portfolio, that is, the distribution of land use within the city, indicates the environmental appeal and the social milieu of municipalities. The land use portfolio of a community is largely a function of public policy measures like zoning, subdivision regulation, redevelopment projects, planning standards such as floor area ratios, and increasingly, private-public development deals involving large-scale projects.

It is possible for a community to exclude certain populations by limiting density and certain types of housing like apartments, town houses, and trailer parks. A community can maintain its social class milieu by having high quality schools and permitting only certain types of land use, for instance, banning liquor stores, laundromats, fast food restaurants, check cashing shops, strip joints, fireworks stores, and the like. This makes real estate so expensive that all but the wealthy are excluded. Other cities with low tax revenue bases may be forced to be more permissive in their land use controls or allow the existence of medium to high-density housing or commercial and industrial activities. Recent fiscalization of land use may have increased the growth of commercial and retail space in these cities. With a growing portfolio of such nonresidential land uses shaped either by historical location decisions or public choice, these cities are not usually located in high-amenity areas. By identifying a set of basic categories of such land use portfolios, we may begin to differentiate the political mosaic of a Tieboutian space that comprises urban sprawl and begin to offer a political-economic perspective on emerging patterns of segregation and inequality.

Our research is based on a cluster analysis of municipality-level land use data for eighty-five of the eighty-eight cities of Los Angeles County. [*Editor's note:* Because of space limitations, details concerning the cluster analysis methodology have not been included; they are available from the authors.] The raw acreage of various land use categories was converted to a percentage breakdown for each city. These percentages were then used to run a simple nonhierarchical cluster analysis with the specification of six clusters, which after a few trials yielded cluster memberships that made intuitive sense while also showing significant differences in the land use profiles of various categories. The six clusters that emerged from the analysis have names based on their dominant land use characteristics.

The *edge cities* (sixteen municipalities) are located at the boundary of the metropolis. Deserts, mountains, or the coast define these cities' borders. Their land use profile includes significant vacant land (slightly more than half the land area) and single-family residential land use. These newer cities have a median age of forty years.

In the *industrial cities cluster* (six cities) more than half the acreage is devoted to industrial activities. This cluster is further distinguished by a distinctive corporate presence. Somewhat older than the first cluster, these cities were incorporated just after World War II in the wake of economic and urban growth, and represent the industrial core of the metropolitan area.

The twenty-six *suburban cities* share some of features of edge cities, although the former are not necessarily located at the boundary of the metropolitan area. Single-family residential homes dominate their land use portfolios; almost two-thirds of the land is devoted to such use. These cities, developed shortly after World War II, devote little space to multifamily housing and for decades have practiced exclusivist, if not exclusionary, zoning policies and practices.

The four *greyfield cities* have a mix of extraction production sites (oil wells, quarries), and industry, some transportation-related. Slightly older than the industrial cities, these were incorporated in the 1940s when extraction and mining activities were still an important component of the southern California economy.

The *apartment cities* cluster of four municipalities contains large concentrations of medium to high-density residential areas. Interestingly, like edge cities, these cities are the youngest, and on average, were incorporated about forty years ago. Unlike edge cities that define the frontiers of metropolitan sprawl, these cities are located at the metropolitan core. The relatively recent incorporation of these core areas validates Tieboutian principles.

The final cluster, *generic cities,* is the largest (twenty-nine cities) and includes some of the county's largest cities, Los Angeles, Long Beach, and Pasadena. It is also the oldest with a median age of incorporation of approximately eighty-five years. The land use profile is most typical with no particular specialization. (This could reflect the fact that these cities include a mixture of communities, for example, rich and poor and the extremes balance out.) All of these cities have a mix of single-family low-density and multifamily higher-density uses, as well as significant acreage devoted to commercial land uses.

The structural differentiation of the land use portfolios of these cities can now be examined against their aggregate socioeconomic characteristics. The 1990 and 2000 Bureau of Census results show that edge and suburban cities have the highest concentration of affluent residents as evidenced by median household incomes ($53,225 and $42,762 respectively). It is interesting to note that the median percentage of Blacks in the edge cities is very close to that of the generic cities suggesting that affluent Blacks have begun to move out of the urban core into the periphery. But this is not true for the Hispanic population. Although the Hispanic percentage share is higher in edge cities and suburban cities (because the overall share of Hispanics is greater than that of Blacks, 45 percent versus 12 percent share for the county), they are concentrated in very high levels in the industrial and apartment cities followed by significant concentrations in the greyfield and generic cities. Indeed, the median level of the share of Hispanics in the generic cities is almost identical to that of the county as a whole. Currently, most of the non-Hispanic white population resides at the perimeter of the metropolis along the hills where the "sprawl has hit the wall." This finding supports the argument made by Bobo et al. (2000) and Ethington, Frey, and Myers (2001). Simultaneously, some of edge and suburban cities have become more diverse as prosperous nonwhites, mainly Asians, have moved in and as the non-Hispanic white population has decreased. Other edge and suburban cities have become less diverse as concentrations of Hispanics have grown in

many of these cities consistent with the resegregation argument presented by Ethington, Frey, and Myers (2001).

Results dealing with changes in ethnic mixing patterns between 1980
and 2000, mainly derived from analysis previously reported by Myers
and Park (2001), are far from clear-cut. Of the eighty-eight cities, about a
third changed racially: thirteen became more racially diverse, while
twenty-one became less diverse (nine in comparison to their 1990 status,
and another twelve in comparison to their 1980 status). Most of this increased mixing occurred in edge cities, suburban cities, and generic cities
clusters. The other clusters—industrial, greyfield, and apartment—became less mixed.

As expected, the six clusters differed with regard to when political
incorporation occurred (Fogelson 1993). Generic cities, the oldest cluster, were incorporated between 1913 and the early 1930s. Suburban, industrial, and greyfield cities were next, incorporated in the late 1930s
and 1940s in response to pressures to maintain existing levels of amenities (particularly in the case of the suburban cities) and, in the case of
industrial and greyfield cities, an emerging economic base of aerospace,
mining, and extraction. Incorporating the industrial cities was an effort
to maintain a high tax base from manufacturing, commercial, and
shipping industries prior to and after World War II. Edge cities, incorporated in the 1950s, were a political response to the contemporary
suburban sprawl. Apartment cities were incorporated at about the same
time (the late 1950s and early 1960s); however, they were not the products of peripheral suburban growth. Prior to their incorporation, these
areas were wards of Los Angeles County. A sense of desperation and
deprivation no doubt led residents and their representatives to assert
their political autonomy.

As mentioned earlier, the 1990 and 2000 median household income
results presented no surprises: edge cities and suburban cities were the
most prosperous and apartment cities the poorest. The same pattern held
true for the 1990 and 2000 poverty rates. The population growth numbers show that the highest growth rates were in greyfield and edge cities
(where there were large stocks of vacant land) while the smallest growth
rate was in apartment cities.

Interestingly, the median commuting time did not vary significantly
different among the clusters. It appears that householders living in the

high-density cities in the metropolitan core spend almost the same time commuting, as do affluent residents in edge cities. The relatively small difference in commuting times among the different clusters attests to Los Angeles' polycentric form and to its ongoing low-density sprawl. These times may also reflect the type of job sprawl recently documented by Joseph Persky and Wim Wiewel (2000).

Our results indicate that land use specialization and social contexts (racial mix, income level, etc.) are related. Cities with a high level of specialization tend to be newer (in terms of incorporation age), but at the same time they are either (1) poorer and Hispanic or nonwhite, or (2) richer and non-Hispanic white. In the former case, land use specialization is more along the lines of nonresidential or higher density residential use, while the latter group's specialization is mainly single-family, low-density residential use. The least specialized cities, the generic types, tend to be older and more mixed in terms of race and income.

Conclusions

We argue that the debate on sprawl, particularly in Los Angeles', has been largely confined to market choice and individual liberty versus environmental quality/aesthetic objectives. Recent writings from social ecology, demography, and environmental planning indicate that overall segregation increased in the past decades and that those living in inner-city ghettos are most likely to experience increased health risks. Up to now, however, these studies have neither linked segregation with urban form characteristics such as land use distribution or residential density, nor have they explained changes in urban form over time.

By building upon and critiquing Charles Tiebout's work on population sorting, we attempt to provide an improved understanding of the link between suburban sprawl and patterns of segregation. Tiebout saw political fragmentation of metropolitan space and decentralized governance leading to more efficient housing markets, but he failed to address issues like income inequality, segregation, and environmental injustice. This omission is linked to Tiebout's club hypothesis, which does not, however, address the nature and effects of specialization and differentiation among clubs.

We attempt to improve upon the earlier work by exploring (1) how these Tieboutian clubs might be differentiated, and (2) how this differentiation may explain the political basis of inequality and segregation. Our cluster analysis of land use portfolios of eighty-five cities shows that it is possible to classify cities according to similarities of their land use portfolios, which begins to explain the specific nature of these communities and their socioeconomic characteristics.

Our analysis shows that the patterns of segregation are related to and even sustained by functional specialization of land use. For instance, a relationship exists between land use specialization and social outcomes as represented by this Tieboutian world of urban sprawl. With less specialization of land use, we see a more diverse and balanced mix of population both in terms of race and income. But with increased specialization of land use, two types of segregation outcomes are possible: (1) a concentration of the affluent and mainly non-Hispanic white population, or (2) a concentration of poorer Hispanic or other non-white populations.

Both Peter Marcuse (chapter 1) and Frederick W. Boal (chapter 2) distinguish between enclaves (which should be left alone since they are a product of voluntary choice) and ghettos (a legitimate target for public policy). Going beyond this dichotomy, William W. Goldsmith (1979) and Lisa Peattie (1994) emphasize the positive values of ghettos. Our typology, which includes such enclaves, questions the desirability of "enclavization" in the Tieboutian world of sprawl. While ethnic solidarity can be seen as a positive outcome of enclaves, this pattern can also lead to bigotry, divisiveness, and territoriality.

Political empowerment comes with affluence, so it is quite possible that with a higher tax base, upper-class enclaves are able to sustain a high quality of life by excluding others and by avoiding their fair share of collective responsibility toward the poor, immigrants, and other dependent populations. [*Editor's note:* By calling upper-income areas "enclaves," Tridib Banerjee and Niraj Verma use the term differently from Ceri Peach and Frederick W. Boal who restrict its use to ethnic clusters.] On the other hand, poor communities, despite their political autonomy, are fiscally incapable of creating opportunities such as better education for their citizens or improving their quality of life.

Though the scope of this chapter does not allow for a review all historical explanations of metropolitan fragmentation (Fogelson 1993), we can say with some confidence that some types of localities, such as greyfield and industrial cities, are more of a market outcome than a public choice. Others, especially low-density, single-family suburban communities, are created and maintained by public choice through incorporation and exclusionary zoning.

It should be noted that almost two-thirds of the cities were classified as "generic." These older, original cities in the region, including the City of Los Angeles at the top of the metropolitan urban hierarchy, tend to be more open and inclusionary, socially heterogeneous, and seemingly more adaptable to changing demography and growth. As older cities, they are also more likely to be ready for more renewal and infill development, and we expect them to bear the brunt of the growing demand for affordable and higher density housing in the future.

We introduced a new methodological approach—cluster analysis—to the study of the sprawl-segregation linkage. As an exploratory study, we are aware that this methodology needs refinement. Future research should be at the community level rather than at the level of the individual municipality. This community-level analysis would take into account the wide diversity within Los Angeles, that is, areas with high incomes and high property values on one end of the extreme and areas with low incomes and low property values, on the other. This type of analysis would address one major weakness of our study—the large portion of the county based on acreage and population that was lumped into an ambiguous generic category. A second refinement would be to extend our study area beyond Los Angeles County, since sprawl does not abruptly stop at the county's borders. Follow-up studies should include the entire Los Angeles urbanized area.

Los Angeles is an aging sprawl city with continuing internal transformations that are the result of immigration, exploding population growth, and a strong economy. As the sprawl continues to hit the wall, much of the future growth of the region (the city was the equal of two Chicagos in 2002), will require higher density development. That much is clear. But the question remains: Will the Tieboutian world respond to the demands of for denser development or will it simply exacerbate current trends?

Note

The authors acknowledge help in documentation and analysis of the data used in this paper from the following individuals: Shahab Rabbani, a doctoral student at USC; Hyung-Cheal Ryu, currently a doctoral student at Texas A and M University; and Deepak Bahl, Associate Director of the Center for Economic Development and the Community Development and Design Forum at USC.

Chapter 12

HOUSING SUBSIDIES AND URBAN SEGREGATION

A Reflection on the Case of South Africa

Marie Huchzermeyer

Introduction

Sociopolitical exclusion in South Africa for most of the twentieth century was distinguished by its racial segregation and the rigorous means by which it was legislated and controlled by the state. The legal framework encompassed racial restrictions on political activity, employment, commercial and investment opportunities, social relations, and spatially, on access to accommodation in the city.

The main apartheid legislation was repealed in 1991 but since then, South African housing policy—especially its subsidy program for developers—has reinforced existing patterns of segregation. This has occurred despite numerous government plans and policy pronouncements promoting greater social integration, greater equity in the provision of public services and the control of urban sprawl (see for example, the Department of Housing's 1997 *Urban Development Framework*). This chapter critiques South Africa's supply-side subsidies and discusses how the country's housing policy must be changed to counter the increasingly socioeconomic underpinnings of segregation.

The Capital Subsidy As a Force Contributing to Spatial Segregation

The current capital subsidy system was first introduced in 1990 through the Independent Development Trust (IDT), a government funded poverty alleviation initiative. Between 1990 and 1994, IDT delivered subsidized serviced sites with freehold title to one hundred thousand households. The subsidy system required developers to prepare project proposals and submit these for approval by the IDT. Capital subsidy funding was released to developers on a project basis, and the completed serviced sites were then transferred to beneficiary households. By 1992, it had become evident to the IDT that "[b]ecause of limited options in accessing available and affordable land, the capital subsidy scheme . . . was having limited impact on urban integration" (Nuttall 1997, 142). Here, the IDT was referring to a poorly defined concept of "re-integrating the social and economic fabric," by locating low-income housing in proximity of employment opportunities and social amenities (Nuttall 1997, 141). The poor location of these capital subsidy developments perpetuated the segregated spatial structure.

In 1994, the IDT capital subsidy scheme became the central mechanism in the new government's housing subsidy scheme, the only operational subsidy mechanism being the project-linked subsidy. While the subsidy amount was increased from the IDT amount, to allow for a minimal house on the serviced site, alternatives to the project-linked developer driven subsidy were only introduced in the following years. Between 1994 and December 1999, 83 percent of all approved housing subsidies were project-linked. By late 1999, 1,162 capital subsidy projects were delivered at an average of 800 units per project, totaling 928,000 units (GCIS 2000). In the absence of a separate subsidy mechanism for informal settlement intervention, the project-linked subsidy is applied also to the so-called upgrading of informal settlements. In effect, informal settlements are replaced by fully standardized and individualized housing developments, in some cases on invaded land (through a "roll-over" procedure), but more frequently on a relocation site. Relocation distances in many cases are in excess of twenty kilometers. The upgrading of informal settlements often led to substantial de-densification with half or more of the original households having to be accommodated elsewhere.

Some recipients of these "free," fully subsidized units have sold them because of the need for cash to cover debt (Boaden and Karam 2000). Prices in this secondary market have been substantially lower than the subsidy amount. While the pattern of these transactions is still poorly understood, the national Department of Housing noted that past beneficiaries were reapplying for subsidies. The Department interpreted this as fraud on the side of beneficiaries who were seen to be exploiting the "give-away" subsidy (Department of Housing 2000; Scheepers 2001). It responded by promulgating an amendment to the Housing Act (Republic of South Africa 2001), which prohibits the sale of subsidized houses for the first eight years after possession, but it is questionable whether this new amendment is enforceable given that such transactions are made informally and at times under pressure by profiteering middlemen or debt collectors (Boaden and Karam 2000).

If enforced, and assuming there actually exists a demand by higher-income groups to buy into the subsidized market, the new amendment would prevent downward raiding or buying up by higher-income groups for the first eight years after the development of a subsidized housing estate. However, the prevention of this downward raiding has the effect of perpetuating these areas as economically segregated. Comparing the South African and Chilean capital subsidy systems, Alan Gilbert (2000, 26) has noted, "the last thing South Africa needs is a housing policy that could accentuate residential segregation."

The current project-linked capital subsidy system has achieved a high level of political credibility and mass support because of the number of units produced and because the standardized home ownership product represents a considerable improvement for residents. However, the project-linked capital subsidy may also be seen to preserve high-income housing markets by directing low-income development onto cheap tracts of land on the urban periphery. Furthermore, the high level of production has served to reduce demands by community-based organizations for more appropriate urban development (Huchzermeyer 2003).

Implications of Segregation and Peripheralization of Low-income Housing

The peripheralization of low-income housing fosters segregation, and in turn, poverty. Residents of these settlements find it difficult to find decent paying jobs within reasonable distance. Bus companies have operated so inefficiently that private minibus taxis have found a commercial niche and have been able to undercut subsidized bus fares. However, the distance between dormitory towns and job centers is such that minibus fares remain prohibitive—a single trip from a housing development to the CBD may cost the commuter more than a good meal.

In the absence of efficient and affordable public transport, segregation between residential areas and economic opportunities impacts significantly on the household economy. While an informal economy exists within segregated low-income areas, low purchasing power minimizes opportunities for income generation. Poor residents travel long distances to domestic-type jobs in higher-income suburbs, to places of informal economic opportunity in central business districts, and to formal employment in industrial zones. The perceived link between the presence of poor people in the central business district and crime in that area is one of the reasons why capital investment has shifted from the CBD to the higher-income suburbs, which are less accessible to the poor.

Planners have responded with metropolitan plans to implement a corridor approach with a vision for mixed land use and intense formal and informal economic activity along major public transport routes backed by high residential densities. However, the project-linked subsidy mechanism has continued to deliver monofunctional, standardized developments on cheap, poorly located tracts of land on peripheral sites, not along corridors.

This type of low-income peripheral development leads to financial and economic problems. The nonrecovery of revenue from these newly constructed areas is recognized to be contributing to local government bankruptcy (Botes 1999; Smit 1999). Municipalities with high rates of housing delivery have drastically increased their urbanized area but they are unable to pay for adequate public services.

The security provided through home ownership assists households in consolidating their stake in the urban economy. However, this commodification may also lead to new forms of vulnerability and displacement. This problem is exacerbated by the context of "resource poverty," increasingly brought about by high rates of HIV/AIDS infection in South Africa. One in every nine people and one in every four women were estimated to be HIV positive in November 2000, with higher concentrations in impoverished areas (Department of Health 2001).

Commodification invariably entails the opportunity, albeit illegal, for converting the housing asset into cash. Motives for the selling of the housing asset include the need to reduce household debt, to finance education, to honor rural kinship obligations, or to maintain an addiction or habit (Boaden and Karam 2000). Thus, for many households, home ownership provides little security as it is easily forfeited through sale in a secondary market. Some South African policy advisors have recommended large-scale government provision of housing made accessible to the destitute at no cost in order to achieve greater security of tenure (R. Tomlinson 2001).

To date, South Africa's housing debate has been limited to two options, "depth" versus "breadth," that is, providing a large number of low quality units (inevitably on the urban periphery) versus providing a smaller number of well-located high-quality units (M. Tomlinson 1998, 139). Patrick Bond (2000, 143) questions the validity of this dichotomy, arguing that the South African economy is capable of delivering higher-quality housing in large quantities, a position also held by the civic movement in the early 1990s (Mayekiso 1996). Provided there is political will to implement this, a significantly larger subsidy amount per unit, at scale, would allow for better land to be utilized and more acceptable housing to be produced, therefore allowing for better spatial integration.

Policy Responses—Redressing the Segregation of Low Income Housing in South Africa

It needs to be emphasized that there are opportunities to reduce income segregation. Employment generation centers exist in many of the higher-income suburbs, as does vacant land. There also exists a desire by impoverished households to have homes in proximity to the domestic and other employment opportunities that these areas offer. The women of the Homeless People's Federation (Budlender 1998) articulated this desire, for instance, through the unsuccessful invasion of the vacant Rondebosch Common in a well-located Cape Town suburb in 1998.

David Dewar (1999, 2) argues that it is necessary "to view housing as an instrument of urban restructuring: [that it is necessary] to use it consciously as a mechanism to promote qualities of urbanism as opposed to townships." To Dewar, the term "urbanism" refers to the qualities of complex urban environments that provide diverse opportunities for income generation and social interaction. He uses the term "township" in the South African sense of monotonously planned, standardized dormitory areas on the segregated urban periphery. Housing policy should, therefore, be conceived of as a program for urban land reform not only on the urban periphery, but also in established parts of the city including the high-income suburbs. Such urban land reform requires appropriate legislation, procedures, and financial mechanisms to ensure implementation.

Would affirmative action in housing, paralleling that in employment, be feasible in South Africa? Could the government require affluent areas to reach a quota of affordable housing units within a set period of time, backed up by a system of penalties for localities that do not comply? The United States offers a number of possible models—fair share plans (Listokin 1976), inclusionary zoning as practiced in Montgomery County, Maryland (see Marcuse, chapter 1 and Pendall, chapter 10, for a discussion of these strategies)—but it is highly uncertain whether these approaches would be politically acceptable in South Africa.

Another issue relates to how these subsidies should be delivered. Should subsidies be supply-side or demand-side, and which form of tenure should be given highest priority? As we have seen, the main approach used in South Africa is a supply-side subsidy for home ownership. South Africa does have a small demand-side program introduced in December 1995 that comprises 10 percent of national housing subsidies. The aim is to allow the householder to purchase an existing property in the market. The problem with this approach is that the government has no control over the location and quality of the units purchased. Such housing tends to be located on the urban periphery.

Judith Yates and Christine Whitehead (1998, 419) note that segregation appears to be less pronounced in countries with a variety of subsidy mechanisms and "where the level of government involvement is greater." In the South African context, this means that a greater mix of subsidy and tenure types could reduce income segregation. While South Africa has introduced a pilot mechanism for subsidized rental housing (M. Tomlinson 2001), a larger scale effort may be needed. Such an effort is hurt by the perception of politicians and government officials that it is too costly to provide rent supplements to low-income households.

Another approach that deserves serious attention is communal or collective development and management of affordable housing. Successful experience may be found in some Brazilian municipalities where organized communities may purchase land through the municipal participatory budgeting system and receive technical assistance from the municipality through a mutual self-help approach.

In South Africa, the Homeless People's Federation is ready to respond at scale to such an opportunity. In 1999, this network, supported by the NGO People's Dialogue, comprised sixty thousand members in twelve hundred autonomous savings groups across South Africa (People's Dialogue 1999). Federation women have proven their ability to manage finances and to construct housing. While the Federation's philosophy supports the idea of communal land ownership in the form of trusts, cooperatives, or property associations, the subsidy mechanism has required individual home ownership. In some developments, family or group titles have been provided for neighboring plots. However, the main obstacle remains the inability to access land for community-managed development, even on the periphery (Mgedezi 1999).

Conclusions

In South Africa, the perpetuation of segregation has been institutionalized through the project-linked capital subsidy system for home ownership. Developed and promoted by the influential business sector and first adopted by the apartheid state in 1990, this subsidy mechanism remains the main mechanism for housing delivery. This approach also continues to deliver segregated housing estates.

The project-linked subsidy mechanism does produce impressive numbers of affordable home ownership units and it, therefore, plays an important role in legitimizing the current government. Spatial inequalities, however, contribute to the maintenance of poverty, as do other factors such as an inadequate educational system.

The South African economy is capable of delivering an alternative that is not spatially segregated and that is responsive to the economic and environmental needs of the poor. What is required is affirmative government intervention in the land market, including (1) low-income housing quotas for middle- and high-income areas; (2) financial incentives for developments that achieve greater income and tenure mix and disincentives for those that are addressed only at middle- and higher-income groups; (3) controls on capital gains to preserve access for low-income households to units in higher-income areas; and (4) the introduction of a wide range of housing subsidy mechanisms linked to different tenure and management forms, including management by community-based organizations.

Chapter 13

SUBURBS AND SEGREGATION IN SOUTH AFRICAN CITIES

A Challenge for Metropolitan Governance in the
Early Twenty-First Century

Alan Mabin

The rise of the suburbs, chronicled most extensively in the United
States, has long ceased to be a matter of the residential structure of the
city. Well within the twentieth century, it left behind the commercial
change that inevitably follows residents with money to spend, to become a question of new structures of work, of society, and of participation in public life. A lesson, also far better documented in American history than elsewhere, is that public policy is central to the development
of suburban forms. Following World War II in the 1950s and 1960s,
public authorities constructed high-rise, multifamily housing for the
poor in places like Chicago, while private developers with government
support constructed suburban communities of single-family housing for
white, male-headed families, such as the three suburban Levittowns in
New York, New Jersey, and Pennsylvania. Dolores Hayden (1996)
argues, this "two-tier policy . . . has separated affluent and poor, white
and black, male-headed households and female-headed households,
young families and the elderly," with the result that the latter groups in
each pair might construe the "other" as the enemy, while the first in
each pair as well as the construction interests, "don't want to deal with
city problems."

That cities and their suburbs are *not* similar across the globe is an old
and classic conception found in various literatures. Perhaps the best way

to gain insight into a classic, but not necessarily a typical European case, is to read François Maspero (1996) and repeat parts of his travels in the Paris suburbs. In some ways the ordinary suburbs of European and Australian working classes resemble the Paris *banlieue* (a word that does not really translate as suburb). Take for example the western suburbs of Sydney (Powell 1995). Patterns of ethnicity are closely associated with some of the implied separations. Just as northeast Paris is more African than other areas, so are the western parts of Sydney more"immigrant" populated and diverse than many other sections of the city.

Describing one of the ultimate pieces of South African suburbanization in the Montecasino complex in the northern suburban reaches of Johannesburg, an *Economist* correspondent (2001) wrote that "the eggs benedict at Montecasino are quite tasty, though smothered a bit too thickly in Hollandaise sauce," sneering at the suburb in a characteristic way. It may be that suburbs in the southern hemisphere not only lack the long-term significance they have in the United States or Australia, but also the new salience they may have in Europe. Indices to books on urban development and management in the South (mostly published in the North) seldom refer to suburbs (Lee 1995). But if suburbs are really expanding in the cities of the South, surely they should be posing similar questions of social change, segregation, and urban management difficulty that they have long posed in parts of the North. Two questions can be asked: are suburbs really areas expanding in significant ways in the South? And, if they are, do they pose the same issues, such as various forms of social segregation, that they do in the North?

Two Different Issues—Segregation and Public Management—with Some Connection

From an urban management perspective, the history of suburban development in countries of the northern hemisphere suggests that the ability of urban government to deliver aspects of good urban life to whole populations, or at least to significant parts of them, can be severely threatened by such development. Does the suburban future bring congestion and difficulty? It certainly imposes new kinds of costs, whether larger or smaller than the older urban ones.

Yet an underlying problem may be that some cities might expect no investment at all if there is no investment in the suburbs. Does the pace of suburban development in many southern hemisphere countries have the potential to undercut the abilities of local governments to deliver services and to assist development in the inner city as well as less formal areas? Or, are the pace of suburban investment and the growth of suburban tax bases actually able to enhance the overall capacity of local government at least at the metropolitan scale? If this investment is stopped, will suburban development and its associated segregations simply go elsewhere in global circumstances leaving the cities without it, but also without any significant level of economic growth presumably vital to their ability to provide for their citizens? Harry Richardson and Peter Gordon, the well-known American critics of loose urban policy thinking, have recently noted that policy makers lack knowledge of the costs and benefits of suburban development to make informed policy choices (Gordon and Richardson 1998). In the cities of the South, the difficult policy choices to which Allen J. Scott (2000) refers, common elsewhere, have become exceedingly tense. Nowhere is this more obvious than in post-apartheid South Africa.

The South African Experience

Any account of urban development in South Africa leads to the conclusion that metropolitan areas now face a particularly uncertain future. So many variables confront the observer that prediction of the future seems foolish. In particular, most observers have grossly underestimated the power of suburbanization and the concentration of new economic activity in the suburbs of the larger cities.

South African urbanism is infamous for its forms of spatial segregation. The end of formal apartheid encouraged many to believe that such segregation would be reduced. But indicators since 1994, when the first democratic elections were held, suggest that old forms of segregation persist, despite some changes. At least as important, new forms of segregation appear in common with segregation in many other parts of the world; facets of change not yet well accounted for in the literature. In particular, most observers have grossly underestimated the power of suburbanization.

Suburban development, symbolized at present by the massive investments and changes underway at locations such as Century City, Cape Town, Fourways, Johannesburg, and the Tongaat-Hulett lands north of Durban, have profound implications for a range of reasons. An extraordinary concentration of new economic activity in the suburbs of the larger cities, and even in many smaller ones, has dashed prospects of new alignments of residence and workplace, (e.g., suburb-to-suburb commutes), substituting new patterns familiar to Australians or North Americans for the old focus on central cities. But these changes are taking place in conditions of continuing rapid urbanization of the society and in conditions of widespread poverty and unemployment. Whatever their consequences elsewhere, they certainly introduce new forms of spatial segregation.

A simple account of the recent past in South Africa's cities would proceed as follows. In the 1970s, surveillance and control began to break down. In the 1980s, racial segregation, never complete, began to dissipate while struggle raged in the townships. A weak attempt to reform apartheid fostered a new discourse on the future of the cities. As the 1990s began, the key issue facing the cities was overcoming the fragmentations of politics and of space. Extraordinarily, ongoing change in local government brought townships and suburbs under single municipalities with none of the fragmentation which characterizes jurisdictions elsewhere, such as those in the United States.

But generally, local government failed to respond to the challenge of dealing with areas of poverty adjacent to suburban development, with consequent land invasion and *favela*-like formation. Local government's most coherent response to the pressures for residential space is often to reproduce the remote, partly serviced, formal-informal settlements of the late apartheid period, in places like Diepsloot north of Johannesburg. Little has occurred in the physical environment to match the accomplishment (unimaginable in its own right ten years ago) of unified and elected town-township local authorities. The notion of socially integrated new developments that somehow physically link towns and townships has received little real support. More significant by far has been the arrival of the private investor and developer in and adjacent to the townships over the last two decades or more. It is this private investment that allows a developer to get away, indeed to do well, with a 2001 billboard in a Cape Town township proclaiming: "Gugulethu is on its way to becoming a SUBURB."

It should, therefore, come as no surprise that the planning system has not yet reached the point where it can constrain an accelerating process of suburbanization. One of the most significant developments of the 1990s was the massive decentralization of offices and office work from older CBDs, something evident in every city (East London is a good example of a smaller city where the process is well advanced), but most developed in Johannesburg. There, the new locations of offices, in ribbons along previously residential major roads and in concentrations around some of the larger suburban commercial nucleations, have moved faster for a number of reasons. Among them are (1) far reaching changes in the organization of work and the division of labor (including subcontracting of service provision) and consequent impacts on desirable office location; (2) the dysfunctionality of older CBDs (with failure on the part of local government to address problems); and (3) white racism that encourages flight to suburban jobs, based on the perception of a black and dangerous CBD. The role of property brokers in stoking these perceptions has belatedly begun to receive some attention in the press (Mnyanda 1998).

This dramatic process of suburbanization and dispersal of work follows the necessary previous stages of commercial and residential dispersion. Once complete, the process will undoubtedly significantly impact on the geographies of cities. In Cape Town, commercial decentralization still has a long way to go, but Century City and the associated residential and commercial developments (Canal Walk) show how it is picking up pace. Suburbanization has, of course, profound meaning for social segregation. Just as it becomes possible for black residents to strike out towards the old centers of wealth and power in the CBDs, and just as that success is symbolized by the location of new public institutions in the CBDs (such as the new provincial capitals), much of the economic opportunity previously concentrated in these centers has fled to the suburbs. A particularly acute example is in Mbombela (Nelspruit), the capital of Mpumalanga province.

Perhaps the greatest impact on the social geography of the cities lies in the residential preferences of the new elites associated with the political, and to some extent, the economic changes in South African society. With the dispersion of upper-income consumption and work opportunities to the suburbs, and with the supposed security advantages of the walled complex, we see a shift to class rather than racial segregation. We also see a shift from state to market forms of segregation, and an entirely new pattern whereby middle-class Blacks have taken up residence in suburban townhouse complexes, which can scarcely be completed fast enough to satisfy the demand. Considering that the first four years of democracy saw a shift from 22 percent of managerial positions in the civil service being occupied by Blacks to 60 percent, that the gross numbers involved are large, meaning perhaps fifty thousand new demands for access to middle-class private housing, that the impact on several cities is exaggerated by the abandonment of old *bantustan* capitals, and that the shifts in the private sector are at least as profound, coming on top of decades of change in the racial division of labor, it follows that the present changes in social segregation are of considerable scale. But it does not follow that the disabilities of the apartheid city are being overcome for a majority of its residents.

Yet it is important to note that urban desegregation has been achieved in several key areas. For example, what has happened in the schools bears commenting. Today, it is quite extraordinary to see processions of black and white children to formerly Whites-only schools in the suburbs with what one might have expected ten years ago. In some respects, what is interesting is that these now shared spaces support the reproduction of the middle classes who increasingly segregate themselves from the less well off. Thus, the segregated township schools remain.

The schools provide symbols both of the division and the sharing of space. What was "white" was never fully so. This space was always, with rare exceptions, open to black involvement as menial servants or otherwise, though strongly defended against the intrusion of Blacks as equals. What was "black space" was indeed black, little open to penetration by Whites. One result can be seen in the familiarity of white children with black skin and the astonishment of very small black children at the presence of *makgowa* (the ones with bleached bones) or *amalungu*. The white spaces of South African cities have been occupied with relative ease by Blacks since 1990 or 1994, but the black spaces remain black, with exceptions like the *shebeens* on tours of Soweto, that are much less penetrable to Whites. What can explain this? It is language to some extent. The knowledge of "white" languages (and cultures) on the part of Blacks gives them an access to white space that Whites do not share in reverse precisely because of the relative lack of linguistic and cultural knowledge. The city appears in limited focus for most Whites.

What lines of unity potentially exist? "*Simunye!* We are one!" was the punning station slogan on public TV1. It is melodious and satisfying and suits the idea that South Africa is a "rainbow nation." But the Truth and Reconciliation Commission process, which often appeared in various languages in the news, told a somewhat different story: the rainbow nation is up against the healing of old wounds," as Cynthia Kros and Shelly Greybe (1994) put it. Yet, as Heribert Adam and Kogila Moodley (1993) argue, South Africa does have points of unity not common to other deeply divided societies, including ones with deep religious divisions.

But what of social and spatial justice? To return to the question of why the post-apartheid period offers little on the restructuring of apartheid urban space, but rather offers the development of new forms of social division, this question fascinates not only because of the empirical trajectories of market driven change in the Pretoria or Durban suburbs, but also because of the enduring appeal of the defeat of apartheid as a symbol for movements of social justice everywhere. Apartheid represented a special form of the urbanization of injustice; the post-apartheid challenge could be called the "urbanization of justice."

It was suggested earlier that one of the features of local negotiation in the dying days of urban apartheid was the emergence of some unifying discourses. Two of those discourses are of particular interest (1) unifying and democratizing divided local government, which I have called "the one city" discourse; and (2) improving the economic and social performance of the cities by means of spatial restructuring, to be termed "the compact city" discourse (Mabin 1999). These discourses, politically articulated, systematic ensembles (not necessarily rigidly defined) of analytical and prescriptive, paradigmatic social texts (verbal and written), assumed or asserted that they could contribute to easing the pain of daily life for ordinary South Africans. These discourses were rooted in a notion of the "exceptionalism" of South African cities, but their implications are far more general.

There are some five hundred urban places in South Africa. In some of the smaller ones, the meaning of the one-city discourse was clear early in the process. The discourse required the incorporation of older town areas, from which Africans were legally, and by policing, largely residentially excluded, with the usually newer township areas consisting in many cases of public housing areas together with extensions consisting of shacks that had grown up after the cessation of public housing construction. One tax base would then exist, instead of the divided situation in which the commercial property taxes overwhelmingly accrued to so-called white local authorities (WLAs). This discourse developed compellingly, contrasting the conditions in towns and townships, explaining the lack of services in the latter through the flow of resources (especially labor and consumer spending) to towns, and the lack of a return flow in the form of public expenditure. The one-city discourse structure allowed for more sophisticated versions, in which the differential costs of services could be closely analyzed and the results found supportive of the need for a single local authority to equalize such costs. The one-city discourse's proposed solution met the problem by offering to share the resources generated by those who saw themselves as different—as residents of different places. The discourse was flexible enough to accommodate the problem of local identities that would not readily bend to a stronger image of unity and integration with different meanings on black and white sides. Thus, except in WLA strongholds of the Conservative Party that defended the divisions of full apartheid, the one-city discourse met with little or no challenge. In this sense, it also displayed another limitation, falling short, for example, of the full import of the slogan the *Partido do Trabaladores* regime adopted in São Paulo, Brazil, in 1989, that is, the city *"para todos,"* for all: for the one-city discourse in South Africa did not suggest that the township must become a town or vice versa, it did not threaten the identity of residents of either space in this way. Instead, it provided the promise of peace to counter the threat to WLA taxpayers. And in so doing, the one-city discourse facilitated the paths of politicians, officials, and service providers into discussions and, in time, into positions of power within altered, though not transformed, local governments. One could argue that the same thing occurred with other discourses (Mabin and Smit 1997).

In the mid- to late-1980s, as the "pass laws" and influx controls were removed, many urban commentators believed that their disappearance would herald a massive movement of people to the cities. At first I sought to persuade readers of various journals that the persistence of circular migration would confound these predictions, not that the disappearance of police harassment and the decline of some stricter boundaries had no impact, but much of that impact had already been felt. Circular migration still persists, since it results from all sorts of economic, cultural, and political sources, tied up with features of apartheid, but is by no means reducible to it. At the heart of the matter, it was hard to overcome the idea that South African urbanism was so exceptional under apartheid that it would lead to immense changes. Just as thinking through the nature of apartheid requires closely specifying continuities and differences from earlier eras, so adequate approaches to its end requires enormous concentrations of energy not only on the changes implied, but also on the continuities in the urban society and its cultures. One of the changes that must receive attention has to do with the acceptability of social hierarchy.

The harsh fact is that the removal of apartheid has done nothing to reduce the acceptability of hierarchy. Indeed, far from the appointment of younger, often black, and sometimes female incumbents to positions of power shaking up the social hierarchy, such appointments have served only to reinforce the structure. One is almost led into a Poulantzian notion of the allocation of agents to places in the class structure (Poulantzas 1975). Those who led the early civic movement may now be members of the new elites who are currently not exactly campaigning for an end to social segregation to match their enthusiasm for an end to political separation and oppression. And as political leaders, their constituency is, above all, a constituency of rising middle-class Blacks who are quite capable of evincing an acceptance of social hierarchy and a sense of just deserts, including a type of residential quality that ironically leads away from, rather than towards, wider social justice.

Attempts to develop greater social justice have had strange results. In Cape Town, the industrial work force has long been mainly colored rather than black, due to apartheid preferences to a certain extent. (The term "colored" in South Africa refers to individuals from India, Pakistan, other countries on the Indian subcontinent, or of Southeast Asian origin.) But many of the industrial sectors that provided employment are now in decline. Clothing and textiles, for example, have been opened up to stronger global competition in recent years. Cuts in the levels of welfare and education spending that previously favored coloreds over Blacks increase the pressures at a time of rising unemployment. Waiting lists for accommodation in public housing estates have been deracialized; this opened up areas, like Retreat, to black residents. In many cases, opportunities are improving for black residents. The immediate experience separates two parts of the Retreat population quite dramatically, though their social and economic positions are similar in many ways. Language, also a segregating factor, still separates *isiXhosa* and Afrikaans (Parnell, Oldfield and Lohnert 1998).

Fragmentation of the urban experience continues for those Blacks that live in the less formal surviving black settlements and who, to some extent, have thrived in spaces formerly considered white. The residentially expensive valley above Hout Bay in Cape Town's suburbs contains one such settlement. But the victory of its residents in overcoming the separations of apartheid and securing access to land in the exclusive Hout Bay valley has done nothing to integrate those residents into the broader patterns of life in the quarter of the city which they occupy (Parnell, Oldfield and Lohnert 1998). Sections like this have sharp edges.

Let me elaborate. There is a long history in which black South Africa watched white South Africa's suburban idylls and thought about reshaping them for themselves (Møller and Schlemmer 1980). Yet change comes in peculiar and limited ways. I live in part of Johannesburg called "Melville." Some shared spaces have appeared in the streets of Melville. Bizarrely, Johannesburg, with its more or less ideal climate for an urban life style, had almost no sidewalk cafés until the 1990s. These cafés might, to some extent, be considered shared spaces. Melville has a more urban feel than most other Johannesburg neighborhoods. English predominates, though older people who have remained often speak Afrikaans. But most consumers in Melville drive in from elsewhere. Very few houses in Melville have been sold to Blacks. I am reasonably certain this is not because real estate agents are reluctant to show and sell houses to black clients, but, and despite a slight fall in Melville's house prices (relative to other parts of the city), black clients are rare. There are no private schools or semipublic schools of perceived quality to attract them. Melville is close to the center of the city, but not to most of the growing office concentrations in the northern suburbs. And though the color transformation of some large employers, such as the national radio and television broadcasting company, is well advanced, Blacks who work in similar occupations to whose who have gentrified Melville, seem to prefer the secured compound, the totally automobile-reliant townhouse, or the cluster house complexes of the newest suburbs. The private development sector and its financial links seem to know how to turn profits from suburban development, albeit no longer of the one house-one plot low-density variety. State policies of uneven financial support for new suburban home ownership, freeway and major road building, and planning practices that essentially favor these developments, encourage and reproduce the social geography, though in color-altered ways. Perhaps these new suburban spaces represent the *métier* of what was denied upwardly mobile Blacks under apartheid. Suburbs of the type to which these occupational classes now move are the backbone (or at least part of the skeleton) of new forms of occupational and class residential segregation in many other parts of the world, from Seattle to Perth and São Paulo to Paris. The failure of neighborhoods like Melville, however, to exhibit residential and social integration, and the preference of critical, economically empowered, occupational groupings for the newest suburbs, are little understood, but highly significant, in understanding developing patterns of urban segregation. A blunt illustration of this phenomenon comes from a black reader of the *Sunday Times* (April 15, 2001):

At a local laundry I was told that we (black girls who live in the suburbs) think we are better. Of course I am better. Hell, I think I am superior to her. I own my own townhouse. I drive my own car, which is more than I can say for her. . . . Why should I be made to feel guilty about my achievements? It is not my fault that other people have ended up where they are . . . I am not asking to be called madam or whatever it is they call white women customers. I am not even asking them to smile at me. All I am asking is that I be afforded the same courtesy they extend to white customers.

Looking to the Future

How will it be possible to bring about increased urban justice in South Africa? The organization of space is obviously central to any answer, but it is clearly not an answer in itself. Building strategies with mass appeal crossing some of the difficult divides in South African cities is no easy political task, as the experience of the ANC in the Western Cape province (from which these Cape Town cases come) explains better than most. As Susan Fainstein (1997) has argued, making and implementing such strategies that foster social justice is something else again. It is undoubtedly true that racial equality, tolerance of diversity, and electoral democracy have all gained a hold in South African cities over the past four years, but new forms of inequality, economically and spatially enforced difference, and autocratic power can be detected and can combine to defeat the fruits of progressive changes.

My argument can be summarized as follows. Take away apartheid, and redistribution continues to favor the wealthy who can segregate themselves from others within a social system with an increasingly unequal distribution of income. Urban life is bleak for most, bleaker certainly than it is for those of us who exercise the privilege of discussing its changes. I suggest that new forms of social differentiation and spatial segregation confound the lines of unity that emerge.

New metropolitan governments in South Africa, elected in December 2000, will increasingly learn that the cities are not simply divided into poor and growing versus rich and stable, but that the interdependencies of all parts become ever more complex. The challenge to researchers is to develop new ways of seeing the nature and significance of segregation. In the face of suburban development, again "we simply do not know enough about the costs and benefits of [suburban development] to make informed policy decisions" (Greater Johannesburg Metropolitan Council 2000, 24).

Chapter 14

CONCLUSION

Desegregating the City

Xavier de Souza Briggs

Inequality and Change: Surveying the Globe

We live in a world more concerned about some inequalities than others. Naturally, these concerns are in part a function of differential awareness. But they also reflect competing priorities and deeply rooted disagreements—first, about what public values *should* guide market-driven economies, particularly in democratic societies, and second, based on those values, about what commitments government, business, and civil society should rightfully expect of each other. There are three distinct but closely connected levels of social and economic inequality on which we can and should focus attention around the globe. Understanding these will help us to put the contributions of this volume in perspective and also to synthesize the disparate lessons of the chapters, which is my primary task here. Synthesizing is a problem-ridden enterprise, of course. We do not want to obscure real divergences in observation or interpretation, but we do want to organize our thinking so as to enable more productive learning. I will focus, in particular, on what can be learned across borders. A number of trends—globalization, rapid urbanization in the global South, and more—suggest that our need for such learning will only increase in the years to come. Following the stage setting section below, I preview the chapter.

Three Levels of Inequality: The Context for Urban Segregation

At the first and broadest level, inequality has increased in recent decades thanks to sweeping, large-scale changes in the nature and organization of work, exploitable technology and patterns of natural resource use, relations between business and government, and the terms of global trade. These changes have contributed to widening, and widely documented, economic inequality, both within and among nations (Rodrik 1999; Stiglitz 2002). Such macro-level transformations, a focus for high-profile activism at WTO, Genoa, and other so-called antiglobalization protests, have helped to renew and intensify important public debates. These debates center on how to reduce poverty and inequality overall, how to manage the usual tensions between growth and equity as economies change, and how, more specifically, to reform wage standards, working conditions, terms of trade, business regulation, and more—in technically promising and politically acceptable ways—on a global, transnational scale.

At a second and much less visible level is the inequality directly tied to rapid urbanization—by the middle of this decade the world will be mostly urban for the first time in history (World Bank 1999)—plus large labor, capital, and material flows *among* key urban economies. There is the endless race among cities for their place on the competitive global stage (Borja and Castells 1997; Sassen 2000). This local dimension involves a hierarchy of its own, not between owners and workers, members of distinct ethnic groups, or technology have's and have-not's in general, but among localities as competing, live-work units. There are high-wage, high-tech "knowledge economy" cities, cheap labor manufacturing cities (not the most desired niche), trade cities with elements of both, and other types.

In the global South, competitive strategic planning and regional economic development offer some logic of response. In the industrialized world, there is a new regionalism, with (broadly) similar tools, motives, and complexities. Metropolitan regions, to act like competitive business units, and to promote the well-being of their residents, must consciously define their niches in a changing world marketplace (Porter 2001). To secure and protect such niches, regions must marshal unprecedented cooperation among market, state, and civil society actors to develop better skills, more attractive business climates, and more. The second level of inequality, thus, defines a game in which, as part of global economic transformations and policy choices, the localities in which we work and live our lives face a wide variety of choices, and complicated fortunes, in the decades ahead. The choices and their impacts have important implications for local markets in labor and land, community identity (self-image), economic redistribution, and other factors that shape spatial segregation (Fainstein 2001).

At a third level, the one on which this volume has focused, there is sorting and inequality *within* localities, whether town, city, or urbanized metropolitan areas. This sorting is not strictly spatial, of course. So-called knowledge-economy cities rely on numerous low-wage workers, in effect a distinct *occupational* hierarchy, to support the labor and life-styles of the more highly skilled and highly paid (Fainstein 2001; Sassen 2000; Waldinger 1996). But linked to occupational and other forces, our central task has been to examine segregation as embodying key spatial dimensions of social and economic inequality at the local level—whether segregation by racial/ethnic identity, socioeconomic status, religious beliefs, or any other difference—and to offer views of a wide array of localities, nested in diverse economic regions and political contexts, around the globe, from Los Angeles to Belfast, from São Paulo to Toronto, Tegucigalpa, and Johannesburg.

Our survey of cities is neither all-encompassing by theme, nor is it geographically comprehensive. There is much more that we need to learn, in particular, about the nature and extent of changes underway in African, Asian, and Latin American cities. Distinct traditions of data collection and analysis, a refusal to collect race or other identity-group data as a matter of policy in some countries, and the scarcity of key statistical data in many developing nations most of all, complicate any comparative project. But in covering a variety of cities and societal contexts, we have distinguished *segregation* (a shorthand for spatial outcomes that indicate "separateness" per se) from questions of *choice and discrimination* (events and processes contributing to separateness) and *access* (what particular groups and individuals may be separated from in cities, thanks to spatial segregation). As we will see, the ghetto versus enclave distinction raises several of these crosscutting issues. Finally, in this volume, we have also identified some of the local patterns that bear the imprint of more global forces, in effect noting links among the three levels of inequality. Much more could be done on this score.

Addressing the third, intralocal level, our agenda has not been to revive simplistic notions of spatial determinism, or to argue that all social problems with spatial dimensions require solutions that "lead" with space. What unites us, rather, is a shared conclusion that space remains a critical dimension along which larger changes in the world continue to produce significant clustering, in some cases with unacceptable barriers to human well-being and opportunity. A more contestable issue, of course, is whether this spatial dimension is *changing* in any fundamental way, that is, in the ways in which, or degrees to which, particular spatial barriers contribute to inequality. As I will review in a moment, our contributors developed no single view on this large question, though we hope we have created a basis for additional comparative dialogue to come. At issue, too, are cultural, political, and other divides that complicate any public response for which we might hope. The contributors vary widely in their specific problem diagnoses and, thus in their prescribed solutions as well. Furthermore, in developing policy recommendations, some applied fairly strict standards of short to medium-term economic and political feasibility, while others ventured further afield with bolder proposals for change.

Preview

Notwithstanding the gaps in empirical evidence, for those concerned about the spatial dimensions of inequality, the central challenge now is less convincing others of the "what" of urban segregation (patterns or conditions), but of the "so what" (causes for alarm) and the "what now"—options for response that are substantively promising (if not always tested) as well as politically legitimate. With that in mind, I will attend both to how the authors in this volume made varied and novel arguments about *different* phenomena and to how we emphasized quite distinct aspects of the *same* phenomena in our partial survey of segregation and cities worldwide. In a number of instances, our concise treatment of complex phenomena and myriad hopes for change has led to rather casual borrowing of policies across borders. Our South African colleagues, for example, identify a number of policy alternatives on which U.S. cities (and state and federal authorities as well) have labored long and with mixed results. It may be that South Africa actually represents more fertile ground for some of these policies, such as area-based fair share housing standards, reforms in tax treatment of home ownership, and varied rental subsidy packages that expand residential options. More specifically, perhaps the United States, as compared to other nations, is long on programmatic know-how and experience—with a rich history of relatively well-documented and highly varied interventions that respond to segregation and its consequences—but short on political will. But whatever the case, it behooves us to excavate the assumptions of these policy tools a bit, if only to leave our conversation across borders a bit more critical and our actions less open to costly surprises.

To organize the disparate concerns of our contributors, I begin by addressing the issue of *choice* that is so central to the causes and consequences of spatial segregation—not to mention assumptions about viable, legitimate responses. I then define the distinct *consequences* (costs and benefits) of spatial concentration on which authors in this volume focus us, respecting the variation in context but asserting some deep parallels in our concerns. Finally, I use these crosscutting concerns to rethink *strategies,* outlining a few simple ways we might think about the hardest problems and the leverage we have (or need) for solving them. The point of this last step is less to blueprint a research agenda, although there is much we would still like to learn, than to suggest what the evidence teaches us so far about *affecting* forms of segregation that we indeed determine to be problematic and worthy of response.

The main argument of this chapter is that the most fundamental choice facing us is that between *lowering* rates of spatial segregation (however it may defined in a given context)—what I call "cure" strategies, on one hand—and, on the other hand, reducing the problematic *links* between space and the social, economic, or other outcomes we care about ("mitigate" strategies) without trying to change spatial patterns themselves to any significant degree. So cures reduce rates themselves, and mitigate strategies reduce social costs that societies may find unacceptable. For many communities, practicality and public values may favor pursuing a bit of both, that is, where significant action can be mounted at all. From immigrant gateways in the United States to post-apartheid South African cities and beyond, the chapters in this volume provide clues, though no easy answers, on how to think about and make these choices.

Perspectives on Choice

The ascendancy of markets, and more specifically of the Western neoliberal model, around the world makes *choice* an appropriate starting point for any discussion of spatial outcomes in cities—and, indeed, makes choice a defining ideal of the world's most influential societies. The problem arises in developing any shared conception of what this much-discussed ideal means or requires. From Gregory D. Squires, Samantha Friedman and Catherine E. Saidat's Washington, D.C. to Alan Mabin's Johannesburg, the contributors to this volume roughly agree that choice and its consequences are not a simple function of buying power, though markets necessarily discriminate on that basis first. Consumers in our subject communities search for housing, but not under conditions of perfect information and not independent of social networks that include coethnics—those who share an income level or (class) lifestyle (regardless of ethnic identification)—and others who inevitably help shape our identities as well as our conceptions of what we want residentially and where best to find it. But in the contemporary lingo of social science, residential search is "embedded" socially; individuals do not walk around searching and comparing like solo buyers in a bazaar. Consumer preferences, for their part, emerge not only as likewise embedded and complex, particularly when assessed across huge differences in cultural and historical context, but such preferences can shift over time, as choices and public values shift.

Mabin's assessment of post-apartheid South African cities illustrates this well: white social and spatial distancing from all Blacks has been transformed into black and white middle class distancing from *poor* Blacks, in part because of the new economic and residential mobility of black professionals and in part because metropolitan development patterns are shifting the choices available to *all* groups. In the most general way, each of these groups makes the most of limited choices and a limited purse, but the practical implications of preference and choice have been transformed in South African cities in less than a decade. Since cities will largely drive the economy and politics of the new South Africa, the new urban segregation shows every sign of being a defining feature of life in a rapidly transforming society.

Mohammed A. Qadeer's Toronto appeals as a checkerboard of small-scale ethnic neighborhoods, segregated at the micro-level but integrated at the level where schools and tax districts are shared. Toronto benefits from its self-image as a place that makes diversity work. But missing is a close analysis of residential preferences by ethnic and income group and of housing prices and other market trends in that famously diverse immigrant gateway. Do current residential choices merely inhibit preferences that would splinter the city into larger segregated districts, or does the relatively generous Canadian welfare state, the historic embrace by government of pluralism rather than the assimilation ideal, and the absence of a large, historically disadvantaged, and stigmatized subgroup (analogous to U.S. Blacks) combine to produce generally more integrative preferences in Canada than in its southern neighbor? Have public policies related to housing, economic development, public education, or other domains been significant contributors, whether for good or bad or both?

Most discussions of choice in housing lead quickly to the phenomena of enclaves, which together create the checkerboard or "mosaic" that the Chicago School recognized as a defining feature of the modern city. Beyond the much-studied inner city (lower-income enclaves of foreign-born immigrants or domestic in-migrants), Frederick W. Boal and Ceri Peach outline a variety of ethnic enclaves. These range from ethno-religious enclaves that Boal defines as "ratcheted up" in levels of segregation, thanks to persistent conflict in the case of Belfast, to "suburban parachuted" Hong Kong Chinese enclaves in Peach's depiction of Vancouver, British Columbia. As David P. Varady outlines in the preface, self-protection, conscious objectives of cultural preservation, less conscious "comfort level" preferences for living among those with shared backgrounds, and considerable buying power—in the case of South Asian immigrants in the United States—all contribute to these spatial concentrations. But *freedom* of choice would seem to be a relative concept where overt conflict or a history of harassment is perceived to threaten one's life and property, where ethnocentrism in the larger society (and not merely the positive attractions of coethnics) motivates self-protective enclaving, and where some members of the enclave may benefit from that residential pattern much more than do other members. The consumers in these cases vary widely in the choice constraints they face, and few of these constraints are a simple matter of inequalities in buying power.

In light of these realities, how should we assess Peter Marcuse's notion that "enclaves" are chosen by their residents and "ghettos" not, that enclaves are mostly good and ghettos usually bad? The first contrary centers on choice, the second on normative judgments we make based, in part, on how we *conceive* of choice. On the one hand, fear of racial harassment and the choice to self-segregate contributes to ghettos, if by that we mean segregated low-status subareas of cities. But as outlined above, this is under an awfully generous rendering of the choices actually available to ghetto residents and of their obligation, relative to that of the rest of society, to overcome fears and make new choices in spite of a painful and costly past. On the other hand, as outlined in chapter 5, enclaves are not good at every point in time, not good for every type of enclave resident, and not equally good for those inside and outside the enclave. In London, Amsterdam, and elsewhere, ethnic enclaves that harbor, and in fact, facilitate, terrorist organizing are a case in point of the latter. So are enclave institutions, religious or other, that may discredit important values of the wider society, such as gender equality in work and civic participation or the separation of church and state, or that do little to encourage literacy in the language and customs of the larger society. As for costs and benefits as a function of point in time (or stage), low-wage laborers, say in New York's Chinatown, benefit from the job networks, credit pools, and other distinctive structures of that enclave—until the same structures inhibit mainstreaming in the wider economy, limiting social, economic, and residential mobility, and contributing to exploitative working and living conditions.

In all of these places and situations, human beings are making choices. They develop preferences, and they act, based on what they observe, what others observe and communicate, and what the choosers decide they are willing to pay. But in practice, choice is a many splendored and much bedeviled thing. Simple analytic distinctions based on "choice" (in the broadest sense of that label), along with normative judgments about what spatial patterns constitute a problem worthy of public intervention and what merely empowers a community to remain distinctive, all too quickly become academic. To be sure, ghettos and enclaves are more than ideal types, especially where there are significant differences between the two in the median buying power of households in each and demonstrable differences in discrimination suffered by those living in a labeled ghetto as compared to a labeled enclave. But the ghetto versus enclave distinction turns out to be an invitation to deeper and much more context-specific questions about the nature of individual and group preferences, actual residential choices available or possible, histories of prejudice and coercion, and societal expectations about what all groups should acquire or share, regardless of background, as part of belonging to a political community—ideally, one that imposes and enforces obligations of all groups even as it extends them rights and due rewards.

Future comparative projects might usefully apply distinct analytic emphases, and distinct conceptions of choice, to the same cases rather than different ones. We are all prisoners of our training and habits of mind, and we all tend to emphasize the features of our local puzzles (the empirical cases) that support our arguments. Moreover, our analytic choices and framing of results are value driven. We agree strongly on some points—for example, some outcomes in cities are largely unintentional (just add up) and not cleverly, let alone diabolically, planned. But the contributors to this volume, sociologists and economists in particular, remain caught in a standoff that precludes what could be a very useful, and policy-relevant empirical consensus on the nature of choice, its limits, and public obligations given the same.[1]

Consequences of Spatial Clustering

One way to read this volume is as an extended commentary on the relevance of the Chicago School model linking social assimilation to spatial incorporation in cities (Park 1926; Massey 1984). Boal and Peach provide the most direct critiques of the rendering of segregation as a merely transitional state leading to assimilation, which in turn would be relatively linear and comparable across identity groups. Using Belfast, Boal shows that segregation can ratchet in the "wrong" direction. Peach reminds us that some groups show persistent ghettoized segregation (Blacks in Chicago) or long- run, apparently voluntary enclaving (Jews in Toronto), both at odds with the Chicago School's core assumptions. Beyond these elements, though, the contemporary era has brought into question the nature and desirability of the assimilation ideal itself, and several of our contributors addressed the pluralist ideal as an alternative to assimilation. In a very real sense, we have shifted our central concern from assimilation (and more recently "convergence"; Briggs forthcoming) that erodes group differences, which may or may not take a widely coveted form, to *access,* for which aspirations are more or less universal.

That is, beyond describing urban choices and their spatial consequences, our normative focus on inequality and the case for intervention center on what segregated patterns mean for access to a host of public and private goods in the city and, through them, to "opportunity" variously defined.

Whatever its form and whatever the causes, what does urban spatial segregation bar access to? Our global roundup confirmed a keen interest, across borders, in access to markets first and foremost. The spatial structure of our cities and of our local labor markets vary widely—for example, Glenn Pearce-Oroz's new towns, built as part of recovery from a massive hurricane, isolate their residents from jobs in Tegucigalpa's urban core, while conversely, the most segregated neighborhoods in urban America create transport, information, and other barriers to jobs that have largely decentralized (headed to the suburbs) in recent decades, and Alan Mabin's and Marie Huchzermeyer's assessments of South Africa emphasize isolation of black townships from a shifting geography of employment (increasingly following the pro-suburban American pattern). But in all these instances, segregation contributes barriers to work. Notably, debates in the United States about a "spatial mismatch" between disadvantaged workers and areas of job growth are largely about the degree of mismatch (how patterns vary by metro context and type of worker) and the how (specific mechanisms) rather than the whether (Kain 1968; reviews in Kain 1992; Ihlanfeldt and Sjoquist 1998). Moreover, recent research indicates that for Blacks, the most job-isolated group in terms of residential locations, a decrease in spatial mismatch between 1990 and 2000 owed mainly to encouraging residential mobility of black households in that period (Raphael and Stoll 2002). While discussions of the "geography of opportunity" in metropolitan America generally lead with these barriers to employment (Galster and Killen 1995; Pastor 2001), European researchers are also tracking spatial and social barriers to consumption markets as evidence of the "social exclusion" of key groups (Lupton and Power 2002). U.S. policy concerns about "under-retailed" urban neighborhoods, a key emphasis of urban economic development proposals late in the Clinton Administration and of Michael Porter's inner-city competitiveness thesis, reflect this concern, albeit rarely with explicit mention of segregation.

If barriers to market participation are priority one, isolation from quality public services represents a close second in many of the city and country contexts assessed in this volume. More than markets, this isolation reflects deliberate policy decisions about the finance, governance, and implementation of public education, safety, welfare, and other public services. Glenn Pearce-Oroz shows that residents of Tegucigalpa's new towns in effect traded away housing in the core that provided better access to urban jobs and consumption for housing on a newly built periphery that offered better access to public services and higher quality housing stock. The long-standing observation in U.S. metropolitan areas that segregation consigns the most disadvantaged young people to the worst public schools continues to hold, but with new wrinkles. Unlike Europe, America's heavy reliance on local property taxes and segregated neighborhood school attendance zones continue to structure school life around residential segregation. But many inner-ring suburbs, especially those with a large minority presence, also show signs of school failure, and charter schools and "choice" proposals formally delink school attendance from neighborhood of residence. These mechanisms function on a limited scale in many metro areas, and early evidence on their impacts is mixed. Unregulated by enrollment balancing mechanisms, charters and choice schemes also reproduce class segregation, and, in some cases, segregation by race as well. In this volume, Robert W. Wassmer defends choice among public service districts in metro America ("Tieboutian clubs") for its efficiency, acknowledging the need for some intervention to curb high social costs.

Where markets and public policy are closely intertwined, as in the siting of land uses with important and controversial spillover effects, spatial access becomes a public health issue as well. Tridib Banerjee and Niraj Verma show, in their chapter on sprawl and segregation in Los Angeles, that black and Hispanic households are more likely to live in core neighborhoods near environmental hazards. Manuel Pastor (2001) argues that the uneven geography of environmental health remains too invisible within the politics of race and spatial segregation in America—not only in L.A., of course, but also in every city where distance from unwanted land uses tracks political and economic power.

As complex and varied as these access issues are, within nations and in comparisons across them, access to a shared political life is more complex and contested still. In the broadest terms, urban spatial segregation not only tends to segregate political jurisdictions (spatially bounded interest communities), for example by race and income in the

United States (Massey and Denton 1993); such segregation also reduces access by the minority poor to extensive, diverse political influence networks and groups, as outlined in the chapter on social capital. Barriers of racial/ethnic identity, socioeconomic status, *and* space compound all too easily to truncate bridging ties, inclusive political groups, and other foundations of democratic life in diverse societies (Briggs 2003a; Putnam 2000). That tendency noted, spatial segregation has historically had a converse effect too, of course, concentrating interest communities in ways that support mobilization. That is, segregation has produced important political enclaves that challenge status quo arrangements. In North and South alike, urban social movements are one important outgrowth of this (Fainstein and Hirst 1995), but so are politically influential, area-based "community development" projects and institutions. The issue becomes how to ensure that political life is not permanently defined by spatial boundaries that correlate strongly with political ones, making political identities partisan and insular, and limiting compromise and learning across groups. Boal's scenarios spectrum, which culminates in the dire euphemism of "cleansing," illustrates the extent of this risk.

Social capital and social stigma represent newer areas for empirical inquiry into segregation. In my chapter, I argued that social capital concepts help explain many of the economic and political consequences of segregation, not as a stand-alone force but as an organizer of public and private choices and their consequences (and see Warren, Thompson, and Saegert 2001). Formal evidence on "space as a signal," that is, social stigmas (or conversely, status enhancement) as a function of place of residence, has been generated primarily in the United States through employer interviews that focus on hiring decisions (Tilly et al. 2001). Keith R. Ihlanfeldt and David L. Sjoquist (1998), in a comprehensive review of the most sophisticated studies of spatial mismatch and employment, note that such signaling and related discrimination are plausible contributors to mismatch impacts. And in this volume, N. Ariel Espino emphasizes segregation as a mechanism for status differentiation with social and psychological, not just economic, motives. It is unclear, based on the assessments in this volume, how or to what degree the space-as-a-signal concept applies outside the United States, where large, racially identifiable ghettos are favorite media subjects and their residents notoriously stereotyped. Alan Mabin's description of a widening class gulf among South African Blacks is at least suggestive of stigmas that may come to separate township Blacks from upwardly mobile black professionals who increasingly live outside the townships. But the American evidence specifically asserts that "ghetto" functions for employers and other brokers of opportunity as a social type and a proxy for a person's reliability, not just as an undesirable physical location. It would be very helpful, particularly as part of our debate over acceptable and unacceptable forms of spatial concentrations—ghetto versus enclave, in the shorthand—to know how much this signaling effect obtains in other nations and whether the effect touches a variety of status groups. Rose Gilroy and Susanne Speak's (1998) work on social exclusion in Great Britain illustrates the type of research that is needed.

Finally, while barriers to opportunity facilitate a comparison of segregation's consequences across contexts, there is clearly more at stake in segregation. The opportunity framework deemphasizes cultural life and sense of place in the city, and the case for policy intervention is rare in connection to those issues. In the sense that culture may seem less urgent than social and economic opportunity, as well as fuzzier or less defined, the oversight is understandable. But it is also curiously at odds with powerful political symbols, specific claims about the costs of certain integrative policies, and even our causal models of how segregation arises in the first place. That is, cultural identity, and the drawing of social boundaries around "us" and "them," remains potent in the symbols, frames, and codes of politics in many places. One lesson of cultural studies is that these boundaries do not in every instance track historical *ethnic* identity differences. Rather, they embrace a class culture emerging in Mabin's upwardly mobile black South Africa and similar status groupings elsewhere. Furthermore, anti-integration activism frequently employs threats to culture, and specifically to cultural preservation, as a rallying cry. And several of us have noted that self-segregation, while not enough to explain segregation outcomes, certainly contributes.

Here again, the U.S. context is instructive and particularly well documented. In the classic juxtaposition, black Americans routinely express to interviewers a desire to live in mixed-race neighborhoods, but define that mix as including a proportion of fellow Blacks that exceeds the apparent comfort zones of similarly surveyed white Americans (Bobo 2001). These findings, on which Whites and Blacks show some convergence in recent decades, probably capture a variety of associations we have with race in America, some of which compete in our decisions: for one, a powerful attraction to coethnics that reflects a variety of shared traits, such as language (or code or dialect), regional or national origin, tastes and normative disposition, physical appearance (physiognomy and/or dress), and more (McPherson, Smith-Lovin, and Cook 2001); but second, the pragmatic observation that mostly white neighborhoods tend to have safer streets, better schools, and better amenities than mostly minority neighborhoods—greater "structural strength," as Ingrid Gould Ellen (2000) summarizes the attraction. Minority suburbanization, a step toward lower segregation in U.S. metro areas, comes fraught with perceived trade-offs among these factors. Squires, Friedman, and Saidat's evidence on the comparatively segregated neighborhoods "chosen" (under constraint) by middle-class Blacks in the Washington, D.C. metro area certainly suggests a strong "net" attraction of living among one's own, and reminds us that even when the multiple dimensions of minority household preferences are kept in view, discrimination too often delimits the options available (and see multicity housing discrimination evidence in Turner et al. 2002; Yinger 1995).

Re-thinking Responses: Policy, Strategy, and Learning Across Borders

The preceding discussion suggests that in spite of cultural and other rationales for protecting separateness, we should take *access*—at once social, economic, and political—as defining the case against forms of spatial segregation that are demonstrably linked to inequality. The discussion further suggests that choice is a powerful ideal, and certainly a powerful force in any market-led society, but not a simple ideal by any means. Choices are embedded and constrained in ways that make it difficult to discern empirical causes and effects as well as the political and moral high ground.

If we turn to implications for policy, the plot thickens from there. The world's cities face a variety of tough policy choices now and in the years ahead, from meeting basic needs to securing much-coveted competitiveness in a global economy and handling new "sustainability" challenges in health and the environment (World Bank 1999). Choices about policy and public action to curb urban spatial segregation, or more precisely to affect segregation of particular kinds, should be thought about in the context of that larger list of priorities. It is not at all clear that affecting segregation in significant ways will rise high on the public agenda on its own; it may well gain momentum if linked to higher priority, "top-of-mind" issues. South Africa may be the ultimate example of this. As Alan Mabin and Marie Huchzermeyer stress, it is the case of a nation very recently transformed by a highly racialized government and social movement, which explicitly identified desegregation as a national priority and yet now shows limited commitment to this policy goal in the face of competing priorities, such as creating jobs, meeting basic shelter needs (regardless of housing location), and combating HIV/AIDS. Likewise, the chapters in this volume that address sprawl (especially Pendall's chapter 10) tackle what has been a very hot public issue in state and local politics in the United States in recent years, hinting at the complex ways in which segregation by race and income may link to these public concerns with much more momentum behind them. And *racial* desegregation enjoys virtually no public attention or support in the United States, while *deconcentration* of poverty (a specific form of income desegregation) enjoys a bit of both—"has legs," as we say in American politics. So lesson one is a reminder not to think about urban spatial segregation in isolation from the larger public agenda, defined by the issues to which the public and policy makers seem willing to attend.

Lesson two is about distinguishing *policies* from the underlying *strategies* of assumed cause and effect that justify policy choices in particular contexts. At their best, strategies embody clear logics of expected cause and effect—why the state of the world will change in a particular direction if some intervention is made. Ideally, these causes and effects can be described in a logical sequence or chain. In the parlance of evaluation, these logics constitute formal or informal "theories of change" (Chen 1990; Weiss 1995), also known in strategic management circles as "logic models." Logic models expose assumptions and contingencies that are critical for policy makers, constituents, implementers, the dilemmas associated with efforts to reduce spatial segregation and evaluators to understand, at least on a basic level.

The enforcement of laws against housing discrimination is a classic example—and one for which more promising logic models are sorely needed. Because a number of our authors have recommended such "fair" housing protections where they are *not* the law of the land, or stronger enforcement where they are (as in the United States), I will outline the logic on which these recommendations depend *as means of reducing segregation*. Clearly, there are other reasons to enact fair housing laws, and I will return to those other reasons in a moment. But in the form of a basic theory of change, fair housing laws, in order to affect spatial segregation patterns, require the following:

- That the "victims" (housing consumers, in this case) be *aware* of their rights under law;
- That the victims be *aware* that they have been victimized (e.g., by real estate professionals, financial institutions, others);
- That the victims be willing and able to *report* their perceived victimization to authorities;
- That adequate *resources* be in place for processing, investigating, and adjudicating claims (the complex operational element of enforcement);
- That *penalties* be adequate for those claims that produce a finding of guilt on the part of alleged perpetrators;
- That ultimately, substantial reductions in housing discrimination (the target process) *will* have a significant impact on residential segregation (the target outcome).

Each step in this logic chain is a potential source of leverage on the ultimate policy targets (designated "problems") and, conversely, a potential breakdown point. First, if the U.S. case is any prologue, victims of housing discrimination are frequently unaware of their rights (so we invest, albeit modestly, in "fair housing education" programs). Next, it is increasingly unlikely that victims will detect wrongdoing when it happens, because discrimination has taken on more subtle forms in recent years. It is harder and harder to police (so we invest, albeit modestly, in random "audit" testing and subpoena records in search of a paper trail of discrimination). Third, some victims, foreign-born immigrants in particular, will be reluctant to report wrongdoing; they may fear reprisal or simply want to avoid inconvenience. Finally, the administrative agencies entrusted to collect, process, investigate, and in some cases adjudicate claims are notoriously underfunded, backlogged, and conflicted about how best to pursue their policy mandates. Some of this is about the contradictions and tensions inherent in regulatory enforcement work, one of the "bad cop" functions of government (Sparrow 2000). But it also reflects a particular ambivalence, at least in U.S. society, about how to handle race and define equal opportunity.

If we assume that penalties, where applied, do in fact change behavior—a bit of a heroic assumption, granted, because discrimination may simply become more clever, but fair housing settlements have run to the hundreds of millions of dollars—then just two hurdles remain. First, reducing discrimination must actually expand the residential choices of potential victims (typically, racial minorities). For reasons outlined above, such reductions may not, at least not in the short run, change self-segregating choices where minorities want to avoid harassment by neighbors or simply enjoy the company of others who are like them. Second, and more problematic still, reducing discrimination faced by minorities (the primary concern of fair housing laws) does nothing to affect white consumers' avoidance of mostly minority neighborhoods. Such avoidance, while perhaps objectionable and certainly costly (in the aggregate) to the society, is perfectly legal. Realtors cannot legally steer clients away from (or toward) mostly minority areas, but clients are perfectly free to steer themselves, that is, to self-segregate.

None of this is to argue against the enactment and vigorous enforcement of fair housing laws, which embody an important commitment to equal opportunity as part of the good society. But this simple logic chain reveals just how precarious and limited fair housing laws can be *as a means of reducing segregation.* Seen in this context, public policy is often thought about quite narrowly as "government mandate," which unduly emphasizes officialdom and often exaggerates the power of government intent alone to affect social conditions. From the standpoint of strategic problem solving, and of prescribing appropriate solutions across disparate contexts, the essence of policy is in: naming conditions in the world that demand attention, money, or other public resources; specifying desired changes or states with respect to those conditions; outlining best-available knowledge about desired causes and effects that might lead to those states; and specifying the mechanisms that will be employed based on the knowledge available.

As a practical matter, policy making is rarely if ever a linear, technical process of choosing among strong alternatives with extensive information on problems in hand. But the preceding distinctions between strategy and policy do enable us to interrogate our authors' policy recommendations and, more specifically, the degree to which supposed solutions might or might not travel well across borders. These distinctions have two broader values as well. First, they help us avoid confounding discussions about policy mechanisms per se with those about assumptions (whys) that underlie those instruments. Second, the distinction highlights the need to generate a wider array of options for implementing particular strategies and, scaling this up, a wider array of strategies for accomplishing complex goals that society deems worthwhile.

In my chapter on social capital and segregation, I outline broad strategies employed in the United States over the past half century to either *lower the rates of spatial segregation* ("cure" strategies), or to *mitigate the social costs of that segregation* without necessarily affecting spatial patterns themselves ("mitigate" strategies). In keeping with the distinction outlined above, each of these *strategies* can be pursued with multiple official *policies* and a host of specific *mechanisms* (consumer incentives, social programs, social marketing, etc.). In table 14.1 here, I expand on this typology to encompass as much as possible the policy ideas of the other contributors to this volume. Note that the role of the fair housing mechanism is now clearer: it targets a problem, which *contributes* to segregation, but other strategies are needed to address proximate problems, such as legal avoidance of particular areas by consumers ("segregative choices" in the left column of the table).

Several tasks are beyond my scope here, such as outlining logic models for each strategy identified in the table, assessing the normative and moral dimensions of each, or even reviewing the bottom-line evidence available on the effectiveness of these strategies. What I can do is focus on a few of the most popular recommendations and the ways in which we have justified them. As previewed above, the contributors to this volume, in developing their policy ideas, begin with varied conceptions of what constitutes "the problem" of spatial segregation (or set of problems) compelling public action. Much of this variation has to do with juxtaposing acceptable social pluralism, which may include some spatial *separateness,* from undesirable *exclusion.* No one provided easy answers on how

TABLE 14. 1. Affecting Segregation: Cure and Mitigate Strategies

Target Problem/sub-problems	Responses
High rates of residential segregation Unequal buying power across groups.	*"Cure" strategies* Targeted economic development, income supports, tax incentives for housing.
Exclusionary land use policies	Fair share housing policies, state/provincial/central overrides of local land use decisions.
Market discrimination by sellers, lenders, brokers	Regulatory (fair housing enforcement) and educational (sellers, consumers, real estate brokers, lenders).
Segregative residential choices by market-rate consumers (including neighborhood avoidance).	Affirmative marketing (to minority and/or majority groups) Housing subsidies, counseling and choice incentives for low-income households. Community development (upgrading), including mixed-income housing development to attract diverse in-movers
Discrimination in public and other subsidized housing.	Affirmative occupancy policy, scattered-site social ("public") housing.
Segregative choices by subsidized consumers.	Community development upgrading of subsidized housing and environs, relocation counseling and assistance, scattered-site housing, equity insurance.
High costs of residential segregation Educational inequality across schools or school districts.	*"Mitigate" strategies* School desegregation by mandatory busing or voluntary choice programs and magnet schools, changes to school governance and attendance boundaries. Fiscal reform to equalize across geographies.
Spatial and space-related barriers to job access.	Reverse commuting (transportation) to jobs Regional workforce development alliances or networks (matching), area-based economic development (grow jobs close to seekers)

TABLE 14. 1. *continued*

Target Problem/sub-problems	Responses
High costs of residential segregation	*"Mitigate" strategies*
Spatially concentrated crime, lower quality housing, lack of public and private amenities, inadequate public services	Community development (upgrading)
	Public service reform and expansion (human services, health, policing, etc.).
Neighborhood stigmas (space as a signal).	Equal employment enforcement and education.
	Workforce development programs (self-presentation, behavioral norms).
	Public education, social marketing ("one city")

Source: Author

much pluralism is acceptable or how to know where exclusion begins. But we do recognize, in particular places, states that seem acceptable or even desirable (Toronto's mixed-income ethnic neighborhoods under multiethnic public service districts) as opposed to undesirable (Chicago's large, high-poverty ghettos or Johannesburg's isolated and poor black townships).

In navigating the boundaries of pluralism and exclusion, recommendations for area-based "fair share" housing requirements, place-based mixed-income housing development, school integration, and expanded people-based (demand-side) housing subsidy options were particularly popular with our contributors. The evidence on these is mixed, of course. Fair share requirements are challenging to sustain politically, and because they tend to rely on new housing development (the requirements are for including affordable units in every locality), fair share policies go nowhere when markets are depressed. (Any basic logic modeling of this strategy highlights the crucial importance of expansion or growth to make the strategy work.) Such policies are, thus, particularly unsuited to segregated communities in which population is declining or where growth is minimal. On the other hand, expanding city regions and parts of same are ideally positioned to include strong fair share principles in larger housing and economic development strategies.

For its part, income mixing can happen at the project, neighborhood, or some larger level. Rolf Pendall emphasizes income mixing as a tool for reducing income segregation or, more modestly, for limiting increase in the same where "smart growth" measures threaten to make price bidding more intense in urban areas. Unless it includes racial/ethnic targeting, though, developments may be income mixed but race segregated. This is the thirty-year-old U.S. experience, at any rate, and race-based occupancy and similar targeting mechanisms tend to be controversial to say the least. Since proximity does not guarantee social contact, let alone tolerance or collective action around shared concerns, making formerly segregated households spatially proximate to one another may fail to meet larger social objectives. But certainly, neighbors often share interests around which mutuality and civic organizing can develop, and spatial mixing addresses the barriers to access (employment, quality public services and shopping) that have a distinctly spatial component independent of any social force.

School integration, where it happens independent of residential desegregation, involves shifts in school enrollment, a structuring of parents' choice options, and often home-to-school transport (i.e., citywide or metropolitan-wide busing) that struggle with logistical problems and political resistance. But as I reviewed in the chapter on social capital, the case for somehow desegregating schools, particularly in the pre-college years, is extremely strong. Disadvantaged minority-group students tend to gain more diverse social networks, better human capital, and the richer psychological resources and cross-cultural skills needed to "make it" in the wide society (Crain and Wells 1994). At the very least, majority-group members gain more diverse networks of the kind needed to curb prejudice and strengthen civic life. Our volume does not present evidence on school-level integration across the globe, but where trends parallel those of the United States (where resegregation of the native-born and high segregation of key immigrant groups are the norms), there is certainly cause for alarm. Frederick W. Boal, citing the so-called Cantle Report (Home Office 2001), indicates that growing segregation (including segregation in the schools) has contributed to rioting in a number of English cities in recent years.

Demand-side housing subsidies, which sometimes come with locational incentives or constraints in tow, have become increasingly popular in recent years, in contexts as disparate as the United States and Chile. Rental housing vouchers and other demand-side tools are thought to embody the efficiencies of the market, and counseling and other services can be attached to the subsidies themselves to encourage particular residential choices. As David P. Varady and Carole C. Walker have shown (in a paper presented at the July 2001 seminar), even comparatively low-cost tenant counseling and placement programs can significantly improve household satisfaction with housing and neighborhood. Larger social impacts, for example, on school or labor performance, are less clear. But long-run evidence from Chicago's Gautreaux program (Rubinowitz and Rosenbaum 2000), along with the early evidence from the five-city Moving to Opportunity (MTO) program of the U.S. government (Del Conte and Kling 2001; Goering, Feins, and Richardson 2003), is certainly encouraging on those dimensions. MTO's recent five-year interim evaluation (Orr et al., 2003), which Varady discusses in his preface, encourages a more cautious optimism, however, and shows why many housing mobility interventions will probably not constitute as dramatic and beneficial a "treatment" (in experimental terms) as Chicago's Gautreaux did. Most "moves to opportunity" will not be from extremely high poverty, racially segregated ghetto neighborhoods (such as those in inner-city Chicago anchored by large, distressed public housing projects) to job-rich, solidly middle-income neighborhoods in which the in-movers are essentially racial pioneers. Most moves will involve more modest transitions, with both the easier adaptation and reduced long-run benefit that implies. Some kids in the mover families will benefit while others will not. Key effects may lag considerably, taking years, or perhaps a decade or longer, to fully register. Finally, some families will stay in lower-risk, higher-opportunity areas, while others will choose to head back to higher-poverty areas. Still others, when offered the "opportunity" to endure immediate and difficult transitions with uncertain benefits that accrue over time, will refuse. Moving involves trade-offs for most families (of any income level or racial/ethnic background). As Varady emphasizes, some of the families that policy makers would like to target will not readily move away from friends and kin, supportive faith institutions, public transportation, and more. Unless policy changes the calculus—the actual trade-offs or the ways in which they are perceived—take-up will be limited in some places.

In general, we have much too little evidence on how to help households adapt to the social and economic transitions they face in moving from what are, typically, high poverty mostly minority neighborhoods to low poverty, mostly white (or racially mixed) ones. In addition, demand-side housing mechanisms are limited where supply becomes constrained, for example, in gentrifying areas where prices spike and supply expansion lags or in sub-markets where discrimination effectively limits the actual stock available to particular groups of consumers. Finally, in lieu of counseling, transportation, and other supports, there is evidence, at least in the U.S. case, that tenants make quite segregative moves if simply "handed" a voucher. Fear of harassment, a lack of information on wider options available, and ignorance of the full cost of segregated living may all contribute to this.

In some instances, otherwise smart policy may generate unintended consequences or pose difficult trade-offs for households and society. Retrofitting, or rounding out, a policy after the fact may help. For example, Pearce-Oroz recommends stronger transportation links to downtown jobs as a way of compensating for the uneven trade that residents of Tegucigalpa's new towns have made (as they started new lives on the urban periphery after the hurricane). My own work on housing mobility and desegregation suggests that transportation likewise helps "brown kids in white suburbs" hang on to social support from the old neighborhood while enjoying advantages of the new (Briggs 1998). And "car vouchers" (a shorthand for car ownership promotion mechanisms such as subsidized loans for purchasing used cars) are probably essential as part of a metropolitan opportunity strategy in the United States and other nations where employment decentralization—"job sprawl," as economists put it—is increasingly the norm. Where access to jobs is concerned, the most immediate resource that many low-income households lack is reliable transportation, and transit has thus far proven inadequate for reaching scattered suburban jobs. Public and charitable resources can help households that lack the ability to make such links themselves, and so could employer-sponsored incentives.

A handful of our contributors, such as N. Ariel Espino, Peter Marcuse, and Robert W. Wassmer, are quite pessimistic about the prospects for significantly reducing economic segregation, a perspective that leads to policy ideas that target buying power and the treatment of housing as a good (i.e., in tax policy or restrictions on sale) rather than locational preferences, locational choices, or discriminatory behavior in the marketplace. These are some of the boldest proposals, as well as the least tested and perhaps least likely to win broad-based public support. But strategies that define these kinds of interventions certainly expand on the alternatives commonly discussed and might find more of an ear in transforming societies than in older, more politically established ones.

Finally, whatever the specific problems we wish to tackle and strategies we develop for tackling them, there remains the thorny policy problem of competing objectives. The South African context presents a number of dilemmas that reflect this—dilemmas faced in a fairly fluid, reformist political environment. The quickest route to expanding shelter may also be the most segregative by race and income. Promoting home ownership by the poor may be at odds with promoting social and economic mobility, especially if spatial mobility or wider spatial choice, are important contributors. Likewise, U.S. housing policies have frequently faced trade-offs between housing affordability and mixing objectives, whether mixing by race or income or both was at issue. Civil rights leaders have rarely been happy when mixed-income housing developments that maintained racial balancing targets kept lines of minority consumers waiting so as to attract the appropriate number of Whites into housing units. Here, too, the challenges are both logistical and political. On the logistical front, units go vacant, revenues are lost, and marketing can be costly. As for politics, strategies that aim for higher social objectives frequently struggle to defend themselves when the public pressures for greater attention to immediate needs. When implementation involves paradoxical double standards, such as "discriminating" in favor of white applicants in the example above, political support and legitimacy are even harder to come by—and harder to hold.

In this volume, we can scarcely claim to have finished the work of developing promising policy in light of such challenges. But we have shown that beyond mere diagnosis of shared or divergent conditions in various places, a more global conversation about segregation and its costs can contribute vital knowledge about how to pin down what we want to change, how to build a more persuasive case for change, and how to make change more likely through substantively savvy strategies. As I write this in the wealthy North of the globe and in a nation particularly eager to export its policy preferences abroad, the need to engage in this conversation more often, and with greater humility and mutual respect, is all too clear.

Notes

Francisco Sabatini and David P. Varady provided helpful advice on this chapter.

1. Most economists analyzing residential choice and its impact on segregation patterns make the standard assumptions that preferences are stable and that individuals can be treated as utility maximizers. Sociologists are interested in how preferences are shaped by social context and how choices are "embedded" in networks, norms, and other socially structured phenomena. Sociologists also tend to see racial/ethnic identity and attitudes as exerting fairly direct influences on how and where we choose to live, while economists are inclined to see race-based preferences as another element of the individual actor's utility function; racial avoidance can be inferred only after the "pure" effects of buying power are accounted for. While buying power gaps among the races do explain some segregation, much remains unexplained, and the survey evidence on racial attitudes about preferred neighbors (e.g., Bobo 2001) is compelling—all the more so when combined with the results of carefully conducted audit tests of housing discrimination (Turner et al. 2002; Yinger 1995). Together, those data indicate that all groups have a hierarchy of preferred neighbors (by race group) and that Blacks and Hispanics in the United States are likely to encounter some form of discrimination from real estate professionals in about one-quarter of all searches (for rental or ownership units). Finally, arguments that Whites avoid certain neighborhoods based on perceptions of "structural strength" (Ellen 2000) rather than racial make-up cannot rule out the existence of a double standard: namely, that judgments about current strength and future viability are filtered through racial attitudes. For example, Whites may well make allowances (qualified judgments) for vulnerable neighborhoods that are mostly white but not do the same for similarly vulnerable neighborhoods that are mostly black. Multidisciplinary work would enable researchers from distinct traditions to build on each other's findings. The assumption of stable preferences, for example, is perfectly reasonable for some analyses but should be "relaxed" for others. Signaling related to structural strength is worth understanding, but so too are the ways in which race may filter signals and interpretations of it.

BIBLIOGRAPHY

Abbott, Carl. 1997. "The Portland Region: Where City and Suburbs Talk to Each Other—and Often Agree." *Housing Policy Debate* 8(1):11–52.

Abrams, Charles. 1955. *Forbidden Neighbors*. New York: Harper.

Achtenberg, Emily Paradise, and Peter Marcuse. 1983. "Towards the Decommodification of Housing: A Political Analysis and a Progressive Program." In *America's Housing Crisis: What Is to Be Done?* Ed. Chester Hartman. Boston: Routledge and Kegan Paul.

Adam, Heribert, and Kogila Moodley. 1993. *The Opening of the Apartheid Mind: Options for the New South Africa*. Berkeley: University of California Press.

Agnew, John. 1982. "Home Ownership and Identity in Capitalist Societies." In *Housing and Identity: Cross-cultural Perspectives*. Ed. James S. Duncan. New York: Holmes and Meier.

Agüero, M. 1998. *Registro de la Propiedad: evaluación del impacto del Registro en el desarrollo de la economía nacional*. Tegucigalpa: II Encuentro del Sector Habitacional y Financiero.

Al-Ahram Weekly. 2003. 10, July, No. 646. http://weekly.ahram.org.eg/2003 /646/ in2htm.

Alba, Richard D., John R. Logan, and Brian J. Stults. 2000. "The Changing Neighborhood Contexts of the Immigrant Metropolis." *Social Forces* 79(2): 587–621.

———. 2001. "How Segregated Are Middle-class African Americans?" *Social Problems* 47(4):543–558.

Alba, Richard D., and Victor Nee. 1999. "Rethinking Assimilation: Theory for a New Era of Immigration." In *The Handbook of International Migration: The American Experience*. Eds. Charles Hirschman, Philip Kasinitz, and Josh DeWind. 137–160. New York: Russell Sage.

Alberti, Marina. 1999. "Urban Patterns and Environmental Performance: What Do We Know?" *Journal of Planning Education and Research* 19(2):151–163.

Alcaldía Municipal del Distrito Central (AMDC), International Organization for Migrations, United States Agency for International Development. 1999. *Censo de población y vivienda en zonas de riesgo*. Tegucigalpa: Alcaldía Municipal del Distrito Central.

Alesina, Alberto, Reza Baqir, and Caroline Hoxby. 2000. *"Political Jurisdictions in Heterogeneous Communities*. Working paper, National Bureau of Economic Research, Cambridge. http://www.nber.org/papers/w7859.

All Things Considered. 2001. *Talk of the Nation:* "Segregation in Cities." May 10. http://search.npr.org.

Altshuler, Alan, and David Luberoff. 2003. *Mega-projects: The Changing Politics of Urban Public Investment.* Washington, DC: Brookings Institution Press.

Arigoni, Danielle. 2001. *Affordable Housing and Smart Growth: Making the Connection.* Washington, DC: National Neighborhood Coalition.

Babcock, Richard F. 1966. *The Zoning Game: Municipal Practices and Policies.* Madison: University of Wisconsin Press.

Balakrishnan, T. R. 2000. "Residential Segregation and Canada's Ethnic Groups." In *Perspectives on Ethnicity in Canada.* Eds. Madeline A. Kalbach and Warren E. Kalbach. Toronto: Harcourt Canada.

Balakrishnan, T. R., and Feng Hou. 1999. "Residential Patterns in Cities." In *Immigrant Canada.* Eds. Shiva Halli and Leo Driedger. Toronto: University of Toronto Press.

Basgal, Ophelia, and Joseph Villarreal. 2001. "Comment on Bruce J. Katz and Margery Austin Turner, Who Should Run the Housing Voucher Program? A Reform Proposal: Why Public Housing Authorities Remain the Best Solution for Running the Housing Voucher Program." *Housing Policy Debate* 12(2):263–281.

Bauman, John F. 1987. *Public Housing, Race, and Renewal: Urban Planning in Philadelphia, 1920-1974.* Philadelphia: Temple University Press.

BBC. 2003. "Father Jailed for 'Honour Killing.'" BBC News. September 29. http://news.bbc.co.uk/1/hi/england/london/3149030.stm.

Becker, Gary S. 1957. *The Economics of Discrimination.* Chicago: University of Chicago Press.

Benvenisti, Meron. 1987. "Polarized Cities." Synopsis of lecture, Salzburg seminar session 267: "Divided Cities." February 11, Salzburg.

Berger, Joseph. 2002. "American Dream Is Ghana Home." *New York Times,* August 21: A17.

Bivins, Ralph. 1999. "Close to the City's Heart. Areas Near Downtown See Home Values Rise." *Houston Chronicle,* October 3: 1D.

Blau, Peter M., and J. E. Schwartz. 1984. *Cross-cutting Social Circles.* Orlando, FL: Academic Press.

Blauner, Bob. 1989. *Black Lives, White Lives: Three Decades of Race Relations in America.* Los Angeles: University of California Press.

Boaden, Bruce, and Aly Karam. 2000. "The Housing Market in Cape Town's Low-income Settlements." Report prepared for the Cape Metropolitan Council. Cape Town: Housing and Community Development Unit, University of Cape Town.

Boal, Frederick W. 1972. "The Urban Residential Sub-community: Conflict Interpretation. *Area* 4(3):164–168.

———. 1981. "Residential Segregation, Ethnic Mixing and Resource Conflict." In *Ethnic Segregation in Cities.* Eds. Ceri Peach, Vaughan Robinson, and Susan Smith, 235–251. London: Croom Helm.

———. 1987. Segregation. In *Social Geography: Progress and Prospect*. Ed. Michael Pacione. 90–128. London: Croom Helm.

———. 1996. "Immigration and Ethnicity in the Urban Milieu." In *EthniCity: Geographical Perspectives on Ethnic Change in Modern Cities*. Eds. Curtis C. Roseman, Hans Dieter Laux, and Günter Thieme. 283–303. Lanham, MD: Rowman and Littlefield.

———. 1999. "From Undivided Cities to Undivided Cities: Assimilation to Ethnic Cleansing". *Housing Studies* 14(5):585–600.

———. 2002. Belfast: "Walls Within." *Political Geography* 21(5):687–694.

Boal, Frederick W., Russell C. Murray, and Michael A. Poole. 1976. "Belfast: The Urban Encapsulation of a National Conflict. In *Urban Ethnic Conflict: A Comparative Perspective*. Eds. Susan E. Clarke and Jeffrey L. Obler, 77–131. Chapel Hill: Institute for Research in Social Science, University of North Carolina.

Bobo, Lawrence D. 2001. "Racial Attitudes and Relations at the Close of the Twentieth Century." In *America Becoming: Racial Trends and Their Consequences. Vol. I*. Eds. Neil J. Smelser, William Julius Wilson, and Faith Mitchell, 264–301. Washington, DC: National Academy Press.

Bobo, Lawrence D., Melvin L. Oliver, James H. Johnson, Jr., and Abel Valenzuela. 2000. *Prismatic Metropolis: Inequality in Los Angeles*. Washington, DC: Russell Sage Foundation.

Boissevain, Jeremy. 1974. *Friends of Friends*. Oxford: Blackwell.

Bollens, Scott A. 1999. *Urban Peace Building in Divided Societies: Belfast and Johannesburg*. Boulder, CO: Westview Press.

———. 2000. *On Narrow Ground: Urban Policy and Ethnic Conflict in Jerusalem and Belfast*. Albany: State University of New York Press.

Bond, Patrick. 2000. *Elite Transition: From Apartheid to Neoliberalism in South Africa*. Pietermaritzburg: University of Natal Press; London: Pluto Press.

Borja, Jordi and Manuel Castells. 1997. *Local and Global: The Management of Cities in the Information Age*. London: Earthscan.

Botes, Sarita. 1999. Personal interview with Marie Huchzermeyer, November 16, 1999. Public Relations Officer for Mr. C. Herandine, MEC for Housing, Western Cape Province.

Bourdieu, Pierre. 1984. *Distinction: A Social Critique of the Judgment of Taste*. Trans. Richard Nice. Cambridge: Harvard University Press.

———. 1990. *The Logic of Practice*. Trans. Richard Nice. Stanford, CA: Stanford University Press.

Bourne, Larry. 2000. *"People and Places: A Portrait of the Evolving Social Character of the Greater Toronto Region."* Toronto: Report to the NEPTIS Foundation.

Brasington, David M. 2000. "The Structure of Local Government: Spatial Considerations in Consolidation and Fragmentation." Working paper. Department of Economics, New Orleans: Tulane University.

Briggs, Xavier de Souza. 1998. "Brown Kids in White Suburbs: Housing Mobility and the Multiple Faces of Social Capital." *Housing Policy Debate* 9(1):177–221.

———. 2002. "The Will and the Way: Local Partnerships, Political Strategy, and the Well-being of America's Children and Youth." Working paper RWP 01-050. John F. Kennedy School of Government, Cambridge, Harvard University, January.

———. 2003a. "Bridging Networks, Social Capital, and Racial Segregation in America." Paper presented at Cambridge University, January 28.

———. 2003b. "Housing Opportunity, Desegregation Strategy and Policy Research." *Journal of Policy Analysis and Management* 22(2):201–206.

———. 2003c. "Reshaping the Geography of Opportunity: Place and Opportunity in Global Perspective." *Housing Studies* 18(6):915–936.

———. 2003d. "Social Capital and Segregation: Race, Connections and Inequality in America." Working paper RWP 02-011. John F. Kennedy School of Government, Cambridge, Harvard University, February.

———. Forthcoming. "Civilization in Color: The Multicultural City in Three Millennia." *City and Community* 3.

Briggs, Xavier Souza de, and Elizabeth R. Mueller with Mercer L. Sullivan. 1997. *From Neighborhood to Community: Evidence on the Effects of Community Development.* New York: Community Development Research Center.

Brown, Karen Destrorel. 2001. *Expanding Affordable Housing through Inclusionary Zoning: Lessons from the Washington Metropolitan Area.* Washington, DC: Brookings Institution Center on Urban and Metropolitan Policy.

Brown, Patricia Leigh. 2001. "With an Asian Influx, a Suburb Finds Itself Transformed." *New York Times* May 26: A1, A8.

Brozan, Nadine. 2004. "Moving Up Without Moving On." *New York Times,* Real Estate February 15. http://www.nytimes.com/2004/02/15/realestate/.

Budlender, Debbie, compiler. 1998. *The People's Voices: National Speak-out on Poverty Hearings, March to June 1998.* Johannesburg: The Commission for Gender Equity (CGE), the South African Human Rights Commission (SAHRC), and the Southern African NGO Coalition (SANGOCO).

Bullard, Robert D. 2001. "Race, Equity and Smart Growth." *Transportation Equity: A Newsletter of the Environmental Justice Resource Center at Clark Atlanta University.* http://www.ejrc.cau.edu/transequnewsvol13.htm.

Bullard, Robert D., Glenn S. Johnson, and Angela O. Torres. 2000a. "Race, Equity, and Smart Growth: Why People of Color Must Speak for Themselves. Environmental Resource Center, Clark Atlanta University, Atlanta http://www. ejrc. cau. edu/.

———, eds. 2000b. *Sprawl City: Race, Politics, and Planning Atlanta.* Washington, DC: Island Press.

Burchell, Robert W., ed. 1998. *The Costs of Sprawl Revisited.* Washington, DC: National Academy Press.

Burchell, Robert W., George Lowenstein, William R. Dolphin, Catherine C. Galley, Anthony Downs, Samuel Seskin, and Terry Moore. 2001. *Costs of Sprawl—2000.* Washington, DC: National Academy Press.

Burtless, Gary. 1996. *Does Money Matter? The Effects of School Resources on Student Achievement and Adult Success.* Washington, DC: Brookings Institution.

Calthorpe, Peter. 1993. *The Next American Metropolis: Ecology, Community, and the American Dream.* New York: Princeton Architectural Press.

———. 2000. "New Urbanism: Condensing the American Dream." CNN. http://www.cnn.com/SPECIALS/2000/democracy/sprawl/views/index.html.

Carey, Elaine. 2001. "High-rise Ghettos." *Toronto Star* February 3: M1, M2.

Caro, Robert. 1974. *The Power Broker: Robert Moses and the Fall of New York.* New York: Alfred A. Knopf.

Case, Karl E. 1992. "Taxes and Speculative Behavior in Land and Real Estate Markets." *Review of Urban and Regional Development Studies* 4:226–239.

Case, Karl E., and Leah Cook. 1989. "The Distributional Effects of Housing Price Booms: Winners and Losers in Boston, 1980–88." *New England Economic Review* (May/June):3–12.

Castells, Manuel. 1998. *End of Millennium.* Malden, MA: Blackwell.

Centro de Diseño, Arquitectura y Construcción (CEDAC). 2001. *Informe de evaluación de los proyectos de OIM en Tegucigalpa con miras a promover mayor participación.* Working Paper. Tegucigalpa: Centro de Diseño, Arquitectura y Construcción.

Centro Latinoamericano de Demografía (CELADE). 2000. *Crecimiento, estructura y distribución de la población, informe conciso.* New York: United Nations.

Charles, Camille Zubrinsky. 2001. "Processes of Racial Residential Segregation." In *Urban Inequality: Evidence from Four Cities.* Eds. Alice O'Connor, Chris Tilly, and Lawrence D. Bobo, 267–271. New York: Russell Sage.

Chaskin, Robert J., Prudence Brown, Sudhir Venkatesh, and Avis Vidall. 2001. *Building Community Capacity.* New York: Aldine de Gruyter.

Chen, Huey-Tsyh. 1990. *Theory-driven Evaluations.* Newbury Park, CA: Sage Publications.

Citizens' Commission on Civil Rights. 1983. *A Decent Home: A Report on the Continuing Failure of the Federal Government to Provide Equal Housing Opportunity.* Washington, DC: The Commission.

Clark, William A. V. 1986. Residential Segregation in American Cities. *Population Research and Policy Review* 5:95–127.

———. 1991. "Residential Preferences and Neighborhood Racial Segregation: A Test of the Schelling Segregation Model." *Demography* 28:1–19.

———. 1992. Residential Preferences and Residential Choices in a Multiethnic Context." *Demography* 29:451–466.

Clotfelter, Charles T. 2001. "Are Whites Still Fleeing? Racial Patterns and Enrollment Shifts in Urban Public Schools, 1987–1996." *Journal of Policy Analysis and Management* 20(2):199–221.

Cohen, Cathy J. 2001. "Social Capital, Intervening Institutions, and Political Power." In *Social Capital and Poor Communities,* Eds. Susan Saegert, J. Philip Thompson, and Mark R. Warren, 267–289. New York: Russell Sage.

Coleman, James S. 1990. *Foundations of Social Theory*. Cambridge: Harvard University Press.

Coleman, James S., and Thomas Hoffer. 1987. *Public and Private High Schools: The Impact of Communities*. New York: Basic Books.

Conley, Dalton. 1999. *Being Black, Living in the Red: Race, Wealth, and Social Policy*. Berkeley: University of California Press.

Crain, Robert L., and Amy S. Wells. 1994. "Perpetuation Theory and the Long-term Effects of School Desegregation." *Review of Educational Research* 64(4):531–553.

Cressey, Paul Frederick. 1938. "Population Succession in Chicago: 1898–1930." *American Journal of Sociology* 44(1):59–69.

Cronon, William J. 1992. "A Place for Stories: Nature, History and Narrative." *Journal of American History* 78(4):1347–1376.

Cross, Malcolm, and Roger Waldinger. 1992. "Migrants, Minorities, and the Ethnic Division of Labor." In *Divided Cities: New York, and London in the Contemporary World*. Eds. Susan S. Fainstein, Ian Gordon, and Michael Harloe, 151–174. Oxford: Blackwell.

Crowder, Kyle D. 2000. "The Racial Context of White Mobility: An Individual-level Assessment of the White Flight Hypothesis." *Social Science Research* 29(2):223–257.

Cullingworth, J. Barry. 1993. *The Political Culture of Planning: American Land Use Planning in Comparative Perspective*. New York: Routledge.

Dahya, Badr. 1974. "The Nature of Pakistani Ethnicity in Industrial Cities in Britain." In *Urban Ethnicity*. Ed. Abner Cohen, 77–118. London: Tavistock.

Dalrymple, Theodore. 2002. "Barbarians at the Gate of Paris." *City Journal* 12(4):63–73.

Danielson, Michael N. 1976. *The Politics of Exclusion*. New York: Columbia University Press.

Darroch, A. G., and Wilfred George Marston. 1972. "Ethnic Differentiation: Ecological Aspects of a Multidimensional Concept." In *Readings in Race Relations*. Ed. Anthony H. Richmond, 107–128. Oxford: Pergamon Press.

Davis, Mike. 1992. *City of Quartz*. New York: Verso.

———. 1998. *Ecology of Fear: Los Angeles and the Imagination of Disaster*. New York: Metropolitan Books.

Dear, Michael. 2001. Review of *Prismatic Metropolis: Inequality in Los Angeles*. *Los Angeles Times* Book Review Sunday (February 11):3.

Del Conte, Alessandra, and Jeffrey Kling. 2001. "A Synthesis of MTO Research on Self-sufficiency, Safety and Health, and Behavior and Delinquency." *Poverty Research News* 5(1). Joint Center for Poverty Research, Northwestern University and the University of Chicago, January–February. http://www.jcpr.org/newsletter/vol5_no1/index.htm.

DeLeon, Richard Edward. 1992. *Left Coast City: Progressive Politics in San Francisco, 1975-1991*. Lawrence: University Press of Kansas.

Dent, David. 1992. "The New Black Suburbs." *New York Times Magazine*, June 14: 18–25.

Denton, Nancy. 1994. "Are African Americans Still Hypersegregated?" In *Residential Apartheid: The American Legacy*. Eds. Robert D. Bullard, J. Eugene Grigsby III, and Charles Lee. Los Angeles: CAAS Publications.

Department of Health. 2001. *Ante Natal Survey November 2000*. Pretoria: Department of Health (March).

Department of Housing. 1997. *Living Cities: Urban Development Framework*. Pretoria: Department of Housing.

———. 2000. "Law To Clamp Down On People Selling RDP Houses." Press release. http://www.housing.gov.za/pages/news/press_releases.htm#2000-5.

———. 2001. "Quickstats (updated April 25, 2001). Subsidies Approved 1994–2001. Department of Housing. http://www/housing.gov.za.

Dewar, David. 1999. "Brave New Frontiers: Housing Challenges of the Future." Paper presented at the Institute for Housing of South Africa Conference, "Developing Housing Environments for the New Millennium," October 17–20, Nelspruit.

Dirección General de Estadística y Censos (DGEC). 2000. *Vigésimo Segunda encuesta permanente de hogares: septiembre 1999*. Comayaguela, M.D.C.: Dirección General de Estadística y Censos.

Doucet, Michael. 2001. "The Anatomy of an Urban Legend: Toronto's Multicultural Reputation." CERIS Working Paper No, 16. Toronto: Joint Centre of Excellence for Research on Immigration and Settlement.

Dowding, Keith. 2001. "Explaining Urban Regimes." *International Journal of Urban and Regional Research* 25(1):7–19.

Downs, Anthony. 1993. "Reducing Regulatory Barriers to Affordable Housing Erected by Local Government." In *Housing Markets and Residential Mobility*. Eds. G. Thomas Kingsley and Margery Austin Turner. Washington, DC: Urban Institute.

———. 1999. "Some Realities about Sprawl and Urban Decline. *Housing Policy Debate* 10(4):955–974.

———. 2000. "How City-planning Practices Affect Metropolitan Area Housing Markets, and Vice-versa." In *The Profession of City Planning: Changes, Images, and Challenges, 1950–2000*. Eds. Lloyd Rodwin and Bishwapriya Sanyal. New Brunswick, NJ: Center for Urban Policy Research, Rutgers University.

Dreier, Peter, John H. Mollenkopf, and Todd Swanstrom. 2001. *Place Matters: Metropolitics for the Twenty-first Century*. Lawrence: University of Kansas Press.

Duncan, Cynthia M. 2001. "Social Capital in America's Poor Rural Communities." In *Social Capital and Poor Communities*. Eds. Susan Saegert, J. Philip Thompson, and Mark Warren. New York: Russell Sage.

Duncan, James S. 1982. "From Container of Women to Status Symbol: The Impact of Social Structure on the Meaning of the House." In *Housing and*

Identity: Cross Cultural Perspectives. Ed. James S. Duncan. New York: Holmes and Meier.

Duncan, O. D., and B. Duncan. 1955. "A Methodological Analysis of Segregation Indexes." *American Sociological Review* 20:210–217.

Duncan, O. D., and Stanley Lieberson. 1959. "Ethnic Segregation and Assimilation." *American Journal of Sociology* 64:364–374.

Eaton, Susan E. 2001. *The Other Boston Busing Story: What's Won and Lost Across the Boundary Lines.* New Haven: Yale University Press.

The Economist. 2001. "A Tuscan Village in South Africa," April 7. www.economist.com/printerfriendly.cfm?story_id=561838ppv=1.

Edley, Christopher, Jr. 1996. *Not All Black and White: Affirmative Action and American Values.* New York: Hill and Wang.

Ellen, Ingrid Gould. 1997a. "Race-based Neighborhood Projection: A Proposed Framework for Understanding New Data on Racial Stability," Taub Urban Research Center Working Paper Series. New York: Taub Urban Research Center, New York University.

———. 1997b. "Welcome Neighbors? New Evidence on the Possibility of Stable Racial Integration." *Brookings Review* 15(1):18–21.

———. 1998. "Stable Racial Integration in the Contemporary United States: An Empirical Overview." *Journal of Urban Affairs* 20(1):27–42.

———. 2000. *Sharing America's Neighborhoods: The Prospects for Stable Racial Integration.* Cambridge: Harvard University Press.

Ethington, Philip J., William H. Frey, and Dowell Myers. 2001. "The Racial Resegregation of Los Angeles County, 1940–2000." Public Research Report No. 2001-04. Population Dynamics Group. University of Southern California. www.usc.edu/sppd/census2000.

Ewing, Reid. 1997. "Is Los Angeles–style Sprawl Desirable?" *Journal of the American Planning Association* 63(1):107–126.

Fainstein, Susan. 1997. "Justice, Politics and the Creation of Urban Space." In *The Urbanization of Injustice,* Eds. Andy Merrifield and Erik Swyngedouw, 18–44. New York: New York University Press.

———. 2001. "Inequality in Global City-Regions." In *Global City-Regions.* Ed. Allen J. Scott, 285–298. New York: Oxford University Press.

Fainstein, Susan, and Clifford Hirst. 1995. "Urban Social Movements." In *Theories of Urban Politics.* Eds. David Judge, Gerry Stoker, and Harold Wolman, 181–204. Thousand Oaks, CA: Sage Publications.

Fair Housing Council of Greater Washington. 1997a. *The Fair Housing Index: An Audit of Race and National Origin Discrimination in the Greater Washington Real Estate Sales Market.* Washington, DC: Fair Housing Council of Greater Washington.

———. 1997b. *The Fair Housing Index: An Audit of Race and National Origin Discrimination in the Greater Washington Rental Housing Market.* Washington, DC: Fair Housing Council of Greater Washington.

———. 1998. *The Fair Lending Index: An Audit of Race and National Origin Discrimination in the Greater Washington Mortgage-lending Marketplace.* Washington, DC: Fair Housing Council of Greater Washington.

Farley, Reynolds, Charlotte Steeh, Maria Krysan, Tara Jackson, and Keith Reeves. 1994. "Stereotypes and Segregation: Neighborhoods in the Detroit Area." *American Journal of Sociology* 100:750–780.

Farley, Reynolds, Elaine L. Fielding, and Maria Krysan. 1997. "The Residential Preferences of Blacks and Whites: A Four-metropolis Analysis." *Housing Policy Debate* 8(4):763–800.

Feagin, Joe R., and Melvin P. Sikes. 1994. *Living with Racism: The Black Middle-class Experience.* Boston: Beacon Press.

Fisher, Robert. 1994. *Let the People Decide: Neighborhood Organizing in America.* New York: Twayne.

Fisher, Ronald C. 1996. *State and Local Public Finance.* 2nd ed. Chicago: Irwin.

Fisher, Ronald C., and Robert W. Wassmer. 1998. "Economic Influences on the Structure of Local Government in U.S. Metropolitan Areas. *Journal of Urban Economics* 43(3):444–471.

Fishman, Robert. 1987. *Bourgeois Utopias: The Rise and Fall of Suburbia.* New York: Basic Books.

Fix, Michael, George C. Galster, and Raymond Struyk. 1992. "An Overview of Auditing for Discrimination." In *Clear and Convincing Evidence: Measurement of Discrimination in America.* Eds. Michael Fix and Raymond J. Struyk, 1–67. Washington, DC: Urban Institute Press.

Fix, Michael, and Raymond J. Struyk. 1992. *Clear and Convincing Evidence: Measurement of Discrimination in America.* Washington, DC: Urban Institute Press.

Fix, Michael, and Margery A. Turner. 1999. *A National Report Card on Discrimination in America: The Role of Testing.* Washington, DC: Urban Institute Press.

Foderaro, Lisa W. 1998. "For Affluent Blacks, Harlem's Pull Is Strong." *New York Times,* September 18: A1, A25.

Fogelson, Robert. 1993. *The Fragmented Metropolis: Los Angeles, 1850–1930.* Berkeley: University of California Press.

Fong, Eric. 1996. "A Comparative Perspective on Residential Segregation: American and Canadian Experience." *Sociological Quarterly* 37(2):199–226.

Ford, R. Glenn. 1950. "Population Succession in Chicago." *American Journal of Sociology* 56(2):151–160.

Franck, Karen A. 1987. "Shared Spaces, Small Spaces, and Spaces That Change: Examples of Housing Innovation in the United States." In *Housing and Neighborhoods: Theoretical and Empirical Contributions.* Eds. William van Vliet—, Harvey Choldin, William Michelson, and David Popenoe. New York: Greenwood Press.

Frankenberg, Erica, Chungmei Lee, and Gary Orfield. 2003. *A Multiracial Society with Segregated Schools: Are We Losing the Dream?* Cambridge, MA: The Civil Rights Project.

Frey, William H. 1979. "Central City White Flight: Racial and Nonracial Causes." *American Sociological Review* 44:425–448.

Frieden, Bernard, and Lynne Sagalyn. 1989. *Downtown Inc.* Cambridge: MIT Press.

Friedrichs, Jürgen, George Galster, and Sako Musterd. 2003. "Neighborhood Effects of Social Opportunities: The European and American Research and Policy Context." *Housing Studies* 18(6):797–806.

Frost, Robert, with an Introduction and Commentary by Louis Untermeyer. 2002. *Robert Frost's Poems.* New York: St. Martin's Press.

Fuchs, Esther R., Robert Y. Shapiro, and Lorraine C. Minnite. 2001. "Social Capital, Political Participation, and the Urban Community." In *Social Capital and Poor Communities.* Eds. Susan Saegert, J. Philip Thompson, and Mark R. Warren. New York: Russell Sage.

Fukuyama, Francis. 1995. *Trust: The Social Virtues and the Creation of Prosperity.* New York: Free Press.

Fulton, William B., Rolf Pendall, Mai T. Nguyen, and Alice Harrison. 2001. *Who Sprawls Most? Exploring and Explaining Urban Density Changes in the U.S., 1982-1997.* Washington, DC: Brookings Institution.

Gabriel, Stuart A., and Stuart S. Rosenthal. 1989. "Household Location and Race: Estimates of a Multinomial Logit Model." *Review of Economics and Statistics* 71(2):240–249.

Galster, George C. 1990a. "Neighborhood Racial Change, Segregationist Sentiments, and Affirmative Action Marketing Policies." *Journal of Urban Economics* 27(3):344–361.

———. 1990b. "White Flight from Racially Integrated Neighborhoods in the 1970s: The Cleveland Experience." *Urban Studies* 27(3):385–399.

———. 1992. "A Cumulative Causation Model of the Underclass: Implications for Urban Economic Development Policy." In *The Metropolis in Black and White: Place, Power and Polarization.* Eds. George C. Galster and Edward W. Hill. New Brunswick, NJ: Center for Urban Policy Research.

Galster, George C., Royce Hanson, and Hal Wolman. 2001. "Multiple Dimensions of Sprawl: How Does Los Angeles Stand Up?" Paper presented at Planning in the Post-Sprawl Era conference, School of Policy, Planning, and Development, University of Southern California, November.

Galster, George C., and Sean P. Killen. 1995. "The Geography of Opportunity: A Reconnaissance and Conceptual Framework." *Housing Policy Debate* 6(1):7–43.

Galster, George C., Ronald Mincy, and Mitchell Tobin. 1997. "The Disparate Racial Impacts of Metropolitan Restructuring. *Urban Affairs Review* 32(6):797–824.

Gans, Herbert J. 1961. "The Balanced Community: Homogeneity or Heterogeneity in Residential Areas?" *Journal of the American Institute of Planners* 27:176–184.

GCIS. 2000. South Africa Yearbook 2000/2001. http://www.gov.za/yearbook/housing/htm.

Gelfand, Mark. 1975. *A Nation of Cities: The Federal Government and Urban America, 1933–1965.* New York: Oxford University Press.

Gilbert, Alan. 2000. "What Might South Africa Have Learned about Housing Subsidies from Chile?" *South African Geographical Journal* 82(1):21–29.

Gilroy, Rose, and Susanne Speak. 1998. "Barriers, Boxes, and Catapults: Social Exclusion in Everyday Life." In *Social Exclusion in European Cities: Processes, Experiences, and Responses.* Eds. Ali Madanipour, Goran Cars, and Judith Allen, 95–113. London: Jessica Kingsley Publishers.

Gittell, Ross, and Avis Vidal. 1998. *Community Organizing: Building Social Capital as a Development Strategy.* Thousand Oaks, CA: Sage Publications.

Glaeser, Edward L., and David Cutler. 1997. "Are Ghettos Good or Bad?" *Quarterly Journal of Economics* 112:827–872.

Glaeser, Edward L., and Jesse M. Shapiro. 2001. *City Growth and the 2000 Census: Which Places Grew, and Why.* Washington, DC: Center on Urban and Metropolitan Policy, Brookings Institution Survey Series, Census 2000.

Glaeser, Edward L., and Jacob L. Vigdor. 2001. "Racial Segregation in the 2000 Census: Promising News." Brookings Institution Survey Series. Washington, DC: April. www.brook.edu/dybdocroot/es/urban/census/glaseer.pdf.

Glazer, Nathan. 1975. *Affirmative Discrimination: Ethnic Inequality and Public Policy.* New York: Basic Books.

———. 1993. "Is Assimilation Dead?" *Annals of the American Academy of Social and Political Sciences* 530:122–136.

Glazer, Nathan, and Daniel P. Moynihan, eds. 1970. Introduction. *Beyond the Melting Pot: The Negroes, Puerto Ricans, Jews, Italians, and Irish of New York City.* Cambridge: MIT Press.

Glebe, G. 1986. "Segregation and Intra-urban Mobility of a High-status Ethnic Group: The Case of the Japanese in Düsseldorf." *Ethnic and Racial Studies* 9:432–441.

Goering, John, and Judith D. Feins, eds. 2003. *Choosing a Better Life? Evaluating the Moving to Opportunity Social Experiment.* Washington, DC: Urban Institute Press.

Goering, John, Judith D. Feins, and Todd Richardson. 2003. "What Have We Learned about Housing Mobility and Poverty Deconcentration." In *Choosing a Better Life? Evaluating the Moving to Opportunity Social Experiment.* Eds. John Goering and Judith D. Feins. Washington, DC: Urban Institute Press.

Goering, John, and Ron Wienk, eds. 1996. *Mortgage Lending, Racial Discrimination, and Federal Policy.* Washington, DC: Urban Institute Press.

Goetz, Edward G. 2002. "Forced Relocation vs. Voluntary Mobility: The Effects of Dispersal Programs on Households." *Housing Studies* 17(1):107–123.

———. 2003. *Clearing the Way: Deconcentrating the Poor in Urban America.* Washington, DC: Urban Institute Press.

Goldsmith, William W. 1979. "The Ghetto as a Resource for Black America." *Journal of the American Institute of Planners* 40(1):17–30.

Goldsmith, William W., and Edward J. Blakely. 1992. *Separate Societies: Poverty and Inequality in U.S. Cities*. Philadelphia: Temple University Press.

Goodman, Paul, and Percival Goodman. 1990. *Communitas: Means of Livelihood and Ways of Life*. New York: Columbia University Press.

Gordon, Milton M. 1964. *Assimilation in American Life*. New York: Oxford University Press.

Gordon, Peter, and Harry W. Richardson. 1997. "Are Compact Cities a Desirable Planning Goal? *Journal of the American Planning Association* 63(1):95–106.

———. 1998. "Prove It: The Cost and Benefits of Sprawl." In *Readings in Urban Economics: Issues and Public Policy*. Ed. Robert W. Wassmer, 114–116. Malden, MA: Blackwell.

———. 2000. "Sprawl: You Love It But Dare Not Speak Its Name." CNN, October 2. http://www.cnn.com/SPECIALS/2000/democracy/sprawl/views/index.html.

Gottdiener, Mark. 1994. *Social Production of Urban Space*. 2nd ed. Austin: University of Texas Press.

Granovetter, Mark. 1974. *Getting a Job: A Study of Contacts and Careers*. Cambridge: Harvard University Press.

Greater Johannesburg Metropolitan Council. 2000. *iGoli 2002: Making Greater Johannesburg Work*. Johannesburg: Office of the City Manager.

Greeley, Andrew. 1971. *Why Can't They Be Like Us? America's White Ethnic Groups*. New York: Free Press.

Greenspan, Alan. 1999. "Mortgage Markets and Economic Activity." Remarks by the Chairman of the Federal Reserve Board before a conference on Mortgage Markets and Economic Activity, sponsored by America's Community Bankers, Washington, DC, November 2. http://www.bog.frb.fed.us/boarddocs/speeches.1999/19991102.

Grillo, Ralph D. 2000. "Plural Cities in Comparative Perspective." *Ethnic and Racial Studies* 23(6):957–981.

Grogan, Paul S., and Tony Proscio. 2000. *Comeback Cities: A Blueprint for Urban Neighborhood Revival*. Boulder, CO: Westview Press.

Grover, Kelly. 1995. The Social Organization of High-rise Neighbourhood: The Influence of Race, Socio-economic Class and Tenure in the Community Sentiment of Kingsview Park. Master's thesis, Queen's University, Kingston.

Guhathakurta, Subhrajit, and Michele L. Wichert. 1998. "Who Pays for Growth in the City of Phoenix? An Equity-based Perspective on Suburbanization." *Urban Affairs Review* 33(6):813–838.

Haar, Charles. 1996. *Suburbs Under Siege: Race, Space, and Audacious Judges*. Princeton: Princeton University Press.

Hadden, Tom, Colin Irwin, and Frederick W. Boal. 1996. *Separation or Sharing*. Belfast: Fortnight Educational Trust.

Hannerz, Ulf. 1969. *Soulside: Inquiries in Ghetto Culture and Community*. New York: Columbia University Press.

Hardin, Garrett, and John Baden. 1977. *Managing the Commons*. San Francisco: W. H. Freeman.

Harrison, Bennett, and Marcus Weiss. 1998. *Workforce Development Networks: Community-based Organizations and Regional Alliances*. Thousand Oaks, CA: Sage Publications.

Harvey, David. 1973. *Social Justice and the City*. London: Edward Arnold.

Harvey, Robert. 1985. "Ethnicity and Neighborhood." In *Gathering Places: Peoples and Neighbourhoods of Toronto, 1843-1945*. Ed. Robert Harvey. Toronto: Multicultural History Society of Ontario.

Hauser, Philip Morris. 1958. "On the Impact of Urbanism on Social Organization, Human Nature, and Social Structure." *Confluence* 7(1):57-69.

Hawley, Amos H. 1972. Population Density and the City. *Demography* 9(4):521-529.

Hayden, Dolores. 1996. "Revisiting the Sitcom Suburbs." *Land Lines: Newsletter of the Lincoln Institute of Land Policy* 14(2):3.

Heikkila, Eric. 1996." Are Municipalities Tieboutian Clubs?" *Regional Science and Urban Economics* 26:203-226.

Henderson, Damien. 2003. "Muslim School Teachers Set Up Pressure Group." *The Herald*, January 2: 1. http://www.theherald.co.uk/news/7292.html.

Hepburn, Anthony C. 1996. *A Past Apart*. Belfast: Ulster Historical Foundation.

Hiebert, Daniel. 1995. "The Social Geography of Toronto in 1931: A Study of Residential Differentiation and Social Structure." *Journal of Historical Geography* 21(1):55-74.

Hirsch, Arnold. 1983. *Making the Second Ghetto: Race and Housing in Chicago, 1940-1960*. New York: Cambridge University Press.

Hirst, Paul, and Grahame Thompson. 1996. *Globalization in Question: The International Economy and the Possibilities of Governance*. Cambridge: Polity Press.

Hise, Greg. 1998. *Magnetic Los Angeles*. Baltimore: John Hopkins University Press.

Hoge, Warren. 2001. "British Life Is Fractured Along Racial Lines, A Study Says." *New York Times*, December 12: A3.

———. 2002. "Britain's Non-whites Feel Un-British, Report Says." *New York Times*, April 4: A6.

Holzer, Harry J. 1991. "The Spatial Mismatch Hypothesis: What Has the Evidence Shown?" *Urban Studies* 28(1):105-122.

Home Office. 2001. *Community Cohesion: A Report of the Independent Review Team*. Ted Cantle, chair. London: Home Office. http://www.homeoffice. gov.uk/reu/community_cohesion.pdf.

Howard, Ebenezer. 1898. *To-morrow: A Peaceful Path to Real Reform*. London: Swan Sonnenschein.

Huchzermeyer, Marie. 2003. "A Legacy of Control? The Capital Subsidy for Housing, and Informal Settlement Intervention in South Africa." *International Journal of Urban and Regional Research* 27(3):591–612.

Huie, Stephanie A. Bond, and W. Parker Frisbie. 2000. "The Components of Density and the Dimensions of Residential Segregation." *Population Research Policy Review* 19:505–524.

Hunter, Floyd. 1953. *Community Power Structure*. Chapel Hill: University of North Carolina Press.

Ihlanfeldt, Keith R., and David L. Sjoquist. 1998. "The Spatial Mismatch Hypothesis: A Review of Recent Studies and Their Implications for Welfare Reform." *Housing Policy Debate* 9(4):849–892.

International Organization for Migrations (IOM). 2001. *Encuesta socioeconómica de beneficiarios del Exit Program en Amarateca*. Working Paper. Tegucigalpa: International Organization for Migrations.

Jackson, Kenneth T. 1985. *Crabgrass Frontier: The Suburbanization of the United States*. New York: Oxford University Press.

Jargowsky, Paul A. 1996. "Take the Money and Run: Economic Segregation in U.S. Metropolitan Areas." *American Sociological Review* 61:984–998.

———. 1997. *Poverty and Place: Ghettos, Barrios, and the American City*. New York: Russell Sage.

———. 2002. "Sprawl, Concentration of Poverty, and Urban Inequality." In *Urban Sprawl: Causes, Consequences, and Policy Responses*. Ed. Gregory D. Squires, 39–72. Washington, DC: Urban Institute Press.

———. 2003. *Stunning Progress: The Dramatic Decline of Concentrated Poverty in the 1990s*. Center on Urban and Metropolitan Policy. Washington, DC: Brookings Institution.

Johnson, Michael P., Helen F. Ladd, and Jens Ludwig. 2001. "The Benefits and Costs of Residential-mobility Programs for the Poor." Paper presented at Opportunity, Deprivation and the Housing Nexus: Trans-Atlantic Perspectives conference, sponsored by *Housing Studies* and the Metropolitan Housing and Community Center, Urban Institute, Washington, DC, May 31, 2001.

Jonas, Andrew E. G. 1998. "Busing, 'White Flight,' and the Role of Developers in the Continuous Suburbanization of Franklin County, Ohio. *Urban Affairs Review* 34(2):340–358.

Kain, John F. 1968. "Housing Desegregation, Negro Employment, and Metropolitan Decentralization." *Quarterly Journal of Economics* 32(2):175–197.

———. 1985. "Black Suburbanization in the Eighties: A New Beginning or a False Hope?" In *American Domestic Priorities*. Eds. John Quigley and Daniel Rubinfeld. Berkeley and Los Angeles: University of California Press.

———. 1992. "The Spatial Mismatch Hypothesis: Three Decades Later." *Housing Policy Debate* 3(2):371–460.

Kantrowitz, Nathan. 1969. "Ethnic and Racial Segregation in the New York Metropolis." *American Journal of Sociology* 7(4):685–695.

Kasarda, John D. 1993. "Inner-city Concentrated Poverty and Neighborhood Distress: 1970–1990." *Housing Policy Debate* 4(3):253–302.

Kazemipur, Abdolmohammad, and Shiva Halli. 2000. *The New Poverty in Canada*. Toronto: Thompson Educational Publishing.

Kearns, Ade, and Michael Parkinson. 2001. "The Significance of Neighborhood." *Urban Studies* 38(2):2103–10.

Kennedy, Ruby Jo Reeves. 1944. "Single or Triple Melting Pot? Intermarriage in New Haven, 1870–1940." *American Journal of Sociology* 49(3):331–339.

———. 1952. "Single or Triple Melting Pot? Intermarriage in New Haven, 1870–1950." *American Journal of Sociology* 58(1):56–59.

Kershaw, Sarah. 2002. "Schenectady's Guyanese Strategy: Mayor Goes All Out For a Wave of Hardworking Immigrants." *New York Times*, July 26: A18.

Keyes, Langley C. 2001. "Housing, Social Capital, and Poor Communities." In *Social Capital and Poor Communities*. Eds. Susan Saegert, J. Philip Thompson, and Mark R. Warren, 136–164. New York: Russell Sage.

Keyes, Langley C., Alex Schwartz, Avis Vidal, and Rachel Bratt. 1996. "Networks and Nonprofits: Opportunities and Challenges in an Era of Devolution." *Housing Policy Debate* 7(2):201–229.

Kiang, Ying-Cheng. 1968. "The Distribution of Ethnic Groups in Chicago." *American Journal of Sociology* 74(3):292–295.

Kirp, David L., John P. Dwyer, and Larry A. Rosenthal. 1995. *Our Town: Race, Housing and the Soul of Suburbia*. New Brunswick, NJ: Rutgers University Press.

Kleit, Rachel Garshick. 2001. "The Role of Social Networks in Scattered-site Public Housing Residents' Search for Jobs." *Housing Policy Debate* 12(3):541–573.

Kluegel, James R., and Eliot R. Smith. 1986. *Beliefs about Inequality: Americans' Views about What Ought to Be*. New York: Aldine De Gruyter.

Knoke, David. 1994. "Networks of Elite Structure and Decision-making." In *Advances in Social Network Analysis*. Eds. Stanley Wasserman and Joseph Galaskiewicz. Thousand Oaks, CA: Sage Publications.

Knox, Paul L. 1992. "The Packaged Landscapes of Post-suburban America." In *Urban Landscapes: International Perspectives*. Eds. J. W. R. Whitehand and P. J. Larkhan. London: Routledge and Kegan Paul.

Korva, Heidi. 2002. "In Large Finnish Cities, Foreigners May Soon Outnumber Swedish-Speaking Finns." *Helsingin Sanomat*, April 3. http://www.helsinki-hs.net/news.asp?id=20020403IE15.

Kostoff, Spiro. 1992. *The City Assembled: The Elements of Urban Form Through History*. Boston: Bulfinch Press.

Kotek, Joël. 1999. "Divided Cities in the European Cultural Context." *Progress in Planning* 52(3):227–237.

Krishnarayan, Vijay, and Huw Thomas. 1993. *Ethnic Minorities and the Planning System*. London: Royal Town Planning Institute.

Kros, Cynthia, and Shelly Greybe. 1994. "The Rainbow Nation vs. Healing Old Wounds." Report 2 of the History Curriculum Research Project. Cambridge: Cambridge University Press; Johannesburg: University of Witwatersrand Press.

Krueckeberg, Donald A. 1999. "The Grapes of Rent: A History of Renting in a Country of Owners." *Housing Policy Debate* 10(1):9–30.

Krysan, Maria, and Reynolds Farley. 2002. "The Residential Preferences of Blacks: Do They Explain Persistent Segregation?" *Social Forces* 80(3):937–980.

Kuhn, Jens. 2002. Personal interview with Marie Huchzermeyer. February 8, Department of Housing, Cape Metropolitan Council Administration, Cape Town.

Kymlicka, Will. 1998. *Finding Our Way.* Toronto: Oxford University Press.

Lazarus, Richard S. 1969. *Patterns of Adjustment and Human Effectiveness.* New York: McGraw-Hill.

Lee, Boon Thon. 1995. "Challenges of Superinduced Development: The Mega-urban Region of Kuala-Lumpur-Klang Valley." In *The Mega-urban Regions of Southeast Asia.* Eds. T. G. McGee and Ira M. Robinson, 315–327. Vancouver: University of British Columbia Press.

Lefebvre, Henri. 1992. *The Production of Space.* Oxford: Blackwell.

Leik, Robert K. 1966. A Measure of Ordinal Consensus. *Pacific Sociological Review* 9(2):85–90.

Lemon, Anthony, ed. 1991. *Homes Apart: South Africa's Segregated Cities.* Bloomington: Indiana University Press.

Lewis Mumford Center for Comparative Urban and Regional Research. 2001a. "Ethnic Diversity Grows, Neighborhood Integration Is at a Standstill." http://mumford1.dyndns.org/cen2000/report.html.

———. 2001b. "Metropolitan Racial and Ethnic Change—2000." Washington, DC-MD-VA-WV PMSA: http://www.albany.edu/mumford/census/.

Lewis, Paul G., and Elisa Barbour. 1999. *California Cities and the Local Sales Tax.* San Francisco: Public Policy Institute of California.

Ley, D. 1995. "Between Europe and Asia: The Case of the Missing Sequoias." *Ecumene* 2:185–210.

———. 2003. "Seeking homo economicus: The Canadian State and the Strange Story of the Business Immigration Program." *Annals of the Association of American Geographers* 93(2): 426–441.

Li, Peter S. 1988. *Ethnic Inequality in a Class Society.* Toronto: Wall and Thompson.

Lieberson, Stanley. 1963. *Ethnic Patterns in American Cities.* New York: Free Press of Glencoe.

———. 1981. "An Asymmetrical Approach to Segregation." In *Ethnic Segregation in Cities.* Eds. Ceri Peach, Vaughan Robinson, and Susan J. Smith, London: Croom Helm.

Lieberson, Stanley, and Mary Waters. 1988. *From Many Strands: Ethnic and Racial Groups in Contemporary America.* New York: Russell Sage.

Lin, Nan. 2001. "Toward a Network Theory of Social Capital." In *Social Capital: Theory and Research*. Eds. Nan Lin, Karen Cook, and Ronald S. Burt, 3–29. New York: Aldine De Gruyter.

Lipset, Seymour Martin. 1986. "Historical Tradition and National Characteristics: A Comparative Analysis of Canada and the United States." *Canadian Journal of Sociology* 11(2):113–155.

———. 1994. "The Social Requisites of Democracy Revisited." *American Sociological Review* 59(1):1–22.

Listokin, David. 1976. *Fair Share Housing Allocation*. New Brunswick, NJ: Center for Urban Policy Research.

Lo, Lucia, Valerie Preston, Shugang Wang, Katherine Reil, Edward Harvey, and Bobby Sui. 2000. *Immigrants' Economic Status in Toronto: Rethinking Settlement and Integration Strategies*. CERIS Working Paper No. 15. Toronto: Joint Centre of Excellence for Research on Immigration and Settlement.

Logan, John R., and Harvey L. Molotch. 1987. *Urban Fortunes: The Political Economy of Place*. Berkeley: University of California Press.

Long, Larry. 1988. *Migration and Residential Mobility in the United States*. New York: Russell Sage.

———. 1991. "Residential Mobility Differences Among Developed Countries." *International Regional Science Review* 14(2):133–147.

Loukaitou-Sideris, Anastasia, and Tridib Banerjee. 1998. *Urban Design Downtown: Poetics and Politics of Form*. Berkeley: University of California Press.

Lupton, Ruth, and Anne Power. 2002. "Social Exclusion and Neighborhoods." In *Understanding Social Exclusion*. Eds. John Hills, Julian Le Grand, and David Piachaud, 118–140. London: Oxford University Press.

Lynch, Kevin. 1981. *A Theory of Good City Form*. Cambridge: MIT Press.

Mabin, Alan. 1999. "From Hard Top to Soft Serve: Demarcation of Metropolitan Government in Johannesburg for the 1995 Elections." In *A Tale of Three Cities: The Democratization of South African Local Government*. Ed. R. Cameron, 159–200. Pretoria: Van Schaik.

Mabin, Alan, and D. Smit. 1997. "Reconstructing South Africa's Cities: The Making of Urban Planning 1900–2000." *Planning Perspectives* 12(2):193–223.

Madden, Janice Fanning. 2000. *Changes in Income Inequality Within U.S. Metropolitan Areas*. Kalamazoo, MI: W. E. Upjohn Institute for Employment Research.

Marcuse, Peter. 1962. "Benign Quotas." *Journal of Intergroup Relations* 3(2):101–116.

———. 1986. "The Beginnings of Public Housing in New York." *Journal of Urban History* 12(4):353–390.

———. 1997a. "Enclave, the Citadel, and the Ghetto: What Has Changed in the Post-fordist U.S. City." *Urban Affairs Review* 33(2):228–264.

———. 1997b. "Walls of Fear and Walls of Support." In *Architecture of Fear*. Ed. Nan Ellin, 101–114. New York: Princeton Architectural Press.

———. 1998. "Historic Preservation, Cultural Tourism, and Planning." *Trialog* 58(1):4–12.

Marcuse, Peter, and Ronald van Kempen. 2000. "Conclusion: A Changed Spatial Order." In *Globalizing Cities: A New Spatial Order.* Eds. Peter Marcuse and Ronald van Kempen, 294–275. Oxford: Blackwell.

———. 2002. *Of States and Cities: The Partitioning of Urban Space.* Oxford: Oxford University Press.

Marris, Peter, and Martin Rein. 1967. *Dilemmas of Social Reform: Poverty and Community Action in the United States.* New York: Atherton.

Marshall, Harvey. 1979. "White Movement to the Suburbs: A Comparison of Explanations." *American Sociological Review* 44:975–994.

Martin, Jonathan D. 2001. "Stein's Legacy: A Just City—Making the Affordable Housing/Diversity Connection in New Urbanism in Portland, Oregon." Master's thesis, Cornell University.

Martinez-Vazquez, Jorge, Mark Rider, and Mary Beth Walker. 1997. "Race and the Structure of Local Government." *Journal of Urban Economics* 41(2):281–300.

Marwell, Nicole P. 2000. "Social Networks and Social Capital as Resources for Neighborhood Revitalization." Ph.D. diss., University of Chicago.

Maspero, François. 1996. *Roissy Express: A Journey Through the Paris Suburbs.* London: Verso.

Massey, Douglas S. 1984. "Ethnic Residential Segregation: A Theoretical Synthesis and Empirical Review." *Sociology and Sociological Review* 69(3):315–350.

———. 1996. "The Age of Extremes: Concentrated Affluence and Poverty in the Twenty-first Century. *Demography* 33(4):395–412.

———. 2001. "Residential Segregation and Neighborhood Conditions in U.S. Metropolitan Areas. In *American Becoming: Racial Trends and Their Consequences. Vol. I.* Eds. Neil J. Smelser, William Julius Wilson, and Faith Mitchell, 391–434. Washington, DC: National Academy Press.

Massey, Douglas S., and Nancy A. Denton. 1988. "Suburbanization and Segregation in U.S. Metropolitan Areas." *American Journal of Sociology* 94(3):592–626.

———. 1993. *American Apartheid: Segregation and the Making of the Underclass.* Cambridge: Harvard University Press.

Massey, Douglas S., and Mitchell L. Eggers. 1990. "The Ecology of Inequality: Minorities and the Concentration of Poverty, 1970–1980." *American Journal of Sociology* 95(5):1153–1188.

Massey, Douglas S., and Mary J. Fisher. 2000. "How Segregation Concentrates Poverty." *Ethnic and Racial Studies* 23(4):670–691.

Massey, Douglas S., Andrew B. Gross, and Kumiko Shibuya. 1994. "Migration, Segregation, and the Geographic Concentration of Poverty." *American Sociological Review* 59:425–445.

Mattoon, Richard H. 1995. "Can Alternative Forms of Governance Help Metropolitan Areas?" *Economic Perspectives* 19(6):20–32.

Mayekiso, Mzwanele. 1996. *Township Politics: Civic Struggles for a New South Africa*. New York: Monthly Review Press.

MacDonald, Heather. 1997. "Comment on Sandra J. Newman and Ann B. Schnare, And a Suitable Living Environment: The Failure of Housing Programs to Deliver on Neighborhood Quality." *Housing Policy Debate* 8(4):755–762.

MacLeod, Murdo. 2003. "Muslims Target Schools for Takeover." *Scotland on Sunday*, November 23: 3.

McLoughlin, Brian. 1969. *Urban and Regional Planning: A Systems Approach*. London: Faber and Faber.

McPherson, Miller, Lynn Smith-Lovin, and James M. Cook. 2001. "Birds of a Feather: Homophily in Social Networks." *Annual Review of Sociology* 27:415–444.

Meo, Nick, and Lucy Adams. 2003. "Jute, Jam and Jihad; Dundee Is Producing a New British Export—Islamic Fundamentalists." *The Sunday Times*, September 21: 23.

Mgedezi, L. 1999. Report, Western Cape Land Convener. February. *UTschani BuyaKhuluma, People's Dialogue Newsletter* 11(March):4.

Miller, John J. 1998. *The Unmaking of Americans: How Multiculturalism Has Undermined the Assimilation Ethic*. New York: Free Press.

Mitchell, Clyde. 1969. "The Concept and Use of Social Networks." *In Social Networks in Urban Situations*. Ed. Clyde Mitchell. Manchester: Manchester University Press.

Mnyanda, Lukanyo. 1998. "There Is No Shortage of Ideas about How Johannesburg's City Centre Can Repave Its Streets with Gold. Stakeholders Must Make It Happen." *Business Day* (Johannesburg) January 29.

Møller, V., and L. Schlemmer. 1980. *Quantity or Quality? A Survey Evaluation of Housing in Relation to the Quality of South African Black Township Life*. Durban: Centre for Applied Social Sciences, University of Natal.

Morris, Nigel. 2003. "Minorities to Outnumber Whites in London's Schools." *The Independent*, December 3:9.

Morrow-Jones, Hazel A. 1998. "Repeat Homebuyers and American Urban Structure." *Urban Geography* 19(8):679–694.

Mphafudi, Lucky. 2001. Personal communication to Marie Huchzermeyer, May. Chief Town Planner, Human Settlements Division, Department of Housing, Pretoria.

Munnell, Alicia H., Lynn E. Browned, James McEneaney, and Geoffrey M. B. Tootell. 1996. "Mortgage Lending in Boston: Interpreting HMDA Data." *American Economic Review* 86(1):25–53.

Murdie, Robert, and Carlos Teixeira. 2000. "Towards a Comfortable Neighborhood and Appropriate Housing: Immigrant Experience in Toronto." Working Paper No. 10. Toronto: Joint Centre of Excellence for Research on Immigration and Settlement.

Murtagh, Brendan. 1995. *Segregated Space in Belfast: Principles and Practice.* Belfast: Community Relations Council.

———. 2002. *The Politics of Territory: Policy and Segregation in Northern Ireland.* Basingstoke: Palgrave.

Musso, Juliet. 1999. *Limits to Tiebout Sorting: City Formation in California.* Institute for Civic Enterprise WP-99-03. School of Policy, Planning and Development, University of Southern California.

Musterd, Sako. 2001. "Urban Segregation, Integration and the Welfare Regime: On Causes and Effects in Multi-layered Contexts." Paper presented at Palme Days, October 6. Malmö, Sweden.

Musterd, Sako, and Wim Ostendorf, eds. 1998. *Urban Segregation and the Welfare State: Inequality and Exclusion in Western Cities.* London: Routledge and Kegan Paul.

Myers, Dowell, and Julie Park. 2001. "Racially Balanced Cities in Southern California, 1980–2000." Public Research Report No. 2001-05. Population Dynamics Group, University of Southern California. www.usc.edu/sppd/census2000.

Myles, John. 2002. "Residential Segregation and Neighbourhood Attainment Among Toronto's Visible Minorities." Toronto: Department of Sociology, University of Toronto.

Nechyba, Thomas. 2001. "School Finance, Spatial Segregation and the Nature of Communities: Lessons for Developing Countries?" Paper presented at the International Seminar on Segregation in the City, Lincoln Institute of Land Policy, Cambridge, July 25–28.

Nelson, Michael A. 1990. "Decentralization of the Subnational Public Sector: An Empirical Analysis of the Determinants of Local Government Structure in Metropolitan Areas of the U.S." *Southern Economic Journal* 57(2): 443–457.

Newman, David. 1985. "Integration and Ethnic Spatial Concentration: The Changing Distribution of the Anglo-Jewish Community." *Transactions, Institute of British Geographers* NS(10):360–370.

Nuttall, Jolyon. 1997. *The First Five Years: The Story of the Independent Development Trust.* Cape Town: Independent Development Trust.

Nyden, Philip, John Lukehart, Michael T. Maly, and William Peterman. 1998. "Neighborhood Racial and Ethnic Diversity in U.S. Cities." *Cityscape* 4(2):1–18.

Nyden, Philip, Michael Maly, and John Lukehart. 1997. "The Emergence of Stable Racially and Ethnically Diverse Urban Communities: A Case Study of Nine U.S. Communities." *Housing Policy Debate* 8(2):491–534.

O'Connor, Alice. 2001. "Understanding Inequality in the Late Twentieth-century Metropolis: New Perspectives on the Enduring Racial Divide." In *Urban Inequality: Evidence from Four Cities.* Eds. Alice O'Connor, Chris Tilly, and Lawrence D. Bobo, 267–271. New York: Russell Sage.

Ogbu, John. 1978. *Minority Education and Caste: The American System in Cross-cultural Perspective.* New York: Academic Press.

Oldham Independent Review Team. 2001. *Oldham Independent Review: Panel Report.* Oldham: Oldham Independent Review.

Oliver, Melvin L., and Thomas Shapiro. 1995. *Black Wealth/White Wealth: A New Perspective on Racial Inequality.* New York: Routledge and Kegan Paul.

Olsen, Donald J. 1986. *City as a Work of Art: London, Paris, Vienna.* New Haven: Yale University Press.

O'Meara, Dan. 1996. *Forty Lost Years: The Apartheid State and the Politics of the National Party, 1948–1994.* Athens: Ohio University Press.

Ong, A., and D. M. Nonini. 1997. *Underground Empires: The Cultural Politics of Modern Chinese Transnationalism.* London: Routledge and Kegan Paul.

Orfield, Gary, and John T. Yun. 1999. "Resegregation in American Schools." Report of Civil Rights Project, Harvard University, Cambridge, June.

Orfield, Myron. 1997. *Metropolitics: A Regional Agenda for Community and Stability.* Washington, DC: Brookings Institution Press; Cambridge: Lincoln Institute of Land Policy.

———. 2002. *American Metropolitics: The New Suburban Reality.* Washington, DC: Brookings Institution.

Orr, Larry, Judith D. Feins, Robin Jacob, Erik Beecroft, Lisa Sanbonmatsu, Lawrence F. Katz, Jeffrey B. Liebman, and Jeffrey R. Kling. 2003. *Moving to Opportunity Interim Impacts Evaluation.* Prepared by Abt Associates Inc. and the National Bureau of Economic Research for the U.S. Department of Housing and Urban Development. Washington, DC: Housing and Urban Development.

Oser, Alan S. 1996. "Immigrants Again Renew Sunset Park." *New York Times,* Real Estate, December 1: 1,6.

Ostrom, Elinor, Charles Tiebout, and Robert Warren. 1961. Organization of Government in Metropolitan Areas: A Theoretical Inquiry. *American Political Science Review* 55:83–184.

O'Sullivan, Arthur. 2002. *Urban Economics.* 5th ed. Boston: McGraw-Hill Irwin.

Pagano, Michael, and Ann O'M. Bowman. 1995. *Cityscapes and Capital: The Politics of Urban Development.* Baltimore: John Hopkins University Press.

Park, Robert Ezra. 1926. "The Urban Community as a Spatial Pattern and a Moral Order." In *Urban Community: Selected Papers from the Proceedings of the American Sociological Society.* Ed. Ernest Watson Burgess, Chicago: University of Chicago Press.

Park, Robert. E., Ernest Burgess, and Roderick D. McKenzie. 1967. *The City,* with an introduction by Morris Janowitz. Chicago: University of Chicago Press.

Parnell, Susan, Sophie Oldfield, and Beate Lohnert. 1998. "Post-apartheid Social Polarisations: The Creation of Sub-urban Identities in Cape Town." *South African Geographical Journal* 80:86–92.

Pastor, Jr., Manuel. 2001. "Geography and Opportunity." In *American Becoming: Racial Trends and Their Consequences.* Vol. I. Eds. Neil J. Smelser, William

Julius Wilson, and Faith Mitchell, 435–468. Washington, DC: National Academy Press.

Pattillo-McCoy, Mary. 2000. "The Limits of Out-migration for the Black Middle Class." *Journal of Urban Affairs* 22(3):225–241.

Peach, Ceri. 1975. "Introduction." In *Urban Social Segregation,* Ed. Ceri Peach, 1–17. London: Longman.

———. 1980a. "Ethnic Segregation and Intermarriage." *Annals of the Association of American Geographers* 70(3):371–381.

———. 1980b. "Which Triple Melting Pot?" *Ethnic and Racial Studies* 3(1):1–16.

———. 1981. "Conflicting Interpretations of Segregation." In *Social Interaction and Ethnic Segregation.* Eds. Peter Jackson and Susan J. Smith. London: Academic Press.

———. 1996. "Good Segregation, Bad Segregation." *Planning Perspectives* 11:379–398.

———. 1998. "Loïc Wacquant's Three Pernicious Premises in the Study of the American Ghetto." *International Urban and Regional Research* 22(3):507–510.

Peattie, Lisa. 1994. "An Argument for Slums." *Journal of Planning Education and Research* 13(2):136–142.

Pendall, Rolf. 1995. "Residential Growth Controls and Racial and Ethnic Diversity: Making and Breaking the Chain of Exclusion." Ph.D. diss., University of California, Berkeley.

———. 1999. "Do Land-use Controls Cause Sprawl?" *Environment and Planning B: Planning and Design* 26(4):555–571.

People's Dialogue. 1999. *Getting to the Highway: The South African Homeless People's Federation, People's Dialogue and the uTshani Fund.* Cape Town: People's Dialogue on Land and Shelter.

Perin, Constance. 1977. *Everything in Its Place: Social Order and Land Use in America.* Princeton: Princeton University Press.

Persky, Joseph, and Wim Wiewel. 2000. *When Corporations Leave Town: The Costs and Benefits of Metropolitan Job Sprawl.* Detroit: Wayne State University Press.

Peterson, George E., and Adele V. Harrell. 1992. "Introduction: Inner-city Isolation and Opportunity." In *Drugs, Crime, and Social Isolation: Barriers to Urban Opportunity.* Eds. Adele V. Harrell and George E. Peterson, 1–26. Washington, DC: Urban Institute.

Philpott, Thomas. 1978. *The Slum and the Ghetto.* New York: Oxford University Press.

Pittenger, William L. 1996. "Managing the Appraisal Component of Fair Lending Compliance." *ABA Bank Compliance* (March/April): 11–15.

Planning and Development Collaborative International (PADCO). 1998. *Diagnóstico rápido: el mercado de terrenos y los barrios marginales, ciudad de Tegucigalpa.* Working Paper. Washington, DC: Inter-American Development Bank.

PolicyLink. 2000. "Beyond Gentrification Toolkit." http://www.policylink.org/gentrification/.

Poole, Michael A., and Frederick W. Boal. 1973. "Religious Residential Segregation in Belfast in Mid-1969: A Multi-level Analysis." In *Social Patterns in Cities*. Eds. B. D. Clark and M. B. Gleave, 1–40. Institute of British Geographers Special Publication No. 5. London: Institute of British Geographers.

Popkin, Susan J., Mary K. Cunningham, and William T. Woodley. 2003. "Residents at Risk: A Profile of Ida B. Wells and Madden Park." Prepared for the Ford Foundation. http://www.urban.org/uploadedPDF/310824_residents_ at_risk.pdf.

Popkin, Susan J., George Galster, Kenneth Temkin, Carla Herbig, Diane K. Levy, and Elise Richer. 2003. "Obstacles to Desegregating Public Housing: Lessons Learned from Eight Consent Decrees." *Journal of Policy Analysis and Management* 22(2):179–199.

Popkin, Susan J., Diane K. Levy, Laura E. Harris, Jennifer Corney, Mary K. Cunningham, and Larry Buron. 2002. *HOPE VI Panel Study: Baseline Report. Final Report. September 2002*. Submitted to the Annie E. Casey Foundation; the John D. and Catherine T. MacArthur Foundation, the Rockefeller Foundation, and the U.S. Department of Housing and Urban Development. Washington, DC: Urban Institute.

Popper, Frank J. 1981. "Siting LULUs." *Planning* 47(4):12–15.

Porter, Michael. 2001. "Regions and the New Economics of Competition." In *Global City-regions*. Ed. Allen J. Scott. New York: Oxford University Press.

Portes, Alejandro. 1998. "Social Capital: Its Origins and Applications in Modern Sociology." *Annual Review of Sociology* 24(1):1–24.

Portes, Alejandro, and Robert Bach. 1985. *Latin Journey*. Berkeley: University of California Press.

Portes, Alejandro, and Ruben Rumbaut. 1996. *Immigrant America*. Berkeley: University of California Press.

Poulantzas, Nicos. 1975. *Classes in Contemporary Capitalism*. Trans. by David Fernbach. London: New Left Books.

Powell, Dianne. 1995. *Out West: Perceptions of Sydney's Western Suburbs*. Sydney: Allen and Unwin.

powell, john. 1999. "Achieving Racial Justice: What's Sprawl Got to Do with It?" *Poverty and Race* 8(5):3.

———. 2002. "Sprawl, Fragmentation, and the Persistence of Racial Inequality: Limiting Civil Rights by Fragmenting Space." In *Urban Sprawl: Causes, Consequences, and Policy Responses*. Ed. Gregory D. Squires. 73–118. Washington, DC: Urban Institute Press.

Priemus, Hugo. 1998. "Redifferentiation of the Urban Housing Stock in the Netherlands: A Strategy to Prevent Spatial Segregation?" *Housing Studies* 13(3):301–310.

———. 2000. "Colourful Districts: West European Cities Moving Towards Multi-ethnicity." In *Ethnicity and Housing: Accommodating Differences*. Ed. Frederick W. Boal, 225–232. Aldershot: Ashgate.

Pulido, Laura. 2000. "Rethinking Environmental Racism: White Privilege and Urban Development in Southern California." *Annals of the Association of America Geographers* 90(1):68–82.

Putnam, Robert D. 1993. *Making Democracy Work: Civic Traditions in Modern Italy.* Princeton: Princeton University Press.

———. 1996. "Bowling Alone: America's Declining Social Capital." In *The Global Resurgence of Democracy.* Eds. Larry Diamond and Marc F. Plattner, 290–306. Baltimore, MD: Johns Hopkins University Press.

———. 2000. *Bowling Alone: The Collapse and Revival of American Community.* New York: Simon & Schuster.

Quillian, Lincoln. 1999. "Migration Patterns and the Growth of High-poverty Neighborhoods, 1970–1990." *American Journal of Sociology* 105(1):1–37.

Raphael, Steven, and Michael A. Stoll. 2002. "Modest Progress: The Narrowing Spatial Mismatch Between Blacks and Jobs in the 1990s." Center on Urban and Metropolitan Policy, The Brookings Institution, Washington, D.C.

Rapoport, Amos. 1979. "Review of *Everything in Its Place: Social Order and Land Use in America,*" by Constance Perin. *Journal of Architectural Research* 7(1):34–37.

———. 1980/81. "Neighborhood Heterogeneity or Homogeneity?" *Architecture and Behaviour* 1(1):65–77.

———. 1990. *The Meaning of the Built Environment: A Nonverbal Communication Approach.* With a new epilogue by the author. Tucson: University of Arizona Press.

Ray, Brian. 1999. Plural Geographies in Canadian Cities: Interpreting Immigrant Residential Spaces in Toronto and Montreal. *Canadian Journal of Regional Science* 22(1/2):65–86.

Reitz, Jeffrey. 1980. *The Survival of Ethnic Groups.* Toronto: McGraw-Hill Ryerson.

Republic of South Africa. 2001. "Housing Amendment Act No. 4." *Government Gazette,* July 15, 432(22388):549.

Rodrik, Dani. 1999. *New Global Economy in Developing Countries: Making Openness Work.* Baltimore: John Hopkins University Press.

Rosenthal, Erich. 1961. "Acculturation Without Assimilation?" The Jewish Community of Chicago, Illinois. *American Journal of Sociology* 66(3):275–288.

Ross, Stephan, and John Yinger. 1999. "Sorting and Voting: A Review of the Literature on Urban Public Finance." In *Handbook of Regional and Urban Economics,* Vol. 3. Eds. Edwin S. Mills and P. Chesire, 281–300. Amsterdam: North-Holland Publishers.

Rubinowitz, Leonard S., and James E. Rosenbaum. 2000. *Crossing the Class and Color Lines: From Public Housing to White Suburbia.* Chicago: University of Chicago Press.

Rusk, David. 1999. *Inside Game/Outside Game: Winning Strategies for Saving Urban America.* Washington, DC: Brookings Institution Press.

Sampson, Robert J., Stephen Raudenbush, and Felton Earls. 1997. "Neighborhoods and Violent Crime: A Multi-level Study of Collective Efficacy." *Science* 277(5328):918–924.

Sandercock, Leonie. 1998. *Towards Cosmopolis*. New York: John Wiley.

Sassen, Saskia. 2000. *Cities in a World Economy*. Thousand Oaks, CA: Pine Forge Press.

Scheepers, Suzette. 2001. "Stop Sale of RDP Houses—By Law." *Housing in Southern Africa*. April:1.

Schill, Michael H., and Samantha Friedman. 1999. "The Fair Housing Amendments Act of 1988: The First Decade." *Cityscape* 4 (3):57–78.

Schuman, Howard, Charlotte Steeh, Lawrence D. Bobo, and Maria Krysan. 1997. *Racial Attitudes in America: Trends and Interpretations*. Cambridge: Harvard University Press.

Schwemm, Robert G. 1996. "Housing Discrimination and the Appraisal Industry." In *Mortgage Lending, Racial Discrimination, and Federal Policy*. Eds. John Goering and Ron Wienk, 365–397. Washington, DC: Urban Institute Press.

Sciolino, Elaine. 2004. "French Assembly Votes to Ban Religious Symbols in Schools." *New York Times*, February 11:A3.

Sclar, Elliott. 2002. "Review of *Place Matters: Metropolitics for the Twenty-first Century*," by Peter Dreier, John Mollenkopf, and Todd Swanstrom. *Dissent* (Spring):120–123.

Scott, Allen J. 2000. "Global City-regions: Economic Planning and Dilemmas in a Neo-liberal World." In *Urban-Suburban Interdependencies*. Eds. Rosalind Greenstein and Wim Wiewell, 119–140. Cambridge: Lincoln Institute of Land Policy.

Scott, Allen J., and Edward Soja, eds. 1996. *The City: Los Angeles and Urban Theory at the End of Twentieth Century*. Berkeley, CA: University of California Press.

Scott, Janny. 2001. "White Flight: This Time Toward Harlem." *New York Times*, February 25:18.

Sellers, Jefferey M. 1999. "Public Goods and the Politics of Segregation: An Analysis and Cross-national Comparison." *Journal of Urban Affairs* 21(2):237–262.

Servon, Lisa J. 1999. *Bootstrap Capital: Microenterprises and the American Poor*. Washington, DC: Brookings Institution Press.

Shepherd, Robin. 2004, "In Europe, Is It a Matter of Fear, or Loathing?" *Washington Post*, January 25:B2.

Shiller, Robert J., and Allan N. Weiss. 1999. "Home Equity Insurance." *Journal of Real Estate Finance and Economics* 19(1):21–47.

Short, Kathleen. 2001. *Experimental Poverty Measures 1999*. Washington, DC: U.S. Census Bureau.

Siemiatycki, Myer, Tim Rees, Rozana Ng, and Khan Rahi. 2001. "Integrating Community Diversity in Toronto: On Whose Terms?" CERIS Working Paper

No. 14. Toronto: Joint Centre of Excellence for Research on Immigration and Settlement.

Sigelman, Lee, and Susan Welch. 1994. *Black Americans' Views of Racial Inequality: The Dream Deferred*. 2nd ed. Cambridge: Cambridge University Press.

Silver, Josh. 2001. Email Message to Membership of National Community Reinvestment Coalition, January 26.

Simmel, Georg. 1955. *Conflict: The Web of Group Affiliations*. Essays translated by Kurt H. Wolff and Reinhard Bendix, with a forward by Everett C. Hughes. Glencoe, IL: Free Press.

Singer, Audrey, Samantha Friedman, Ivan Cheung, and Marie Price 2001. *The World in a ZIP Code: Greater Washington, DC as a New Region of Immigration*. Washington, DC: Center on Urban and Metropolitan Policy, Brookings Institution Survey Series.

60 Minutes. 2002. "Going home." [October 27] Transcript. Burrelle's Information Services. CBS Worldwide, Inc.

Small, C. 2000. "National Identity in Quebec's Changing Society: Spatial Differentiation in Montreal." Research Paper 57. Oxford University, School of Geography.

Small, Mario Luis, and Katherine Newman. 2001. "Urban Poverty after the Truly Disadvantaged: The Rediscovery of Family, the Neighborhood, and Culture." *Annual Review of Sociology* 27(1):23–45.

Smit, J. A. 1999. "Developing Housing Environments for the New Millennium." Paper presented at the Institute for Housing in Southern Africa Conference, Nelspruit, October 17–20.

Smith, David J., and Gerald Chambers. 1991. *Inequality in Northern Ireland*. Oxford: Clarendon Press.

Soja, Ed, and Allan Scott. 1998. *The City: Los Angeles and Urban Theory at the End of the Twentieth Century*. Los Angeles: University of California Press.

South, Scott J., and Kyle D. Crowder. 1997. "Escaping Distressed Neighborhoods: Individual. Community, and Metropolitan Influences." *American Journal of Sociology* 102:1040–1084.

———. 1998. "Leaving the 'hood': Residential Mobility Between Black, White, and Integrated Neighborhoods." *American Sociological Review* 63:17–26.

Sparrow, Malcolm. 2000. *The Regulatory Craft*. Washington, DC: Brookings Institution Press.

Sprawl Hits the Wall: Confronting the Realities of Metropolitan Los Angeles. 2001. Southern California Studies Center, University of Southern California. Los Angeles and Washington, DC: Brookings Institution and Center on Urban and Metropolitan Policy.

Squires, Gregory D. 1994. *Capital and Communities in Black and White: The Intersections of Race, Class, and Uneven Development*. Albany: State University of New York Press.

———, ed. 1997. *Insurance Redlining: Disinvestment, Reinvestment, and the Evolving Role of Financial Institution.* Washington, DC: Urban Institute Press.

———. 2002. *Urban Sprawl: Causes, Consequences and Policy Responses.* Washington, DC: Urban Institute Press.

Squires, Gregory D., Samantha Friedman, and Catherine E. Saidat. 2001. "Housing Segregation in the United States: Does Race Matter?" Paper presented at the International Seminar on Segregation in the City, Lincoln Institute of Land Policy, Cambridge, July 25–28.

Squires, Gregory D., Sally O'Connor, Michale Grover, and James Walrath. 1999. "Housing Affordability in the Milwaukee Metropolitan Area: A Matter of Income, Race, and Policy." *Journal of Affordable Housing and Community Development Law* 9(1):34–73.

Stack, Carol. 1974. *All Our Kin: Strategies for Survival in a Black Community.* New York: Harper and Row.

Starr, Kevin. 1991. *Material Dreams: Southern California Through the 1920s.* New York: Oxford University Press.

Stein, Clarence S. 1957. *Toward New Towns for America.* Rev. ed. New York: Reinhold Publishing.

Stiglitz, Joseph E. 2002. *Globalization and Its Discontents.* New York: W. W. Norton.

Stoker, Gerry. 1995. "Regime Theory and Urban Politics." In *Theories of Urban Politics.* Eds. David Judge, Gerry Stoker, and Harold Wolman, 54–71. Thousand Oaks, CA: Sage Publications.

Stone, Clarence N. 1989. *Regime Politics: Governing Atlanta, 1946-1988.* Lawrence: University of Kansas Press.

Sunday Times, Johannesburg, 2001, Letter to the editor, April 15.

Swarms, Rachel. 2002. Mingling despite mistrust in South Africa. *New York Times* December 9:A1, A10

Taeuber, Karl E., and Alma Taeuber. 1964. "The Negro As an Immigrant Group." *American Journal of Sociology* 69(4):374–382.

———. 1965. *Negroes in Cities.* Chicago: Aldine.

Thernstrom, Stephan, and Abigail Thernstrom. 1997. *America in Black and White: One Nation, Indivisible.* New York: Simon & Schuster.

Thomas, June Manning, and Marsha Ritzdorf, eds. 1997. *Urban Planning and the African American Community: In the Shadows.* Thousand Oaks, CA: Sage Publications.

Thomas, Liz, and Jenny Howard. 1998. "AIDS and Development Planning." In *Implications of AIDS for Demography and Policy in South Africa.* Ed. Alan Whiteside. Pietermaritzburg: University of Natal Press.

Thompson, Heather Ann. 1999. "Rethinking the Politics of White Flight in the Postwar City: Detroit, 1945–1980." *Journal of Urban History* 25(2):163–198.

Tiebout, Charles. 1956. "A Pure Theory of Local Expenditures." *Journal of Political Economy* 64:415–424.

Tilly, Chris, Philip Moss, Joleen Kirschenman, and Ivy Kennedy. 2001. "Space as a Signal: How Employers Perceive Neighborhoods in Four Metropolitan Labor Markets." In *Urban Inequality: Evidence from Four Cities*. Eds. Alice O'Connor, Chris Tilly, and Lawrence D. Bobo, 304–338. New York: Russell Sage.

Tomlinson, Mary. 1998. "South Africa's New Housing Policy: An Assessment of the First Two Years, 1994–1996." *International Journal of Urban and Regional Research* 22(1):137–146.

———. 2001. "New Housing Delivery Model: The Presidential Job Summit Housing Pilot Project." International Union for Housing Finance: http://www.housingfinance.org/Whatsnewframe.htm.

Tomlinson, Richard. 2001. "Housing Policy in Context of HIV/AIDS and Globalization." *International Journal of Urban and Regional Research* 25(3): 649–657.

Troper, Harold. 2000. *History of Immigration Since the Second World War: From Toronto "the Good" to Toronto "the World City."* CERIS Working Paper No.14. Toronto: Joint Centre of Excellence for Research on Immigration and Settlement.

Turner, Margery Austin. 1998. "Moving Out of Poverty: Expanding Mobility and Choice Through Tenant-based Housing Assistance. *Housing Policy Debate* 9(2):373–394.

Turner, Margery Austin, Stephern L. Ross, George Galster, and John Yinger. 2002. *Discrimination in Metropolitan Housing Markets: National Results from Phase I of HDS 2000*. Report prepared for the U.S. Department of Housing and Urban Development. Washington, DC: Urban Institute Press.

Unidad de Programas y Proyectos de Vivienda (UPPV). 2001. *Sector vivienda y ordenamiento urbano: reunión de seguimiento de la reconstrucción y transformación nacional*. Tegucigalpa: Secretaría de Obras Públicas, Transporte, y Vivienda (SOPTRAVI).

United Nations Development Program (UNDP). 2000. *Informe sobre desarrollo humano: Honduras 2000*. Tegucigalpa: United Nations.

U.S. Bureau of the Census. 1997. *United States Census 2000 Participant Statistical Areas Program Gidelines: Census Tracks Block Groups (BGs), Census-designated Places (CDPs), Census County Divisions (CCDs)*. Washington, D.C.

U.S. Bureau of the Census. 2000. Unpublished data derived from March Current Population Survey, 1997–1999. Ethnic and Hispanic Statistics Branch, Population Division, Bureau of the Census, Washington, D.C.

———. 2001a. *Profiles of General Demographic Characteristics — 2000 Census of Population and Housing: United States*. Washington, D.C.

———. 2001b. *Profiles of General Demographic Characteristics — 2000 Census of Population and Housing: District of Columbia*. Washington, D.C.

———. 2001c. *Profiles of General Demographic Characteristics — 2000 Census of Population and Housing: Maryland*. Washington, D.C.

——. 2001d. *Profiles of General Demographic Characteristics—2000 Census of Population and Housing: Virginia.* Washington, D.C.

——. 2001e. Table IE-1. Selected Measures of Household Income Dispersion: 1967 to 1999. April 23. http://www.census.gov/hhes/income/histinc/ie1.html.

U.S. Department of Housing and Urban Development. 2002. "HUD Releases Report: Discrimination in Metropolitan Housing Markets 1989-2000." Report shows housing discrimination declining but more work to be done. News release 7 November. www.hud.gov:80/news/release.cfm?content=pro2-138.cfm.

U.S. Federal Housing Administration. 1938. *Underwriting Manual.* Washington, DC: GPO.

U.S. General Accounting Office. 1995. *Poverty Measurement: Adjusting for Geographic Cost-of-living Differences.* Washington, DC: GPO.

Van Davidson, William. 1994. "Honduras." In *Latin American Urbanization: Historical Profiles of Majors Cities.* Ed. G. Greenfield. New York: Greenwood Press.

Van Kempen, Eva. 2002. "Poverty Pockets and Social Exclusion: On the Role of Place in Shaping Social Inequality." In *Of States and Cities: The Partitioning of Urban Space.* Eds. Peter Marcuse and Ronald van Kempen, 240-257. New York: Oxford University Press.

Van Kempen, Ronald A., and Sule Özüekren. 1998. "Ethnic Segregation in Cities: New Forms and Explanations in a Dynamic World." *Urban Studies* 35(10):1631-1656.

Vandell, Kerry D. 1995. "Market Factors Affecting Spatial Heterogeneity Among Urban Neighborhoods." *Housing Policy Debate* 6(1):103-139.

Varady, David P., 1979. *Ethnic Minorities in Urban Areas: A Case Study of Racially Changing Communities.* Boston: Kluwer.

Varady, David P., and Carole C. Walker. 2003a. "Housing Vouchers and Residential Mobility." *Journal of Planning Literature* (18)1:17-30.

——. 2003b. "Using Housing Vouchers to Move to the Suburbs: How Do Families Fare?" *Housing Policy Debate* 14(3):347-382.

——. 2003c. "Using Housing Vouchers to Move to the Suburbs: The Alameda County, California, Experience." *Urban Affairs Review* 39(2):143-180.

Varady, David P, Carole C. Walker, and Xinhao Wang. 2001. "Using Housing Vouchers to Open Up the Suburbs: Do the Poor Become Better Off?" Paper prepared for the International Seminar on Segregation in the City, Lincoln Institute of Land Policy, Cambridge, July 25-28.

Varenne, Herve. 1996. "Love and Liberty: The Contemporary American Family." In *A History of the Family,* introduced by Claude Lévi-Strauss and Georges Duby; translated by Sarah Hanbury Tenison, Rosemary Morris, and Andrew Wilson, Vol.2. Eds. André Burguire, C. Klapisch-Zuber, M. Segalen, and F. Zonabend. Cambridge: Belknap Press of Harvard University Press.

Von Hoffman, Alexander. 1998. "High Ambitions: The Past and Future of American Low-income Housing Policy." In *New Directions in Urban Public Housing.*

Eds. David P. Varady, Wolfgang F. E. Preiser, and Francis Russell, 3–22. New Brunswick, NJ: Center for Urban Policy Research.

Wacquant, Loïc. 1997. "Three Pernicious Premises in the Study of the American Ghetto." *International Journal of Urban and Regional Research* 21(2): 341–353.

Wacquant, Loïc, and William Julius Wilson. 1993. "The Cost of Racial and Class Exclusion in the Inner City." In *The Ghetto Underclass: Social Science Perspectives.* Ed. William Julius Wilson, 76–101. Annals of the Academy of Political and Social Studies, Newbury Park, CA: Sage Publications.

Waldinger, Roger. 1986. *Through the Eye of the Needle: Immigrants and Enterprise in New York's Garment Trade.* New York: New York University Press.

———. 1990. "Ethnic Business in Sunset Park, Appendix E." In *New People in Old Neighborhoods,* Ed. Louis Winnick. New York: Russell Sage.

———. 1996. "Ethnicity and Opportunity in the Plural City." In *Ethnic Los Angeles.* Eds. Roger Waldinger and Mehdi Bozorgmehr, 445–470. New York: Russell Sage.

Waldman, Amy. 2001a. "In Harlem's Ravaged Heart, Revival." *New York Times,* February 18: 1, 14–15.

———. 2001b. "Lines That Divide, Ties That Bind." *New York Times,* February 21: 1, 14–15.

———. 2002. "How in a Little English Town Jihad Found Young Converts." *New York Times,* April 24: A1,12.

Warren, Mark R., J. Philip Thompson, and Susan Saegert. 2001. "The Role of Social Capital in Combating Poverty." In *Social Capital and Poor Communities.* Eds. Susan Saegert, J. Philip Thompson, and Mark R. Warren, 1–28. New York: Russell Sage.

Wassmer, Robert W., and Ronald C. Fischer. 2000. *Tiebout, Time, and Transition in the Structure of Local Government in U.S. Metropolitan Areas.* Working paper. Sacramento: Graduate Program in Public Policy and Administration, California State University, Sacramento. http://www.csu.edu/indiv/w/wassmerr/wpaperou.htm.

Waterman, Stanley, and Barry A. Kosmin. 1986a. "Residential Patterns and Processes: A Study of Jews in Three London Boroughs." *Transactions, Institute of British Geographers,* NS(3):79–95.

———. 1986b. "Mapping an Underenumerated Ethnic Population: Jews in London." *Ethnic and Racial Studies* 9(4):484–501.

Weiss, Carol H. 1995. "Nothing as Practical as Good Theory: Exploring Theory-based Evaluation for Comprehensive Community Initiatives for Children and Families." In *New Approaches to Evaluating Community Initiatives: Concepts, Methods, and Contexts.* Eds. James Connell, Anne Kubisch, and Lisbeth Schorr. New York: Aspen Institute.

Wellman, Berry, and Kenneth Frank. 2001. "Network Capital in a Multi-level World: Getting Support from Personal Communities." In *Social Capital: Theory and Research*. Eds. Nan Lin, Karen Cook, and Ronald S. Burt, 233–273. New York: Aldine de Gruyter.

White, Paul. 1998. "The Settlement Patterns of Developed World Migrants in London." *Urban Studies* 35(10):1725–1744.

Wilson, Alan. 2003. "'Hitman' Tells Court of Threat to Kill Daughter." *Dundee Courier and Advertiser*, November 5:1–2.

Wilson, Franklin D., and Roger B. Hammer. 2001. "Ethnic Residential Segregation and Its Consequences." In *Urban Inequality: Evidence from Four Cities*. Eds. Alice O'Connor, Chris Tilly, and Lawrence D. Bobo, 267–271. New York: Russell Sage.

Wilson, James Q. 2004. "What Makes a Terrorist?" *City Journal* 14(1): 24–35.

Wilson, William Julius. 1978. *The Declining Significance of Race: Blacks and Changing American Institutions*. Chicago: University of Chicago Press.

———. 1987. *The Truly Disadvantaged: The Inner City, the Underclass, and Public Policy*. Chicago: University of Chicago Press.

———. 1991. "Studying Inner-city Social Dislocations: The Challenge of Public Agenda Research." *American Sociological Review* 56(1):1–14.

———. 1996. *When Work Disappears: The World of the New Urban Poor*. New York: Knopf.

———. 1999. *The Bridge Over the Racial Divide: Rising Inequality and Coalition Politics*. Berkeley: University of California Press.

Winnick, Louis, ed. 1990. *New People in Old Neighborhoods*. New York: Russell Sage.

Wirth, Louis. 1928. *The Ghetto*. Chicago: University of Chicago Press.

———. 1938. "Urbanism as a Way of Life." *American Journal of Sociology* 40(1):1–24.

Woolcock, Michael. 1998. "Social Capital and Economic Development: Toward a Theoretical Synthesis and Policy Framework." *Theory and Society* 27(2):151–208.

Woolcock, Michael, and Deepa Narayan. 2000. "Social Capital: Its Significance for Development Theory, Research, and Policy." *World Bank Research Observer* 15(2):225–249.

World Bank. 1999. *Entering the 21st Century: The 1999/2000 World Development Report*. New York: Oxford University Press.

Yardley, Jim. 1998. "Brooklyn's Russian Residents Fnd a 'Suburb' in a Neighborhood Next Door." *New York Times*, September 23: A29.

Yates, Judith, and Christine Whitehead. 1998. "In Defense of Greater Antagonism: A Response to Galster's 'Comparing Demand-side and Supply-side Housing Policies.'" *Housing Studies* 13(3):415–423.

Yinger, John. 1995. *Closed Doors, Opportunities Lost: The Continuing Costs of Housing Discrimination.* New York: Russell Sage.

Zhou, Min. 1992. *New York's Chinatown: The Socioeconomic Potential of an Urban Enclave.* Philadelphia: Temple University Press.

CONTRIBUTORS

TRIDIB BANERJEE is the James Irvine chair of urban and regional planning at the University of Southern California's School of Policy, Planning, and Development. His most recent book is *Urban Design Downtown: Poetics and Politics of Form* with Anatasia Loukaitou-Sideris (Berkeley: University of California Press, 1998).

FREDERICK W. BOAL is professor emeritus at Queen's University's School of Geography in Belfast, Ireland; his latest book is *Ethnicity Housing: Accommodating the Differences* (Aldershot, Hampshire: Ashgate Publishing Company, 2000).

XAVIER DE SOUZA BRIGGS is an associate professor of public policy at Harvard University and Martin Luther King, Jr. Visiting Fellow in urban studies and planning at MIT (2002–2004). He is a former senior policy official and White House adviser at the U.S. HUD. A sociologist by training, he has published widely on housing desegregation, social networks, neighborhood change, and urban poverty.

N. ARIEL ESPINO is a Ph.D. candidate at Rice University's Department of Anthropology; he has his own architecture and planning practice in Panama.

SAMANTHA FRIEDMAN is an assistant professor at George Washington's University's Department of Sociology.

MARIE HUCHZERMEYER is a senior lecturer and coordinator of the postgraduate housing program at the University of Witwatersrand in Johannesburg. Her research interests are the sociopolitical aspects of housing policy and informal settlements, in particular the comparison between South Africa and Brazil.

ALAN MABIN is a member of the faculty at the University of Witwatersrand's Graduate School of Public Policy and Development Management in Johannesburg.

PETER MARCUSE is a professor of urban planning at Columbia University's Graduate School of Architecture, Planning, and Preservation; his most recent book with Ronald van Kempen is *Of States and Cities: The Partitioning of Urban Space* (London: Oxford University Press, 2002).

CERI PEACH is professor of geography at Oxford University's School of Geography and a Fellow at St. Catherine's College. His chapter, "Geographers and the Fragmented City," appears in R. J. Johnston and M. Williams, eds., *A Century of British Geography* (London, Oxford University Press, 2003).

GLENN PEARCE-OROZ is the Urban and Municipal Development officer of the United States Agency for International Development in Tegucigalpa, Honduras.

ROLF PENDALL is associate professor of city and regional planning at Cornell University and has written numerous reports for the Brookings Institution, the most recent of which is "Transition and Renewal: The Emergence of a Diverse Upstate Economy" (2004).

MOHAMMAD A. QADEER is professor emeritus of Queen's University's School of Urban and Regional Planning, Kingston, Ontario.

CATHERINE E. SAIDAT is a master's student in the Department of Sociology at George Washington University.

GREGORY D. SQUIRES is chair of the Department of Sociology at George Washington University. His most recent book is *Organizing Access to Capital: Advocacy and the Democratization of Financial Institutions* (Philadelphia, PA: 2003).

DAVID P. VARADY is professor of planning in the College of Design, Art, Architecture, and Planning at the University of Cincinnati. He has published numerous books and articles on public housing and housing vouchers.

NIRAJ VERMA is an associate professor of planning and management at the University of Southern California's School of Policy, Planning, and Development, Los Angeles.

ROBERT W. WASSMER is professor in the graduate program in public policy and administration at California State University, Sacramento. His most recent working paper is titled "Urban Sprawl in a U.S. Metropolitan Area: Ways to Measure and Comparison of the Sacramento Area to Similar Metropolitan Areas in California and the U.S."

INDEX

access, 6, 111, 118, 120, 149, 214, 217, 235, 241–244, 246, 255
access deficiency, 120
accessory apartments, 146
activist judges, 173
Adam, Heribert, 227
Adams, Lucy, xi
advocacy planning, 78
affirmative action, 78, 144, 218–220, 256
affirmative marketing, 99, 101, 131, 163, 250–251 table 14.1
affirmative occupancy policies, 251 table 14.1, 252–253. *See also* benign quotas
African Americans. *See* Blacks
agriculture, 198
air pollution. *See* environment
Al Qaeda, x
Alba, Richard D., 32
Albanians, viii
Alesina, Alberto, 165
Algerians, viii–ix
American Dream, 148
Amsterdam, viii, 1, 240
Anchorage, Alaska, 199 n.6
Anglo-Canadians, 60
anti-Semitism, ix, 44
apartheid. *See* South Africa
    American, 102
apartment cities, 206–209
Arabs, 21
Ashby, W. Ross, 76
Asians, 128, 132–133, 202–203, 207
assimilation, x, 31–33, 35–36, 46, 48, 58, 60, 72–73, 241–242

assimilation-diffusion model, 35, 41, 45, 47, 71, 239
    spatial, 58
Atlanta, Georgia, xiii–xiv, 200
audit testing. *See* testing
Australia, 222, 224

Balakrishnan, I. R., 54
Baltimore, 140
Banerjee, Tridib, 9, 243
Bangladeshis, viii, 40, 48, 53
Baqir, Reza, 165
Barrett, Tom, Senator, 142
Beirut, 72
Belfast, Northern Ireland, 4, 62–63, 66, 70, 71–75, 235, 239, 241
    Catholics and Protestants, 34, 63–64
    Policy Appraisal for Separation and Sharing (PASS), 75–76
benign quotas, 18
Benvenisti, Meron, 71–72, 77
Berlin, 72
big-box, *See* zoning, large-lot
Birmingham, England, xi, 147
black migration, 38
Blacks, 21, 52, 54–55, 128–129, 132
    African, 40, 51, 55, 58
    African Americans, xiii–xix, 2, 4, 6, 23–25, 33, 35, 37–43, 45–48, 60, 66, 70, 73, 82–83, 89, 96, 98–99, 127, 130–131, 133–142, 147, 153, 163, 166, 176–177, 181–184, 186, 189, 191–192, 202, 207, 221, 239, 241–243, 246, 257 n.1

synagogues, 67, 102

Taeuber, Karl and Alma, 41–42
Taiwan, 55
Taliban, xi
Tamils, 60
taxes, 9, 27, 29, 153–155, 160, 162,
    166, 169–172, 198, 203–205,
    210, 223, 228, 237, 239, 243,
    255
  antispeculation, 27
  appropriate tax prices, 160
  capital gains taxes, 27, 154, 220
  capitalization, 171–172
  land value taxation, 155
  metropolitan tax systems, 169
  progressive income taxes, 29
  property taxes, 8, 171, 204, 228, 243
  real estate transfer taxes, 196
  redistribution within states, 169–170
  sales tax, 204
  tax incentives, 27, 251 table 14.1
  tax increment financing, 203–204
  tax policies, 255
  tax revenue base, 203, 205, 210,
    223, 228
  tax treatment of home ownership,
    236
Tegucigalpa. See Honduras
Terrorism, 240
  Bali bombing, xi
  "Tipton Taliban," xi
testing, 129, 248
Tiebout, Charles, 7, 159–165, 168,
    201, 209–211
  Tiebout-sorting, 166–170, 201,
    203, 209
  "Tieboutian clubs," 9, 204–205,
    207, 209–210, 243
tipping point, 57–58
tolerance, 253. See also prejudice
Toronto, 1, 3, 44, 49, 52–55, 57–60,
    73, 235, 238–239, 241, 252

Agincourt, 53
Bathurst, 53
begum pura, 55
Bloor-Ossington, 55
Brampton, 53
Centre for Equality in Accomoda-
    tion (CERA), 56
Crescent Town, 53
Dawes Road, 53
Dundas West, 53
Etobicoke, 57
Greater Toronto Area (GTA), 49,
    53
Jaffaria Islamic Society, 59
Jane/Finch high-rise corridor, 60
Lawrence West, 53
Malton, 53
Markham-Richmond Hill, 53, 59
Mississuaga, 55, 59
North York, 59
public housing, 60
Regent Park, 60
Rosedale, 59
Scarborough, 53
Thorncliffe Park, 56
Toronto Metropolitan Municipality
    (TMM), 53
Torres, Angela D., 201
trade cities, 234
tragedy of the commons, 203
transportation, 7, 25, 28, 117–118,
    121, 123, 134–135, 142, 146,
    177, 215–216, 235, 242, 251
    table 14.1, 254–255
triple melting-pot, 34
Trudeau government, 51
Tse-Tung, Mao, 66
Turks, 87

Ukrainians, 51, 54
United Kingdom. See Great Britain
U.S. Bureau of the Census, 184, 186–
    188, 198–199 n.1, 207

Printed in the United States
45852LVS00003B/212

9 780791 464595